Gar[...]
of British [...]
Columbia
Gardening to Attract, Repel and Control

Janice Elmhirst, Ken Fry
and Doug Macaulay

LONE PINE

Lone Pine Publishing

The Publisher: Lone Pine Publishing
10145–81 Avenue
Edmonton, AB
T6E 1W9
Canada

Website: www.lonepinepublishing.com

Library and Archives Canada Cataloguing in Publication

Elmhirst, Janice Ferne, 1953-
　　Garden bugs of British Columbia / main author, Janice Elmhirst ; with Ken Fry and Doug Macaulay.

Includes bibliographical references and index.
ISBN 978-1-55105-591-6

　　1. Insects—British Columbia—Identification. 2. Garden pests—British Columbia—Identification. I. Fry, Kenneth McNichol, 1961- II. Macaulay, Doug, 1975- III. Title.

QL476.E45 2007　　　　595.7'09711　　　　C2007-906016-1

Editorial Director: Nancy Foulds
Project Editor: Gary Whyte
Editorial: Wendy Pirk, Nicholle Carrière, Carla MacKay
Technical Consultant: Don Williamson
Photo Coordinator: Carol Woo
Production Manager: Gene Longson
Book Design and Layout: Heather Markham
Production: Michael Cooke, Trina Koscielnuk, Heather Markham
Cover Design: Gerry Dotto
Cover Photo: Monarch larva (JupiterImages Corporation)
Anatomy Illustrations: Frank Burman
Illustrations and Photographs: please see p. 4 for a complete list of credits

We acknowledge the financial support of the Government of Canada through the Book Publishing Industry Development Program (BPIDP) for our publishing activities.

PC: P15

Table of Contents

Acknowledgements

Any book of BC garden bugs is bound to leave out many fascinating creatures. British Columbia has such varied climate and ecology, that, by necessity, we've focused primarily on the south coastal region, although, along the way, we've tried to note some of the major bugs in other parts of the province. I would like to thank my fellow authors, and the editorial staff at Lone Pine Publishing, Gary Whyte, Wendy Pirk and Nancy Foulds for their help and encouragement in preparing this book.

–Janice Elmhirst

I would like to thank the excellent editorial and production staff at Lone Pine, my wife for her support and forbearance, and the myriad of insects that serve as an inspiration and source of wonder every day.

–Ken Fry

I would like to thank my family for their loving support and encouragement of my entomology pursuits: my wife Sherri, my parents Allan and Karen, my brothers Stacy and Roger, and my nephew Blake Mackey. Special thanks go to Greg Pohl for his enthusiasm and for inspiring me to pursue this career. From the University of Alberta in my early teenage years, I thank Dr. Ronald Gooding, Dr. John Spence and Gerald Hilchie; and from my entomology studies and summer student work I thank Dr. Lloyd Dosdall, Dr. Jan Volney, Greg Pohl and Dr. Dave Langor. Also, thanks to Charlie Bird, Chris Schmidt, Gary Anweiler, Felix Sperling, Ernest Mengerson, Rob Hughes and other members of the Alberta Lepidopterists Guild for their inspiration and for their continuing work on Alberta Lepidoptera. Thanks to Cal and Charity Dakin for their input and support up here in the Peace Country. Lastly, thanks to my coworkers Toso Bozic and Martine Bolinger who have supported my interest in entomology.

–Doug Macaulay

Illustration and Photo Credits

Illustrations: **Charity Briere** 24, 53, 60, 61, 63, 69, 72, 76, 78, 79, 82, 84, 85, 109, 184a; **Frank Burman** 14, 15, 16, 17, 165; **Ivan Droujinin** 21b, 49, 51, 52, 55, 58, 59, 62, 64, 66, 67, 68, 75, 81, 83, 87, 91, 95, 96, 97, 98, 99, 100, 104, 112, 113, 115, 118, 120, 122, 123, 125, 126, 130, 132, 133, 135, 136, 137, 138, 139, 140, 141, 142, 143, 144, 146, 149, 151, 154, 155, 157, 158, 159, 162, 163, 164, 166, 169, 170, 174, 175, 182, 188a, 188b, 189, 205, 206; **George Penetrante** 26b, 147, 148, 150, 152, 171, 172, 173, 178, 180, 192, 202; **Ian Sheldon** 1, 21a, 25, 26a, 34, 42, 43, 44, 45, 46, 47, 48, 50, 54, 56, 57, 70, 73, 74, 77, 80, 86, 88, 89, 90, 92, 93, 94, 101, 102, 103, 105a, 105b, 106, 107, 108, 110, 111, 114, 117, 121, 124, 128, 129, 131, 134, 156, 160, 161, 167, 176, 177a, 177b, 181, 183, 184b, 185, 186, 190, 191, 194, 195, 196, 197, 198, 199, 200, 201, 203, 204.

Photographs: **Tamara Eder** 15a, 37a, 37b, 93a, 110; **Derek Fell** 116b; **JupiterImages Corporation** front cover, 12, 13, 41, 165; **Liz Klose** 39, 116a; **Doug Macaulay** 20a, 20b, 22, 23, 29, 145; **Tim Matheson** 15b, 18a, 31, 32, 47, 71a, 71b, 179, 187, 207; **Allison Penko** 35, 122; **Laura Peters** 108, 153; **Robert Ritchie** 18b, 103; **Gary Whyte** 193a, 193b; **Don Williamson** 93b.

Quick Reference Guide

Meadowhawks &
Dragonflies, p. 42

Mosaic Darners
p. 45

Spreadwings
p. 46

Bluets
p. 48

Grasshoppers
p. 49

Field Crickets
p. 50

Ambush Bug
p. 51

Damsel Bugs
p. 52

Plant Bugs
p. 53

Stink Bugs
p. 54

Lace Bugs
p. 55

Boxelder Bug
p. 57

Minute Pirate Bugs
p. 58

Aphids
p.59

Cooley Spruce Gall
Adelgid, p. 61

Mealybugs
p. 62

Scale Insects
p. 63

Oak Leaf Phylloxera
p. 64

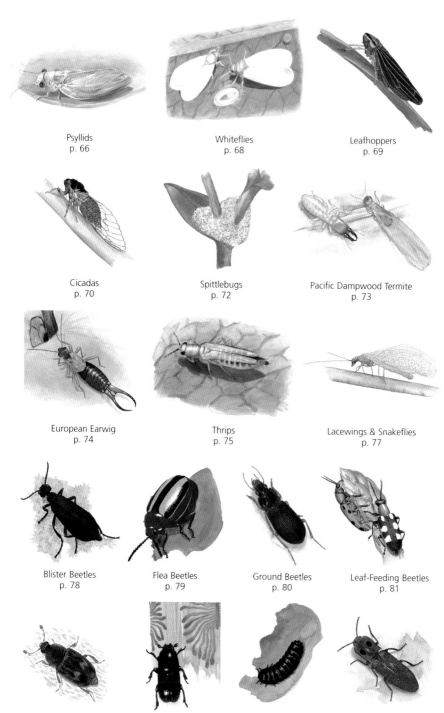

Psyllids
p. 66

Whiteflies
p. 68

Leafhoppers
p. 69

Cicadas
p. 70

Spittlebugs
p. 72

Pacific Dampwood Termite
p. 73

European Earwig
p. 74

Thrips
p. 75

Lacewings & Snakeflies
p. 77

Blister Beetles
p. 78

Flea Beetles
p. 79

Ground Beetles
p. 80

Leaf-Feeding Beetles
p. 81

Sap Beetle
p. 83

Elm Bark Beetles
p. 84

Carrion Beetles
p. 85

Click Beetles / Wireworms
p. 86

Bark Beetles
p. 87

Rove Beetles
p. 88

June Beetles & European
Chafer, p. 89

Dung Beetles
p. 91

Lady Beetles
p. 92

Tiger Beetles
p. 94

Root Weevils
p. 95

Terminal Weevils
p. 96

Bronze Birch Borer &
Jewel Beetles, p. 97

Poplar Borer
p. 98

Banded Alder Borer
p. 99

Poplar & Willow Borer
p. 100

Swallowtails & Tiger
Swallowtails, p. 101

Cabbage Butterfly
p. 103

Admirals
p. 104

Mourning Cloak
Butterfly, p. 106

Azures & Blues
p. 107

Monarch
p. 109

Painted Lady
p. 111

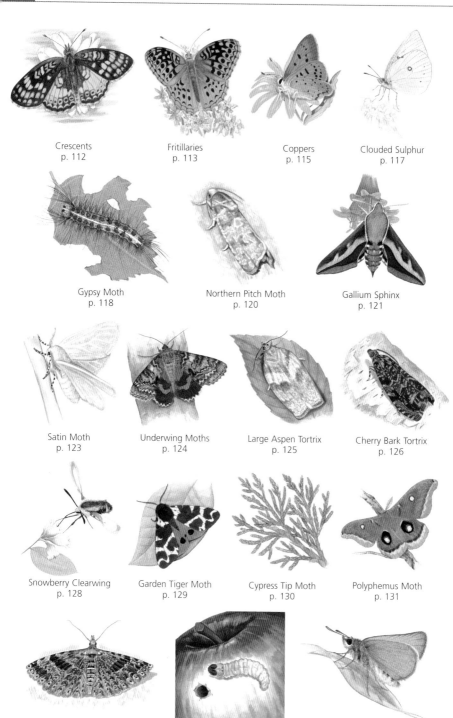

Crescents
p. 112

Fritillaries
p. 113

Coppers
p. 115

Clouded Sulphur
p. 117

Gypsy Moth
p. 118

Northern Pitch Moth
p. 120

Gallium Sphinx
p. 121

Satin Moth
p. 123

Underwing Moths
p. 124

Large Aspen Tortrix
p. 125

Cherry Bark Tortrix
p. 126

Snowberry Clearwing
p. 128

Garden Tiger Moth
p. 129

Cypress Tip Moth
p. 130

Polyphemus Moth
p. 131

Plume Moth
p. 132

Codling Moth
p. 133

European Skipper
p. 134

Peach Tree Borer
p. 135

Raspberry Crown Borer
p. 136

Peach Twig Borer
p. 137

Lilac Leaf Miner
p. 138

Speckled Green
Fruitworm, p. 139

Carpenterworms &
Carpentermoths, p. 140

Sod Webworms
p. 141

Western Spruce Budworm
p. 143

Obliquebanded Leafroller &
Blueberry Leaftier, p. 144

Bruce Spanworm &
Winter Moth, p. 146

Uglynest Caterpillar
p. 147

Tent Caterpillars
p. 148

Silverspotted Tiger Moth
p. 151

Armyworm Moth &
Army Cutworm, p. 152

Root Maggots
p. 154

Crane Flies
p. 156

Fruit Flies
p. 157

Carrot Rust Fly
p. 158

Tachinid Flies
p. 159

Hover Flies
p. 160

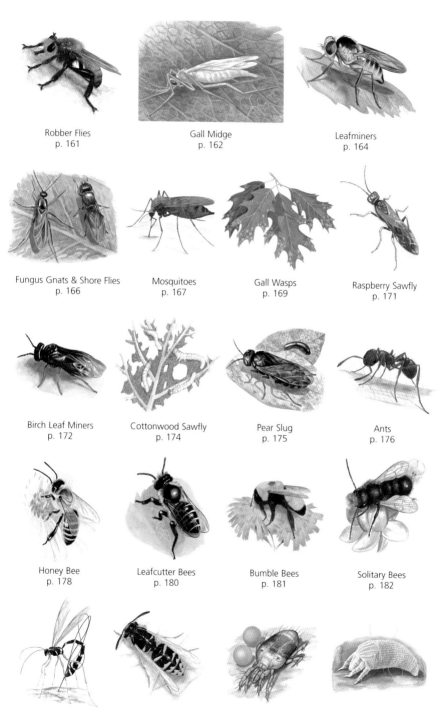

Robber Flies
p. 161

Gall Midge
p. 162

Leafminers
p. 164

Fungus Gnats & Shore Flies
p. 166

Mosquitoes
p. 167

Gall Wasps
p. 169

Raspberry Sawfly
p. 171

Birch Leaf Miners
p. 172

Cottonwood Sawfly
p. 174

Pear Slug
p. 175

Ants
p. 176

Honey Bee
p. 178

Leafcutter Bees
p. 180

Bumble Bees
p. 181

Solitary Bees
p. 182

Parasitoid Wasps
p. 183

Yellow Jackets
p. 185

Spruce Spider Mite
p. 188

Eriophyid Gall Mites
p. 189

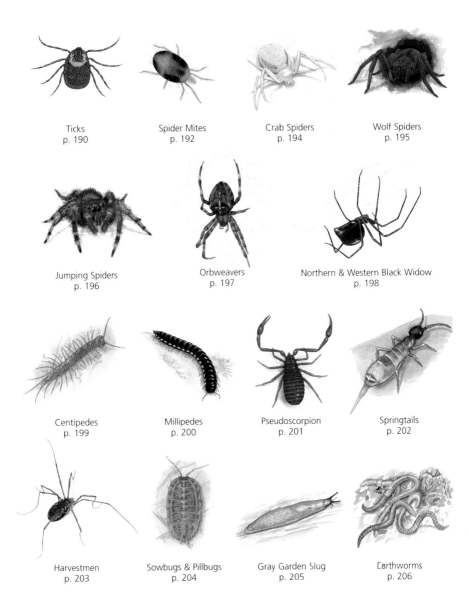

Ticks
p. 190

Spider Mites
p. 192

Crab Spiders
p. 194

Wolf Spiders
p. 195

Jumping Spiders
p. 196

Orbweavers
p. 197

Northern & Western Black Widow
p. 198

Centipedes
p. 199

Millipedes
p. 200

Pseudoscorpion
p. 201

Springtails
p. 202

Harvestmen
p. 203

Sowbugs & Pillbugs
p. 204

Gray Garden Slug
p. 205

Earthworms
p. 206

Lacewing

Introduction

No healthy garden is complete without a plethora of bugs—all bugs, including the beneficial, the beautiful and the nasty. Some bugs we enjoy watching, some we just ignore. Other bugs we consider nasty little creatures, and we lose sleep over them as we plot their demise, just as they haunt our minds and gardens!

On the bright side, there are many more species of bugs in the garden than just the nasty, beneficial or beautiful critters. If we look closely enough for them and spend some time learning about them, bugs will delight us when we see them. Some bugs are like mini-superheroes in the garden, battling the evil pests. Yes, it is difficult to overcome our fears of some of these little garden beasties, but many gardeners realize that having a variety of bugs is good, that having biodiversity in your garden or on your farm is crucial to how well plants will do. It is just a matter of recognizing the

good from the bad and understanding the roles each one plays—for example, are they pollinators or defoliators? In this book we hope to welcome you to the world of garden bugs and provide some tools to help you understand, recognize and appreciate them.

What Are Bugs?

The bugs covered in this book belong to three different groups—known as phyla—the Annelida, the Mollusca and Arthropoda. The creatures we call bugs—earthworms, slugs, insects and the like—lack backbones (vertebrae). To make things a little more clear and to keep our entomology buddies happy, we should mention that some insects are known as true bugs, from the order Hemiptera. But for all you non-entomologists out there, we will refer to "bugs" in this book generically, using the above criteria.

Bugs rule the world. They outnumber all other life forms. Even if we were to combine all the numbers of other described species together into one group, that group would be a small fraction of the total species pie. Arthropods in particular dominate, occupying all areas of the globe on land, in the air, in the sea and in our gardens and fields.

Without bugs we are doomed. They are important food sources for many animals such as fish, birds and small mammals. They are pollinators, responsible for the success of many of our crops. They are decomposers, building our soils and filling them with nutrients. Many are predators of pests that would otherwise eat us out of house and home.

Bugs are so successful owing to a number of different abilities. They are extremely adaptable and have morphological traits that help them survive some of the most severe environments on our planet including freezing temperatures and droughts. If one species can't handle an environment, you can be certain that eventually another species will. Some have tough exoskeletons that act like suits of armour, allowing the bugs to resist many conditions that other organisms cannot. Bugs can reproduce prolifically and go from being scarce to quite common in a matter of weeks. Just think of mosquitoes in the spring— a few large females survive the winter, and their offspring send us running for repellent a few weeks later. Some species are even parthenogenic, meaning that they can reproduce without mating.

The following sections describe the characteristics of annelids, molluscs and arthropods, so we can get a feel for their strengths and weaknesses.

Phylum Annelida

The phylum Annelida has about 9000 known species and includes critters like earthworms, leaches and polycheate worms. Most annelids are aquatic with a few, such as the earthworm, that are terrestrial. They like moist environments and have soft bodies.

The most noticeable thing about these critters is that they are segmented from one end to the other. This segmentation makes earthworms unique in that they can localize muscle movement within the segments, giving them the ability to move in all directions rather freely. The body wall of annelids is special as well: it has both circular and longitudinal muscles, giving annelids a wider range of motion than many other creatures.

It is important to understand that in the garden, a wrong decision could lead to a series of long-lasting consequences such as pest outbreaks, poor crop yields or sterile soil. Losing bug diversity is a bad thing, so when we look at pest management, we want to be sure we are dealing with the problem and not just the symptom.

Just watch them crawl around—they are quite amazing. These animals also maintain their bodies' rigidity by having a pressurized body cavity that is something like the hydraulics on a tractor. Those of you who have held an earthworm know what we're talking about; they are like little liquid-filled tubes. Their bodies are soft to the touch, as well, and can compress quite easily, unlike the other bugs covered in this book.

Annelids have well-developed internal organs. The digestive system is complete with a mouth, gut and anus. Respiration is through the skin, and they have no true respiratory organs. The circulatory system is closed, with a dorsal vessel and a ventral vessel connected by a series of vessels that pump blood into the dorsal head region. In the anterior, they also have a series of hearts that help circulate blood. The nervous system consists of a ventral nerve cord with a series of ganglia. In the head, concentrations of these ganglia form a small brain.

Reproduction in earthworms is simple: they contain both male and female sex organs. Despite having both sets of sex organs, they do mate with other worms and exchange genetic material. Overall, worms have some pretty neat features. In this book, they are the simplest of all species covered but are the only phylum that has a closed circulatory system.

Phylum Mollusca

The phylum Mollusca, with 50,000 described species worldwide, tends to be primarily aquatic: e.g., octopus, clams, snails and slugs. Land-dwelling slugs and snails are in the class Gastropoda. Most have a shell of some sort that they retract into when threatened. All are soft bodied and none have exoskeletons, as do most other bugs in this book.

Gastropods have a muscular foot that they use for creeping along. They are rather smart creatures and are likely the smartest invertebrates described in this book. They have a well-developed nervous system, well-developed eyes and a large brain. The digestive system is simple, with a mouth, stomach, intestine and anus. They tend to be grazers and feed on detritus and plant

Simple Anatomy of an Earthworm

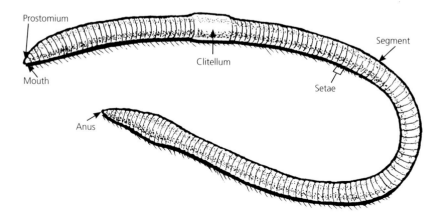

Prostomium

Segment

Clitellum

Mouth

Setae

Anus

Simple Anatomy of a Slug

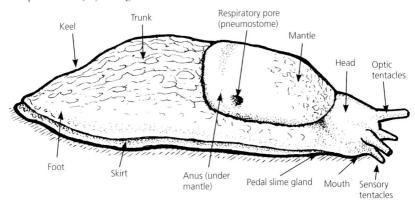

Keel · Trunk · Respiratory pore (pneumostome) · Mantle · Head · Optic tentacles · Foot · Skirt · Anus (under mantle) · Pedal slime gland · Mouth · Sensory tentacles

material. The circulatory system is open, with the heart circulating blood into the body cavity. The respiratory system consists of gills that collect oxygen and release carbon dioxide, which is transported in the blood. These terrestrial species breathe through gills and need to be wet, otherwise their system doesn't work; this is why they are most active on overcast days or at night.

Mollusc reproduction is similar to that of other bugs, with the majority of species being dioecious (individuals are either male or female), though some of our common garden slugs are monoecious (they have both sex organs). In many molluscs, eggs are fertilized externally and are laid in a sheltered location.

Phylum Arthropoda

The phylum Arthropoda, which dominates the globe, includes insects, spiders, crabs and centipedes. The species in this phylum outnumber all other phyla combined. Arthropods are major contributors to the suffering of humans as well—it is said that arthropods are responsible for most of the major plagues and famines recorded in history. Therefore, it is important that we learn about the many arthropods that we are likely to encounter in our gardens.

We cover four classes of Arthropod in this book. The largest class is the insects, followed by arachnids, millipedes and centipedes. The insects are the most successful of the classes and are the

most diverse, with around one million described species. Arachnids are next, with around 60,000 known species. The millipedes come in next with 8000 species, then the centipedes with 2500.

Arthropods are the most successful phylum for a number of reasons. They are covered in a durable suit of armour made out of a protein matrix called chitin, which gives them a protective advantage over many other organisms. Also, they are bilaterally symmetrical, so if you cut an arthropod in half from the head downwards, you would end up with two virtually identical halves. Arthropod bodies are segmented as well as jointed, with a distinct head, thoracic and abdominal region with jointed appendages. Most arthropods also have a series of eyes, known as compound eyes, or ocelli; in many cases they have both. They also have a variety of other sensory organs they use to smell, taste, hear and touch their environment.

Their body cavity, or hemocoel, contains the muscles, innards and circulatory systems. Arthropod blood is called hemolymph, and a heart circulates it throughout the hemocoel. Their gut or digestive system is complete, not open as is the circulatory system. A nervous system with a simple brain is connected to the central nerve ring, which is connected to the two ventral nerve cords. The respiratory system is unique—tracheal canals are found all over the body, and most spiders and some other arachnids also have a pair of gill-like structures known as "book lungs."

The arthropod reproductive system is one of the most advantageous of all living things and is one of the reasons arthropods dominate the globe. Some arthropods are monoecious, and others

Simple Anatomy of a Spider

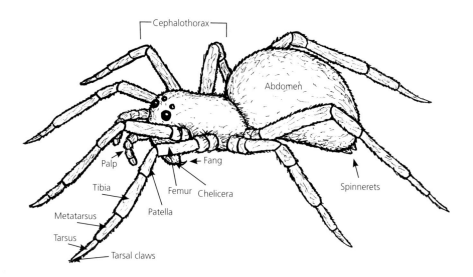

Cephalothorax

Abdomen

Palp

Fang

Tibia

Femur   Chelicera

Metatarsus

Patella

Tarsus

Spinnerets

Tarsal claws

are dioecious. Fertilization of eggs is mostly internal, and most species lay eggs that hatch and develop through different growth stages, from juvenile or larva to adult.

In some insects, such as moths and butterflies, the larva (caterpillar) transforms into a much different-looking adult. This transformation, which takes place in the pupa, is called complete metamorphosis. However, many other arthropods, such as grasshoppers, hatch already looking like miniature adults and go through a series of growth stages until they reach maturity. This type of development is known as incomplete metamorphosis.

The external body structure—the exoskeleton, often referred to as the cuticle—is one of the strongest parts of an arthropod's body. It has three layers—a thin outer layer and two thicker inner layers—made up of

Some chemical companies have produced insecticides that disrupt moulting hormones. As well, a biological control called diatomaceous earth, made of sharp particles of fossilized algae, cuts up many arthropods' cuticles, creating wounds that are often fatal. Diatomaceous earth is recommended for species such as ants.

the protein chitin, which gives it its strength. The outer layer is a hard, waxy armour. This layer is the strongest. It makes the insects rigid and gives them that crunching sound when stepped on. As immature arthropods grow, they must shed this outer layer and form a new, larger one.

A hormone called ecdysone triggers the moulting process, during which a new outer layer forms underneath the old one and moulting fluid is produced. This fluid digests part of the outer layer, which is then absorbed. Once this

Simple Anatomy of an Insect

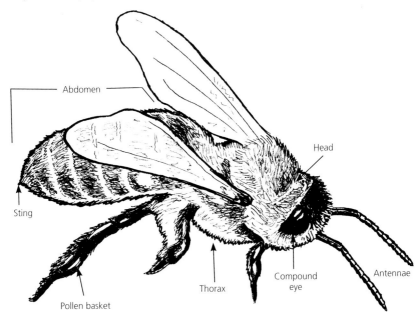

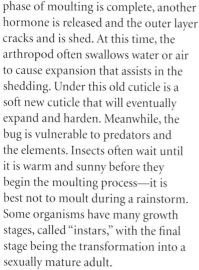

Caterpillar on roses

Beetles

phase of moulting is complete, another hormone is released and the outer layer cracks and is shed. At this time, the arthropod often swallows water or air to cause expansion that assists in the shedding. Under this old cuticle is a soft new cuticle that will eventually expand and harden. Meanwhile, the bug is vulnerable to predators and the elements. Insects often wait until it is warm and sunny before they begin the moulting process—it is best not to moult during a rainstorm. Some organisms have many growth stages, called "instars," with the final stage being the transformation into a sexually mature adult.

Arthropods need oxygen to breathe. The main difference between arthropods and other animals is that the arthropods' respiratory system is completely separate from the circulatory system where oxygen is transported in the blood. Because most of our garden residents are insects, we will discuss their respiratory system, which is known as the tracheal system. The tracheal system is composed of a series of canals that run from the outer cuticle into the inner system. The outer openings are called spiracles and can be observed using a microscope. These air-filled canals are branches that join larger canals and then split into smaller ones. There are two types of tracheal systems—an open system, which is found in most terrestrial garden arthropods, and an enclosed system, which has gills instead of spiracles and is found in aquatic species. In the open system, oxygen travels from the outer spiracles into the canals and then into the tiny branches that are attached to muscles and organs. Carbon dioxide produced in the muscles and organs is transported out through the canals and then the spiracles.

This open system has disadvantages, and predators or parasites of many insects use them to advantage. Creatures such as parasitic mites can get into the system through spiracles and can reduce the vigour of many susceptible insects—the tracheal mite, for example, has become a pest for beekeepers. Fungal spores can also penetrate these canals when conditions are right. Insecticides disrupt this system as well, and substances such as oils can coat the outer cuticle and block the spiracles.

Arthropods do have blood, even though it is different than ours. Most have an open circulatory system, meaning the blood basically circulates freely around and amongst the organs. The blood of insects is responsible for transporting materials such as nutrients, hormones, waste and a few other things. It does not carry oxygen to tissues as it does in other animals. The blood is clear, sometimes with a yellowish or greenish colour. It travels along the dorsal blood vessel located along the top of the body chamber. The vessel runs from the end of the abdomen to the head. The pulsating of the heart, which is the central region of the dorsal vessel, moves the blood by pushing and pulling it through the dorsal vessel. Blood is dumped into the head region and flows back through the body chamber toward the abdomen, where it is then sucked back into the dorsal vessel in the abdomen. Body muscle contraction also aids in the movement of blood through the body. The hemolymph does have some blood cells. These vary in shape, size and function and make up about ten percent of the blood volume. Many parasites of bugs live in the hemolymph, where they feed on tissues and nutrients. Sometimes the insect's immune system will build a cyst of blood cells around the unwelcome guest and may even be successful in killing it, but more often than not the parasite persists.

Because eating is the favourite pastime of garden arthropods, it is important that we understand their digestive system. As with most animals, insects have a mouth during at least one stage in their life, and this mouth varies in shape, size and function. The mouth region has appendages that help the insects grab, suck or chop up their food. Digestive juices are even pumped onto food in many instances to help soften things that would otherwise be too tough to swallow.

Once food is swallowed, it travels into three main sections of the bug before returning to the outer world. First it enters the foregut, then the midgut and finally the hindgut. The foregut's job is to grind, soften and macerate the food into smaller, more manageable particles. So, a particle of food enters the mouth, then travels into the pharynx, then the esophagus. The pharynx is the chamber located immediately behind the mouth, and the esophagus is the canal that travels inward to the crop. After the

When using biological insecticides—and in fact for most biologicals that involve viruses and bacteria—such as Bacillus thuringiensis (B.t.) *in your garden, cover the bugs' food source thoroughly. It is more important to coat the foliage the insects are feeding on rather than the insects themselves. Note that the younger the insect's stage, the less food it needs to consume, and therefore the better this biological control is going to work.*

crop, there is a chamber called the proventriculus that contains a valve that separates the midgut from the foregut. This separation is important because the proventriculus acts like a gizzard and sometimes contains teeth that further grind up and prepare food for the journey. This proventriculus valve opens periodically and releases food into the midgut. The midgut is like the stomach, where food is digested and is bombarded with enzymes. After digestion, nutrients in the far reaches of the stomach are absorbed into the body. The digested food eventually travels along the stomach and into the hindgut, where it begins its journey outward. The intestine and the rectal region continue to extract valuable material, and the rectum sucks out any remaining water. Finally, the solids are passed out the anus. Some species, such as aphids, eat food with a high water content and excrete much of the liquid; for other species, water is much more valuable and most of it is retained.

For many bugs, the digestive system is their biggest weakness and is how they contract many diseases. Harmful bacteria, viruses and other deadly microorganisms are gobbled up and enter the insect's mouth, then travel into the stomach where they become active and infect the insect. In the year following a tent caterpillar outbreak, for example, the entire population crashes because viruses and bacteria have taken advantage of this digestive weakness.

One of the arthropods' best assets (and the reason they outnumber all other creatures on Earth combined) is their ability to reproduce. All arthropods produce an egg, but not always with a male and female.

Reproductive organs of garden bugs are often located near the rear of their bodies, so look there when sexing these creatures. Males have a set of external claspers, whereas females often have an egg-laying ovipositor. This ovipositor can be quite elaborate and long, as it is in some parasitoid wasps. Once eggs are fertilized, they may be deposited in a mass or individually. In rare cases, the insects hold onto the fertilized eggs. For example, some parasitic tachinid flies hang onto the fertilized eggs until they hatch and then deposit live larvae onto hosts.

Mountain Pine Beetle in gallery

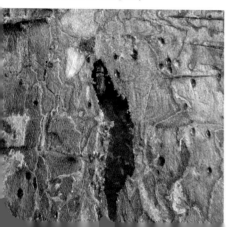

Primary pest (Lilac Leaf Miner damage)

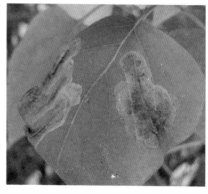

Integrated Pest Management

Integrated Pest Management (IPM) is a method of dealing with pests that is in widespread use in agriculture and horticulture. Its origins can be traced back to the dawn of agriculture, around 10,000 BCE (Before the Common Era). Many different definitions of IPM exist, but we will adopt the following definition from *Concepts in Integrated Pest Management* (Norris, et al., 2003):

Migrant pest (Painted Lady butterfly)

> A decision support system for the selection and use of pest management tactics singly or harmoniously coordinated into a management strategy, based on a cost benefit analysis that takes into account the interests and impacts on producers, society and the environment.

In short, IPM requires you to gather information before you take action. Some questions you should ask include whether a pest is present. Is the pest causing enough damage to warrant action? What actions should I take? When and where should I take action? Did the action have any effects? Do I need to do it again?

With IPM, you must have a plan with objectives. IPM requires knowledge of the ecology of the system and is informed or determined not just by profitability, but also by effects on the environment and society.

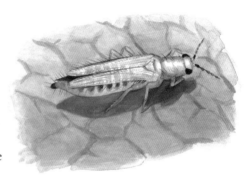

Occasional pest (Western Flower Thrips)

What is Ecology?

Ecology is the study of organisms, their relationships with each other and with their biotic and abiotic (or nonliving) environments. You need to understand your plants, not just the pests. You also need to understand the interactions of the plant with the soil, the sun, water and other plants.

You must take a systems approach to understanding and managing the landscape. Nothing grows in isolation. All organisms, water, air and nutrients—everything in your yard—are connected, and action taken to affect one component will affect each of the others.

What is a Pest?

A pest is commonly defined as anything that is detrimental to or interferes with human activities and desires. Here, a pest is not restricted to the traditional definition, in which an organism affects yield; instead, nearly any organism that negatively affects humans is considered a pest.

For a pest to negatively affect humans, all four of the following conditions—known as the pest tetrahedron—must be met. First, the host plant or plant part has to be present for the insect to feed on; e.g., you do not have problems with leaf-feeding insects when there are no leaves. Second, the pest must, of course, be present. Third, the weather conditions must be right; it cannot be too hot or too cold for either the pest or the plant. And fourth, it must be the right time of year. Some pests only feed in spring, whereas others do most of their damage in fall. You must know what is required of the plant and the pest to diagnose a problem and address it in a timely and efficient manner.

Types of Pests

Not all pests are present year-round or every year. And not all pests are pests all the time. There are primary or key pests that you can set your clock by; they come back every year and damage the same plants. Examples include aphids on nearly everything, the Black Vine Weevil on rhododendrons and leaf miners on birch.

Insects that are present year in and year out but do not cause substantial damage are called minor pests. Many of the showy moths with large caterpillars are considered minor pests. For example, the woolly bear caterpillars of the Garden Tiger Moth feed on a variety of woody and herbaceous plants but rarely, if ever, cause significant harm to the landscape.

Some insects are a problem only if the conditions are right. These are potential, or secondary, pests that cause damage if you plant their preferred host (e.g., strawberries or potatoes planted after sod will be damaged by wireworms, the larvae of click beetles that laid their eggs in the grass). These secondary pests can sneak up on you from other hosts (e.g., plant bugs that were feeding on weeds or pasture may move into vegetable crops when the hay is cut or the weeds begin to die in late summer). Secondary pests might be waiting for you to change

Mountain Pine Beetle damage

a growing practice to favour them. For example, failure to prune trees and shrubs or remove suckers and dead branches can create attractive sites for borers. Sometimes the weather is ideal for a secondary pest outbreak (e.g., grasshoppers thrive under drought conditions; otherwise, they lurk in the background, barely noticed).

Secondary pests happily munch away in your yard in relative obscurity. They are often out-competed by the primary pests and do not reach the high numbers needed to do much damage or be immediately noticeable. But if the primary pest is knocked out or the secondary pest's community of natural enemies is eliminated by the use of pesticides, then the secondary pest can fill in the gap left by the primary pest or increase to primary pest status because of the lack of natural control. For example, applying a broad-spectrum garden insecticide early in the summer for aphid control will kill natural enemies, and can lead to an outbreak of spider mites.

Two other forms of pest common in British Columbia are the migrant pest and the occasional pest. An example of a migrant pest is the Painted Lady butterfly. This butterfly flies up from the southern United States in years of great abundance down there. Several generations may occur in British Columbia but all will die out come winter. In years following a season when weather is favourable and food is abundant, a mass migration northward will occur and it seems every other butterfly you see is a Painted Lady.

Occasional pests are blown in with storms from as far south as California and include aphids, thrips and leafhoppers.

Ants and aphids

An animal can be the prey of a predator. If you know a particular insect is prey, you may be able to introduce its predator to help manage its population. Predators are usually generalists, feeding on many different kinds of insects. For example, lady bird beetles will feed on aphids, thrips and spider mite eggs, scale insects and mealybugs, among others.

Types of Damage

A pest can affect a plant in many ways. In agriculture, reduction in yield is usually the main measure of damage by a pest. In home gardens, "yield" might be measured by visual appeal, enjoyment by your children or how many birds are attracted to your yard. If we know the types of damage that can happen, then we can learn what might have caused the damage. We can then determine what threat the insect poses to our plants and act accordingly. Damage can be characterized in the following ways.

Physical damage harms the plant, compromising structural integrity or allowing for entry of pathogens. Wood-boring beetles can weaken branches

Green Peach Aphid

and stems. Leaves shredded or holed by leaf beetles allow fungi and bacteria to enter the wounds. Roots chewed by weevil grubs expose the plant to invasion by fungi.

With *cosmetic damage,* the pest can cause lesions, chew holes or deposit frass, all of which reduce the aesthetic value of the plant without leading to its death.

With *vectoring,* the pest may transmit pathogens, i.e., disease-causing organisms such as phytoplasmas (bacteria-like organisms that infect plants), viruses, bacteria or fungi. For example, many common plant viruses are transmitted by aphids. The most commonly known plant phytoplasma is aster yellows, which is notoriously transmitted by leafhoppers.

Direct contamination is when whole insects, body parts or frass contaminate the plant, reducing its appeal. For example, lady beetles can spoil a fruit harvest, or black widow spiders can live in a grape cluster.

Economic damage includes the cost of management measures such as equipment and products applied to manage the pests. Training in the correct use of pesticides is included here as well (think of the cost of this book or a session at a horticultural show).

The broad category of environmental and social costs includes groundwater contamination from excess pesticide run-off, or real or perceived harm to a neighbour from exposure to pesticide application.

Insects and their relatives can cause characteristic damage, known as arthropod-specific damage, which differs from disease or abiotic causes in the following ways.

Biting/Chewing/Boring: plant material is removed. It may be in bite-size chunks or by skeletonizing the leaf.

Mining: this form of biting/chewing takes place within a leaf.

Piercing/Sucking: fluid is removed, or individual plant cells below the epidermis are digested and removed.

Protection of Other Insects: some species of ants protect aphids while the aphids feed. The ants collect honeydew from the aphids in return for this protection.

Frass: in some cases (e.g., aphid honeydew) frass causes or contributes to the development of disease. More often, frass reduces the visual appeal of the plant without directly harming its health.

Ecological Roles

To appreciate the influence of pest and plant biology, we need to approach pest management from an ecological perspective. Ecology ranges from the individual to populations (a group made up of members of the same species), communities (assemblages of different species in a geographic area), ecosystems (community and abiotic factors), ecoregions (areas of similar ecosystems) and finally the biosphere we call Earth.

Basic principles or characteristics in ecology allow us to make informed decisions based on simple observations. Organisms can be classified into specific roles in the environment. If we can assign an arthropod to a role, then we will know something about it and how to deal with it. For example, a plant or arthropod can be a host—it is fed on or parasitized by other animals. A plant can be a host to a plant-eating insect. An insect can be a host to a parasitoid. Knowing a plant is host to a particular insect means you will have to manage for that insect. Knowing that a particular insect is host to a parasitoid means you may be able to exploit that relationship and include biological control in your management plan.

Parasitoids are insects that kill their host. They are different from parasites, which benefit from its host without killing it. Parasitoids deposit eggs onto or into their host, and the resulting larva(e) devours the host from the inside out. In general, parasitoids are very host-specific, attacking one or just a few different species. If we know the pest in question is host to a parasitoid, we can use the parasitoid to control the pest.

Selectivity of Feeding

Insects exhibit a range of selectivity when it comes to food choice. An insect may have a very narrow range of acceptable food types. It may feed on only one species of plant or animal; for example, the caterpillars of the Old World Swallowtail butterfly feed only on wild tarragon, also called dragon's-wort in British Columbia. An insect might have a moderate range of food preferences. For example, the Cabbage Butterfly feeds on plants in the family Brassicaceae. Other insects have a wide range of acceptable foods. For example, during an outbreak, the Forest Tent Caterpillar will consume the leaves of nearly any woody plant.

Food Webs

If we look at the energy flows of organisms, we can see what is commonly called a food web. Note that we use the term food web instead of food chain. "Food chain" implies

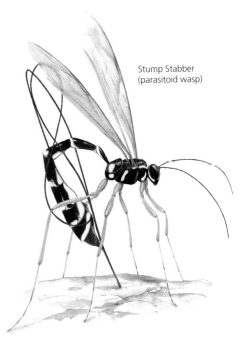

Stump Stabber
(parasitoid wasp)

a linear relationship, but in nature, relationships are often much more complex. An insect may help us by preying on a pest but harm us by feeding on plant material in the absence of its prey. If we disrupt one part of the food web, say by knocking out a predator, we risk upsetting the equilibrium in our yard. We should also recognize that weeds or other plants can serve as alternate hosts for pests and, therefore, should be managed to reduce pest numbers. We can also exploit the food web by including plants in our yard that attract beneficial bugs. Parasitic wasps and predatory hover flies need nectar to fuel their flight. You can entice these beneficial bugs into your yard by planting many nectar-bearing flowers.

Why Some Bugs Are So Good at Being Pests

Being short lived, producing large numbers of offspring and having poor competitive ability doesn't make some bugs better pests; rather, it means they do not like to reside in established ecosystems where they have to duke it out with many other species. Instead, most pests generally tend to exploit a recently disturbed site, such as the artificial landscape in a yard or garden, where there is likely to be few if any competitors. These organisms become pests because they use a "get in fast, and eat as much as you can until competitors arrive and push you away" strategy—the "live fast, exploit resources rapidly and die young" strategy. Adults invest very little in their offspring, and the species relies on high numbers of offspring rather than quality of parental care to ensure its survival. The populations can build up rapidly, overwhelming the host plant and the suppressive pressure of natural enemies. For example, many weeds are well adapted to invading disturbed sites, and aphids and spider mites are well adapted to exploiting annual plants and disturbed sites.

Bugs with the opposite survival strategy are long lived, have few offspring, are good competitors and prefer to live in stable environments. This strategy is characteristic of many predators. They require a reliable source of prey to be successful. Because they have a high-quality food source (i.e., other insects), they do not need to produce as many young to ensure the survival of the species.

Cabbage Butterfly

Tent Caterpillar adult

IPM Decision-Making Process

Development of a sound integrated pest management plan depends on several pieces of information that together are used to make a management decision. The following are the critical steps to take when making IPM decisions.

1. Pest Species Identification. Correctly identifying the pest to ecological role, feeding habit or order, family or genus level is the first priority. If the pest is not properly identified, information on biology and ecology will be incorrect and could lead to a damaging decision. For example, if you know the type of damage is wood-boring, you then know that it is likely a beetle or moth, it is the immature stage that is doing most of the damage and the adult stage is the one that can be monitored outside of the tree. You have options on whether to treat the host, prevent the adult from attacking the host or deal with the larva directly.

2. Understanding the Biology of the Pest and Host. You need to characterize or put into context what the pest is doing. What is the pest population size? Is it high enough to warrant action? What is the status of the pest population, its population dynamics? Is the pest population increasing, steady or decreasing? Is there potential for future harm?

What about beneficial arthropods? Are they present? Are there enough to suppress the pest population without you taking action?

What is the status of the host plant? Is it water-stressed, diseased or in otherwise poor condition? If a plant is stressed, it is less able to compensate for insect damage or attack and is therefore more susceptible.

Lastly, you must consider the economics of the plants that need to be protected. Are they high-value plants that you can justify expending effort and money to protect? Or are the plants in a low-visibility area, which would allow for a higher tolerance for damage? It is a good idea to prioritize the areas of your yard—what needs immediate attention or a high degree of management and what area is fine just being green—a bit chewed up maybe, but still essentially green.

3. Evaluate the Potential for Damage. Will this pest cause damage? Is the pest density greater than the economic or action threshold for that pest? The economic or action threshold (discussed in detail later) is the go/no-go point for taking action against a pest. IPM is about being proactive, not just reactive. If the pest is not an immediate or future threat, there is no need to act. However, if you allow the population of some pests to increase, it may cause a much bigger problem in following years. Therefore it might be prudent to manage the pest when you first notice it.

4. Evaluate Available Tactics. Determine which management methods will be best for this pest and situation. Consider cost (including labour), effectiveness and environmental impact. If one method is not satisfactory alone, consider combining two or more methods to achieve your goals.

5. Evaluate Possible Interactions. Is the pest the key pest? By suppressing this pest, will you free up other pests to take its place (remember secondary pests)? Will the tactic negatively affect other members of the ecosystem, such as beneficial arthropods or pollinators?

This step is crucial to "integrated" pest management.

6. Legality. Once you have chosen a tactic, make sure it conforms to regulations in your community. Many municipalities have pesticide bans in place.

7. Decide. If the pest population size does not warrant action, then you can decide to take no action at all. We should not live by the credo "see bug, kill bug." A little pruning often does not harm a plant. Instead, it can make the plant stronger by stimulating it to grow more leaves or send out more shoots, or it can cause the plant to release defensive chemicals.

You can reduce how vulnerable the plant is to the pest population by changing some aspect of plant culture. For example, you make sure the plant is well watered or fertilized, or spaced far enough from other plants to encourage airflow.

You can reduce the pest population size directly by releasing biological control agents, spraying with an insecticide or physically removing the pest.

In most circumstances, you will likely choose a combination of options. IPM relies on integrating multiple tactics for the best effect and the least negative impact. When considering the economics of a plan, keep in mind that short-term loss may be acceptable to prevent total loss in the future or if multiple seasons are taken into account.

If steps 5 and 6 are omitted, problems often arise with insecticide resistance, resurgence of a pest, environmental contamination or illegal pesticide residues.

8. Measure Success. This step is often overlooked in IPM decision-making. Make sure you evaluate whether a given tactic or method worked. Did it have a short-term or lasting effect? Were there side effects? Was it worth the time and effort? Knowing how well or poorly a tactic works feeds back into steps 4 and 5 so that you can make a better decision next time.

Monitoring or Scouting for Insects

How do we know there is a problem in the first place? How do we find the pest if there is a problem? We need to monitor the landscape to detect problems before or as they arise. Monitoring requires a sampling plan. There are two different pest-specific variables to be measured: pest stage present (egg, larva/nymph, pupa or adult) and pest density (how many insects there are in a given area).

What else is there to measure? To put pest stage and pest density into context, we also need to measure developmental events of the plant and pest. Phenology is defined as the sequence of growth and development of an organism over time. We can track phenology by observing plants and animals, or we can predict phenology by monitoring degree-days.

In cold-blooded animals such as arthropods, and in plants, outside temperatures regulate the rate of metabolism or physiology. There are lower and upper thresholds to development (too cold or too hot to grow or develop), and you can predict an organism's development rate based on heat units accumulated. A degree-day is defined as $°D = temp\ 1°$ (C or F) above lower threshold for 24 hours, and is calculated using the following formula: $°D = ([Max + Min]/2) - T_{low}$, where Max is the daytime high temperature, Min is the overnight low temperature and T_{low} is the lower developmental temperature threshold for the organism in question.

You can use weather information from Environment Canada to calculate degree-days, but it is best to use data collected on-site using a dedicated weather monitoring station. If you do not know the lower developmental threshold for a pest, use the default value of 10° C.

With degree-days known, you can predict what life stage a pest will be in, what developmental stage a plant is in or when to take action to manage a pest. Degree-day models have been developed for many agricultural pests. You can record degree-days beginning April 1 and see for yourself when various insects emerge. This way you track what goes on in your yard, and you will be prepared each year when a specific pest arrives.

How Many Are There?

To determine the population density, count the number of pests. There are two different counts that can be made: absolute and relative. An *absolute count* is a measure of pests per unit area; for example, the number of aphids per leaf or beetles per branch. A *relative count* is a measure of pests per sampling unit; for example, the number of thrips per sticky card.

Insects are usually distributed in the environment in clumps corresponding to their food source. Often, if you see one insect, you will see others nearby. Patches of insects are difficult to detect because there are often large gaps

between patches. To overcome this obstacle, you can go through your yard in a systematic fashion, inspecting each plant individually. This inspection will take you a long time. Alternatively, you can sub-sample your yard by inspecting every fifth plant, or some similar fraction. Be sure to inspect a representative of each species of plant in your yard because different insects specialize in different plants.

Because many insects can fly, they can invade your yard from distant infestations. The following are some points to ponder regarding where you may find pests:
• a point-source infestation will look patchy in the early establishment stage
• arthropods are distributed differently on the edge of an area than they are in the centre (there are alternate food hosts near the edges and usually an increase in relative humidity and temperature at the centre of a group of plants)
• prevailing winds and windbreaks may affect how or where flying insects enter your yard or move around in it
• soil conditions can affect how well ground insects will spread in your yard or garden.

Pest density

Monitoring Methods

When deciding which of the monitoring methods you are going to use, keep in mind the following points:

• Do you require actual numbers or just need to know presence/absence?

• What time were the samples taken? Are the insects of interest active at that time of day?

• What is the weather like (rainy, windy, cold, warm; will it affect the activity level of the insects)?

• What is the phenology of the plant and the pest? Was the damaging stage of the pest present at the time of sampling? Is the susceptible stage of the plant present (flowers, fruit)?

• What surrounding plants are present? Will they act as a refuge for the pest or a source of re-infestation?

There are four categories of monitoring methods: direct observation, damage evaluation, trapping and soil sampling. In *direct observation* you are looking for the pest itself, which is best accomplished by inspecting the plants for pests.

With *damage evaluation*, you are looking for indirect evidence of the pest. You can look for stunted plants, mottled or yellowed leaves, curled leaves, necrotic spots, wilted plants, swollen or galled plant parts or other forms of physical injury. You may also observe a reduction in yield or number of blooms.

A less labour-intensive method is to *use a trap* to collect samples. Trapping works well to determine whether the pest is present but it is not always reliable for population numbers. Traps can be affected by wind, and they may be inaccurate because they catch pests in transit and not on the plant. Traps can come in many forms and can be passive or active. Passive traps do not attract the pest. Active traps have some form of attractant such as visual cues (colour or shape) and can be baited with host odours or pheromones. Active traps tend to reduce the amount of by-catch (unintended victims).

Lastly, you can *sample the soil* in a region, a method that is particularly useful when detecting overwintering populations or root-feeding pests.

The mobility of a pest will affect how and when you monitor. How fast the

---

Monitoring Methods

Method	Target
Visual inspection	Foliage feeders
Frass counting	Non-nest building caterpillars
Honeydew patch counts	Aphids, psyllids
Pheromone traps	Adult moths, bark beetles
Sticky traps	Psyllids, winged aphids, adult thrips
Double sticky tape	Crawler stage of scale insects
Foliage beating	Beetles, mites, thrips, plant bugs, leafhoppers
Burlap bands	Gypsy moth larvae
Boards/refugia	Snails, weevil adults
Degree-day models	Indicator of when to begin monitoring

pest disperses from an alternate host or an overwintering site will determine how often you have to resample your yard to ensure you detect the pest at the earliest moment.

Knowing where the pest is likely to come from can help you determine where you should begin your sampling. Is there a neighbouring area that has the pest and could serve as a source of infestation?

The timing of your sampling effort is important. When should you begin sampling to be assured the pest is there to be captured? The frequency of your sampling will depend on how rapidly a pest population can change. You must sample for many-generation insects such as aphids far more often than single-generation insects such as white grubs or lygus bugs.

Record Keeping

It is important to maintain records of your monitoring. Records allow you to track trends in populations and determine if they are increasing or decreasing, and they let you see whether your management methods are working. Do you see a long-term upward or downward trend?

You should record the site of collection (where on the plant, where in the landscape); the number of pests in the sample and what life stage they are in; the condition of the host plant; the weather, date and time; and whether any beneficial arthropods are present.

Paying attention to trends will allow you to predict future pest infestations so you can prepare accordingly. You should also keep an eye on what is going on in your neighbour's yard or around your block to be aware of what may enter your yard in the future.

Sticky pheremone traps are useful for monitoring insect populations.

Thresholds

Once you have determined pest identity, pest density, and pest and plant phenology, you can make a pest-management decision. When an insect causes little or no damage, the impact on the plant is usually low. If the pest causes low levels of cosmetic damage, the plant is considered to tolerate the pest. At slightly higher levels of attack, some plants exhibit "compensatory" behaviour—they increase growth or physiological activity to compensate for what was damaged or lost. Beyond this tolerance or compensation, we observe real damage and loss.

Lygus bug on cosmos flower

The necessity of defining acceptable levels of damage has led to the development of thresholds. The concept of low densities of pests resulting in low levels of damage is central to pest management. It is assumed that a few pests will only cause a little damage and with increasing density comes increasing damage.

There are different kinds of thresholds. The most basic threshold is that of *discovery*. If you can detect the insect, at least you know that you have a situation that demands a decision be made. You may take an extreme position by choosing to act on this threshold because you cannot tolerate any damage at all. Often you and your plants can tolerate a wee bit of damage, and just because the pest is present is

not necessarily cause for alarm. Recall that beneficial insects are likely present to suppress the pest.

Another type of threshold is called the *economic injury level*: the pest density at which you lose money because of damage caused by the pest. If you take action above this threshold, you may prevent or reduce further loss, but you will have lost more than if you had acted earlier.

The threshold most commonly used is called the *economic* or *action threshold*. This threshold is the pest density at which action must be taken to prevent the pest population from reaching the economic injury level. If you act at this threshold, you will reduce or prevent further damage. Although you are spending time, effort or money to treat the plants, the cost of treating is much less than what you would lose if you did not act. The economic threshold is lower than the economic injury level because with any tactic you use, there will not be a 100 percent reduction in the pest, and it follows that injury will continue to occur after the management action is taken.

There are limitations to using thresholds. Environmental conditions may change threshold levels from year to year or region to region. For example, drought or wet years affect thresholds.

A strategy of pre-emptive release (releasing the predator or parasitoid before you detect the pest) is commonly used with biological control agents. When this strategy is used, there is usually no need of a threshold because you have already taken action.

Thresholds are of no use when there are no effective tactics available to treat or react to the pest. In this case, prevention is the only option. Thresholds are also of little value in cases where once the pest has reached a detectable stage, it is too late for action. For example, cyclamen mites are usually detected after the damage is done. Another limitation of thresholds is when there is no economic tactic available.

Tactics

There are several ways you can manage a pest. The tactics or methods to choose from fall under one of three categories:

- With *pest manipulation*, you directly target the pest. You can use prevention, pesticides, biological control, behavioural control or physical control.
- With *plant manipulation*, you indirectly affect the pest by using cultural methods (agronomy) or by modifying host-plant resistance.
- With *environmental manipulation*, you modify the environment to indirectly affect the pest. It can be on a micro scale (humidity within the canopy, plant thinning, etc.) or a macro scale (shelterbelts).

Managing Beneficial Insects in the Landscape

A "natural enemy" is defined as any organism that directly suppresses another organism. For the purposes of this book, only beneficial organisms that affect pest species will be considered. A natural enemy can be a predator, parasitoid or disease. Natural enemies should not be ignored when developing an IPM plan because they can contribute significantly to pest management. In this book, we distinguish between natural enemies and biological control organisms. Biological control organisms are commercially produced for use in an IPM program; natural enemies are predators, parasitoids or pathogens that occur naturally in the environment. Natural enemies and commercially obtained biological control organisms can be considered synonymous depending on their use within an IPM program. For example, strategies such as conservation, augmentation and habitat diversity can be applied to enhance the effectiveness of natural enemies and commercial biological control organisms.

Natural enemies can be manipulated in several ways to enhance their impact. The principle method is through conservation of pre-existing populations of natural enemies. Local populations can be increased through augmentation and by various physical and cultural practices.

1. Conservation is the practice of preserving pre-existing populations of natural enemies in a local area. The most effective method of conservation is to limit or eliminate the use of broad-spectrum chemical pesticides. As a result of indiscriminate pesticide use, a mutation occurs providing populations of resistant pests with the ability to somehow survive exposure to the pesticide. The insect does not adapt to the chemical; instead, a pre-existing condition allows it to survive and become the one to reproduce (the pesticide has little or no effect on the pest as a result of years of pesticide use). Natural enemies usually do not have the same degree of chemical resistance as do their prey or hosts and are therefore more susceptible to pesticides. By spraying narrow-spectrum pesticides only when action thresholds have been surpassed and only in areas where absolutely necessary, you contribute to the conservation of natural enemies by limiting their direct exposure to pesticides and pesticide residues.

Thirteen-spot Ladybug adult

Another conservation strategy is to provide for the successful reproduction and overwintering of natural enemies. Provide plants that offer shelter and nectar for adult feeding, and use mulches and hedgerows to provide overwintering sites.

2. Augmentation is the process of supplementing existing numbers of natural enemies with releases of wild-collected natural enemies. Augmentation can be achieved in two ways: inoculation or inundation. The practice of inoculation involves introducing natural enemies to an area where they were not originally present or were wiped out through the use of pesticides or other practices. The homeowner relies on the natural enemy to reproduce on its own to increase its population. The introduced natural enemy and its offspring help suppress the pest species. For example, when you clear your yard of old turf and later re-seed it, you could collect predatory beetles and reintroduce them into the newly planted turf for control of white grubs and other pests.

Augmentation may be required after natural enemies have been reduced or eliminated because of pesticide use. Most natural enemies have not been selected for resistance to pesticides. As a result, pest species' populations often explode after pesticide use because of the lack of natural controls. A common example of this phenomenon can be seen in spider mite outbreaks on fruit trees after pesticides are directed at the mites or other pests. The pesticides severely reduce predatory mite populations, allowing pest mite populations to increase. Another example is the loss of predatory rove beetles and ground beetles when a soil drench is used against white grubs.

Inundation is the practice of repeated introductions of a natural enemy with reliance on only the enemies released for pest suppression. There is no expectation that the introduced natural enemy will reproduce and increase its population. The season may not be long enough for the natural enemy to reproduce, or it may be incapable of surviving the winter. You can purchase insects from suppliers, and this option may work for large acreages.

3. Habitat diversity enhances pest management and adds to the beauty and longevity of the landscape. A uniform or large planting of only one or a few plant species is not ideal for recruiting or maintaining natural enemies. Planting several different species of vegetation provides for multiple hosts, nectar and pollen sources, and microhabitats for resting or overwintering. Use caution when selecting food or habitat plants to ensure the pest does not also feed on that plant. Keep an eye on which bugs are eating what and adjust your plants accordingly to achieve a landscape populated by "selective food plants." A complex canopy with many available layers, heights and textures will usually result in increased success in recruitment and overwintering of natural enemies.

In some instances, natural enemies can prey on alternate hosts feeding on the secondary planting and then switch to the pest on the primary planting. This phenomenon is called using "banker" plants in biological control. It is an effective method for maintaining natural enemies in the absence of the primary pest. Natural enemies can be lured to a landscape, or the probability of their survival can be increased, by adding organic matter such as manure.

Habitat diversity must also be considered in the context of time. Choose plants that provide resources to natural enemies throughout the growing season. Pay particular attention to early flowering plants to provide the bugs with a head start in spring.

4. Impact of Management Practices. The use of pesticides can have a significant negative impact on natural enemies. If you wipe out the natural enemies, the pest species may come back in much

Beneficial bugs: ladybug (above), ladybug larvae (below)

greater numbers—a phenomenon called resurgence. Timely and careful use of pesticides limits their impact on natural enemies. Opt for soft or narrow spectrum pesticides and apply at the lowest concentration recommended on the product instruction label.

Alternatives to pesticides, such as mechanical or physical practices, can also affect natural enemies. Traps, barriers, screens and other physical methods may reduce or inhibit natural enemies. The use of steam or other temperature-related management practices may reduce natural enemy populations. To offset some of these potential impacts, alter the time or duration of the practices to allow natural enemies to re-colonize or escape the threat. Alternatively, apply the measure when the target pest is most vulnerable and not when natural enemies are.

5. Impact of Maintenance and Cultivar Selection. Many maintenance and cultural practices directly affect pest and natural enemy performance. Excessive fertilization promotes succulent growth, resulting in rapid pest build-up, which in turn may lead to pest species populations that are too large for the natural enemies to control. By setting the blades higher on your lawn mower, you will reduce pest problems by providing a refuge for natural enemies. Selecting resistant cultivars will help suppress disease and keep pests at levels with which natural enemies can cope.

Consider that almost any action taken will have an impact on the plant, its pests and their natural enemies. A good gardener observes what these impacts are and adjusts accordingly.

The garden and yard are every bit as complex and vibrant as any natural area. Protecting your yard and garden is a challenging but rewarding task. To best prevent, reduce or eliminate pests, an integrated management approach is warranted. The objective is to obtain a balanced and healthy landscape ecosystem that will ensure long-term plant health. You don't have to eliminate pests, but instead reduce stress of any sort to the plants and maintain individual pests at levels below an injurious or economic threshold. All sorts of pests are present at all times, whether in the soil, on the plant or in surrounding areas; therefore, a program based on eradication is not sustainable and rarely, if ever, achievable. An integrated pest management program can be used successfully to maintain a healthy ecosystem.

Pesticides

Synthetic pesticides are a relatively recent innovation in pest management. Inorganic chemicals such as sulphur and arsenicals have been used for centuries, but synthetic organic chemicals have only been used since the middle of the 20th century. Because of their ease of use and effectiveness in areas where there were no inorganic pesticides owing to worker safety or phytotoxic (harmful to plants) effects, synthetic chemical pesticides were quickly and widely adopted.

There are, arguably, some advantages to using pesticides. They come in handy when all else fails, but they need to be used sparingly and carefully. Pesticides really reduce the amount of effort required when compared to manual weeding. They provide rapid remedial action and typically do not require detailed knowledge of plant and pest biology. But most commonly, gardeners remark that pesticides provide a relatively predictable level of control.

There are three main types of pesticides: *inorganic chemicals, organic chemicals* and *biopesticides*. There may be some confusion surrounding the definition of organic and inorganic pesticides. Inorganic pesticides contain elements such as sulphur, arsenic or mercury. "Organic" is a term applied to any compound that is carbon-based. Therefore, many of the synthetic pesticides in use today, such as organophosphates, chlorinated hydrocarbons and carbamates, are organic chemicals. Organically certified pesticides, on the other hand, are pesticides of organic, inorganic or biological origin that have been evaluated by a regulatory body and are "certified" to meet the standards of that body for use in organic agricultural production.

Biopesticides are pesticides that are made up of or are derived from living organisms. Examples include living systems such as bacteria (*Bacillus thuringiensis* var. *kurstaki* [B.t.k.] for use against caterpillars), fungi (*Streptomyces griseoviridis* for protection of plant roots from root rot), predatory nematodes (*Steinernema* and *Heterorhabditis* spp. for use against white grubs in lawns or root weevil larvae), fermentation products (isolated proteins from *Bacillus thuringiensis* or *Saccharopolyspora spinosa*) and botanicals (pyrethrum from flowers of the pyrethrum daisy, rotenone from roots of tropical legumes such as *Lonchocarpus* and *Derris*, nicotine from tobacco, sabadilla from the seeds of a tropical lily plant and azadirachtin or "neem" from leaves and seeds of the neem tree).

Regardless of whether a product is referred to or labelled as "conventional" or "organically certified," it is still a chemical. Make sure you use it according to the label instructions and only when absolutely necessary. Have you taken steps to promote a healthy plant that can compensate for insect attack? Can you tolerate a little damage to your plants and let the pests live? Have you tried alternatives to chemical insecticides, such as selecting resistant cultivars, mulches, pruning or hand picking? Applying a pesticide is usually considered to be a last resort.

There are many different kinds of insecticides, including compounds that attack the nervous, respiratory or digestive systems, disrupt chitin (a component of the hard outer shell)

Dill with sunflowers and others

synthesis or development, and cause physical damage to the surface wax layer or thin cuticle. The active ingredient, the chemical that causes the harm, can be the same in many different brands of insecticide. Read the product label to determine the active ingredient and help you decide which product to use to ensure insecticide resistance does not occur.

An insect is considered resistant to a pesticide if the insect has the ability to prevent entry of the chemical, can rapidly bind up or excrete the poison, or has changed the nature of the site of action of the poison such that the poison no longer has any effect. When this happens, the insecticide has less and less impact. One strategy to avoid selecting for resistant members of a pest population is to rotate among insecticides that have different modes of action, that is, target different sites or systems in the insect. Be careful though: different active ingredients can have the same mode of action.

Chief among the disadvantages to pesticide use are what are called non-target effects. A responsible gardener will take great care in selecting the products he or she uses. How specific a pesticide is has a bearing on how damaging it can be to the environment. In general, the more specific the action of the product, the fewer non-target organisms will be affected. More discriminating pesticides, such as insect growth regulators, interfere with how an insect moults. These pesticides are specifically targeted to insects, although some other arthropods can also be affected. Some insecticides affect only a narrow range of insects. B.t.k., for example, only affects caterpillars.

Conversely, the less specific the product, the more collateral damage there is, with potentially toxic effects to the applicator or bystanders. If a product kills indiscriminately, there is the potential for toxic effects to humans—the weakness of many of the conventional insecticides such as organophosphates is that they are nerve poisons; they affect insect and human alike. Toxicity to the user is a primary health concern. Residues on plants and vegetables can affect not only the applicator but also anyone who comes in contact with the product. The chemicals may move outside of your yard and into ground or surface water or into the air. They can also move up the food chain in a process called bioaccumulation. Pesticide residues may accumulate on food and ornamentals, posing a risk to you, your family and your pets. However, if used according to the label instructions, the risk of exposure to residues should be minimal.

Active Ingredients and Modes of Action

Active Ingredient	Mode of Action	Notes
Traditional Synthetic Insecticides		
Organophosphate, e.g., malathion	Nerve poison, Ach (short for acetylcholinesterase) inhibitor	Mildly persistent, broad spectrum, toxic to vertebrates
Carbamate, e.g., carbaryl	Nerve poison, Ach inhibitor	Broad spectrum, not as toxic to vertebrates
Pyrethroids, e.g., deltamethrin	Nerve poison, sodium channel inhibitor	Low persistence, highly toxic to aquatic organisms
Organotins	Affects energy production	Specific for mites
Neonicotinoids, e.g., imidacloprid	Nerve poison, Ach inhibitor	More specific for insects therefore less toxicity to humans
Biological Insecticides – isolated from micro-organisms		
Bacillus thuringiensis	Stomach poison	Toxin derived from a soil bacteria, specific for caterpillars (B.t.k.) or flies (B.t.i.)
Spinosad	Nerve poison, Ach inhibitor	Derived from a soil fungus
Avermectin	Nerve poison, chloride channel activator	Derived from a soil bacteria
Growth/Development Regulators		
Chitin synthesis inhibitors	Block production of chitin	Slow acting, non-toxic to humans but toxic to other invertebrates (e.g., shellfish)
Insect Growth Regulator	Block action of developmental hormones, check for specific hormone blocked	Specific to insects
Botanicals – isolated from plant material		
Pyrethrum	Nerve poison, sodium channel modifier	Very short persistence
Rotenone	Affects energy production	From Derris and Lonchocarpus, highly toxic to fish
Nicotine	Nerve poison, Ach inhibitor	From tobacco, highly toxic to mammals
Limonene	Nerve poison, Ach inhibitor	From citrus, non-toxic to mammals
Azadiractin	Block action of developmental hormones	From Neem, non-toxic to mammals
Oils and Others		
Mineral oil	Suffocation	Dormant oils can harm plants, summer oils less harmful to plants
Sulphur	Contact poison	Effective against mites
Boric acid	Contact poison	Do not allow contact with skin
Diatomaceous earth	Abrasive	Do not inhale
Potassium salts of fatty acids, e.g., insecticidal soap	Desiccation, strips surface wax off insect	Non-toxic to mammals, most effective on soft-bodied insects

Improper use of pesticides can create pest problems such as resistance, resurgence or secondary pests. Prolonged use of the same active ingredient (the poison that is responsible for killing the insect) regardless of manufacturer or formulation (powder, spray) often results in the insect developing resistance to the product. When you spray an insecticide, it kills most of the insects that are susceptible to the poison. Insects that have a pre-existing mutation that allows them to survive the poison live on to reproduce. This phenomenon results in a pest population that has an increasing number of individuals that are no longer harmed by the poison, rendering the poison less and less effective as a management tool. Eventually you might just as well hit the insects with the insecticide container for all the harm it does to the resistant pests.

An insecticide's effect on non-target organisms can have a huge impact on beneficial insects and other organisms, reducing their ability to suppress pest insects. The result may be a situation in which the pest resurges to a level much higher than it was before you applied the insecticide. In this case, you may be irrevocably tied to the pesticide treadmill, where no other option will suffice unless you are willing to allow the pest to build up until it crashes and something resembling normality returns (i.e., natural enemies return to your yard and resume their role as guardians).

Remember that your overall goal should be to limit or eliminate the use of insecticides—they should be used only as a last resort. Responsible use of pesticides (i.e., only when necessary, least toxic or most narrowly targeted compounds, and applied only when and where the pest is doing damage) will result in less harm to the environment and you, and will also lead to the preservation of the community of natural enemies in your yard.

A Final Word

Overall, bugs are pretty amazing creatures! They have all sorts of adaptations that make them successful. If we learn to understand them, we can learn to appreciate them in our gardens. The more we know about bugs, the better we can prevent or manage outbreaks. To do this, we need to understand what groups they come from. Are they arthropods, annelids or molluscs? How do they function? Are they beneficial or pests? If they are pests, what are they harming?

This book is a tool to help you identify bugs and understand them better. Knowing their anatomy helps us understand how they live. It can give us clues on where to find them and how to control them, if need be. It can also give us clues on how to attract them and create favourable habitats. Learning about Integrated Pest Management will help you analyze potential pest problems and decide whether to control the pests or leave them alone. The key is creating a place where bug diversity is high and balanced so that the opportunity for pest outbreaks is limited. A garden with a great diversity of insects is a wonderful and healthy place.

Garden Bug Directory

Meadowhawks & Whiteface Dragonflies

Leucorrhinia spp., *Sympetrum* spp.

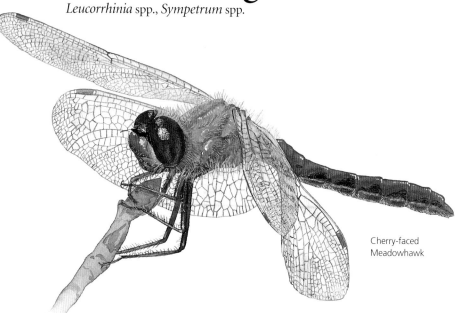

Cherry-faced
Meadowhawk

Meadowhawks and whitefaces are beautiful, beneficial predators of many smaller insects, especially pests such as mosquitoes. These small, bright red or yellow dragonflies are hard to miss when they are perched on flowers or skimming over a flowerbed and are welcome additions to any garden. The two genera are easy to tell apart.

Whitefaces, as their name suggests, have white faces, whereas meadowhawks do not. Some common species found across BC include the Cherry-faced Meadowhawk *(S. internum)*, Variegated Meadowhawk *(S. corruptum)*, Saffron-winged Meadowhawk *(S. costiferum)*, Black Meadowhawk *(S. danae)*, Red-waisted Whiteface *(L. proxima)* and the Hudsonian Whiteface *(L. hudsonica)*.

ID: *Adult:* long, narrow body marked with red, black or yellow, and wide, double wings. *Nymph:* small and brownish with big eyes and retractable mandible; looks alien-like but resemble wingless dragonfly with compressed abdomen; tiny, bud-like wings protrude slightly from thorax.
Size: *Adult:* 3–4 cm. *Nymph:* variable, but no larger than about 3 cm.

Habitat and Range: sunny openings in gardens, often near ponds or slow streams.
Scouting: Adults are often observed either perched in the garden or cruising for prey. Whitefaces are present in gardens in spring, whereas meadowhawks appear much later, in summer. Both genera can survive until the first hard frost.

Black Meadowhawk

Dragonflies and damselflies undergo incomplete metamorphosis during their lifetime. Females lay eggs in the vegetation or soil around a pond. Female whitefaces often deposit eggs in floating mats of vegetation, while many meadowhawks drop or fling their eggs into emergent vegetation. The nymphs of all dragonflies and damselflies are aquatic and need wetlands to complete their life cycle. Nymphs later hatch from these eggs and begin to feed on anything that is smaller than them. This includes free-swimming insects such as mosquito larvae, other dragonflies and damselfly nymphs and, as the dragonfly nymphs get bigger, sometimes even tadpoles.

The nymphs go through a number of moults, growing and changing a little with each one. This stage can last anywhere from several weeks to several years depending on the species of damselfly or dragonfly.

How to Attract: If you live close enough to a waterbody, you may not have to do anything to attract dragonflies. If you don't have a natural wetland nearby, you can build a dragonfly pond. It should be about 6 metres across and at least 60 centimetres deep in the centre, with shallow edges and a few flat rocks along the edge. Also, support the protection of riparian areas in your neighbourhood.

Meadowhawks & Whiteface Dragonflies (continued)

Hudsonian Whiteface

One study revealed that on average, one adult female meadowhawk eats about 14 percent of its body weight each day. That is the equivalent of about six mosquitoes, so an entire squadron can devour hundreds every day.

Once nymphs mature, they climb out of the waterbody onto emergent vegetation and begin a process called transformation, in which they turn into adults. The nymphs swallow air continuously and split their larval skin, slowly rising out of their shells, which are known as exuviae. Once the nymphs are out, their new body hardens and their wings inflate.

This newly hatched individual, also known as a teneral, feeds until it is sexually mature. This is when adults are seen in gardens, especially away from wetlands. Sexually mature adults later return to the shorelines, patrolling for a mate. Males are often seen guarding their small territories when they are courting females. Mating pairs can be observed flying in tandem, though some species perch while mating. The males also stay nearby or, in some cases, remain connected to the females while the females lay their eggs. Adults live for only a few months.

Dragonflies have many predators. Eggs are attacked by many foraging critters such as mice, birds and beetles, and are even parasitized by wasps. Birds and other dragonflies prey on adults, especially tenerals. It is also common to see adults with mites attached to their bodies. These red mites drink the dragonfly's blood.

Mosaic Darners

Aeshna spp.

Variable Darner

One of the swiftest insects on the planet, a dragonfly can reach speeds of up to 34 kilometres per hour as it cruises through our gardens. This voracious predator eats any smaller insect, especially flies. Horseflies are often victims of darners. On cool mornings, darners can be seen basking on fences or tree trunks and can be observed closely as they warm their muscles before their daily activities. At times, I've had a couple of darners circling me, grabbing a pesky horsefly or two. Darners occasionally land on a person's chest or shoulder thinking it is a nice place to bask in the sun. Common species seen in our gardens include the Lake Darner (*A. eremita*), Variable Darner (*A. interrupta*), Shadow Darner (*A. umbrosa*) and Sedge Darner (*A. juncea*).

Darners require wetlands to complete their life cycle but, unlike many other dragonflies, can travel far from them. Females use their ovipositor to insert their eggs into the vegetation or soil around a pond. In ponds without fish, *Aeshna* nymphs are at the top of the food chain, eating everything within reach. *Aeshna* nymphs and nymphs of the genus *Anax* have long slender abdomens. Other genera's nymphs tend to be stouter.

ID: *Adult:* large, swift dragonflies with long, narrow, blue or green patterned body; wide double wings; face has dark T-shaped spot called a "T-spot." *Nymph:* large and brownish with big eyes and retractable mandible; looks alien-like, but resembles wingless dragonfly with compressed abdomen; tiny, bud-like wings protrude slightly from thorax.

Size: *Adult:* 7–8 cm. *Nymph:* variable, but no larger than about 5–6 cm.

Habitat and Range: sunny openings in gardens, often near ponds or slow streams throughout British Columbia.

Scouting: Darners are often observed perched on fence posts, higher up on tree trunks or even on garage walls. They are also often seen cruising over gardens in search of prey.

How to Attract: If you live close enough to a waterbody, you may not have to do anything to attract these gorgeous predators. Otherwise, consider constructing a dragonfly pond.

Spreadwings

Lestes spp.

Common Spreadwing

When perched, it holds its wings half spread, hence its name. Unlike its bigger relatives the dragonflies, this little guy hunts within the garden vegetation rather than patrolling for prey above the garden canopy. It is beneficial to gardeners because it preys on insect pests such as grasshopper nymphs and lygus bugs. The commonly observed species in British Columbia are the Common

The spreadwing is one of our most elegant damselflies and is often observed resting among garden vegetation. The spreadwing can be easily separated from other garden damselflies by the position of its wings.

ID: *Adult:* small dragonfly-like insect with slender, delicate, blue or brown body with metallic emerald or bronze markings on thorax and along abdomen; 2 pairs of narrow wings, held half spread when resting. *Nymph:* small, slender and brownish with big eyes, retractable mandible and feather-like gills at end of abdomen; looks alien-like but

resembles wingless damselfly with elongated abdomen; tiny, bud-like wings protrude slightly from thorax.

Size: *Adult:* approximately 4 cm. *Nymph:* variable, but no larger than about 4 cm.

Habitat and Range: throughout the province, in gardens near wetlands.

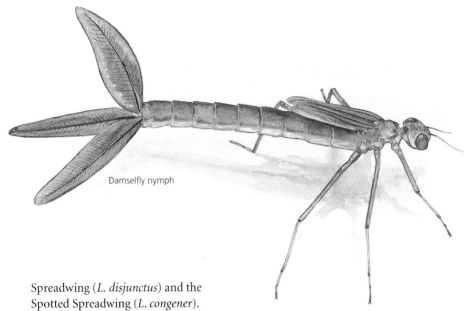

Damselfly nymph

Spreadwing (*L. disjunctus*) and the Spotted Spreadwing (*L. congener*).

Spreadwings court their mates and females lay their eggs in shallow water around the borders of small ponds. Spreadwing nymphs have the unique ability of being able to live in temporary ponds with high salinity. This adaptation allows damselfly eggs to survive through drought years when these ponds are absent. When the water returns a year or two later, from either snowmelt or heavy rains, the eggs hatch. However, if these dried up areas are cultivated or disturbed, the eggs are often killed, and spreadwing populations can be decimated. The protection of riparian areas during droughts is vital to this species' survival.

A favourite environment of spreadwings

Scouting: If your garden is by a wetland, you may find these damselflies among shoreline vegetation and in bordering garden plants. They especially like wet sedge meadows.

How to Attract: Avoid mowing, spraying or clearing the native sedges and cattails near bodies of water. If you do not have a wetland, you can construct one. (see p. 43).

Bluets

Coenagrion spp., *Enallagma* spp.

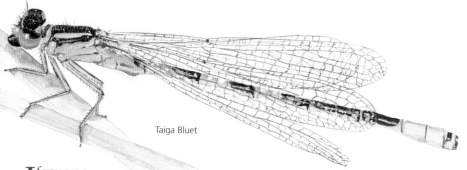

Taiga Bluet

If you see a slender, blue insect zipping through your garden, it is probably a bluet. This mighty hunter is often observed perched among the flowers, munching on little flies. The bluet is considered a typical damselfly; it perches with its wings held over its back. Some of our common species are the Taiga Bluet (*C. resolutum*), the Prairie Bluet (*C. angulatum*), the Boreal Bluet (*E. boreale*) and the Northern Bluet (*E. cyathigerum*).

The bluet inhabits areas bordering wetlands. It inserts its eggs into emergent plant tissue. Nymphs hatch within four weeks. Most Odonata nymphs have a retractable mandible (labium) they use to snatch prey. Nymphs sit motionless and ambush prey, which are grabbed with the labium. I suspect that the makers of the movie *Alien* must have observed this remarkable behaviour. Damselfly nymphs can be easily separated from dragonfly nymphs because they have external feather-like gills at the end of their abdomens. The nymphs swim differently than dragonfly nymphs, basically wiggling their bodies and using the gills to propel them through the water. Often, all nymphs complete their transformation at about the same time. It's possible, in some years, for your yard to come alive with thousands of damselflies and when this happens the birds rush in to fill their beaks.

ID: *Adult:* small dragonfly-like insects with slender, delicate, blue body and black markings on thorax and abdomen; 2 pairs of narrow wings, held over back when resting. *Nymph:* small, slender and brownish with big eyes, retractable mandible and feather-like gills at end of abdomen; looks alien-like but resembles wingless damselfly with elongated abdomen; tiny, bud-like wings protrude slightly from thorax.

Size: *Adult:* approximately 3.5 cm. *Nymph:* variable, but no larger than about 4 cm.

Habitat and Range: throughout the province along shorelines of wetlands that have plenty of emergent vegetation such as sedges and cattails.

Scouting: Look in the vegetation along shorelines and among the garden plants in gardens that border wetlands.

How to Attract: Avoid mowing, spraying or clearing the bordering native sedges and cattails near a body of water. If you do not have a wetland, you can construct one (see p. 43).

Grasshoppers

Camnula pellucida, Melanoplus spp.

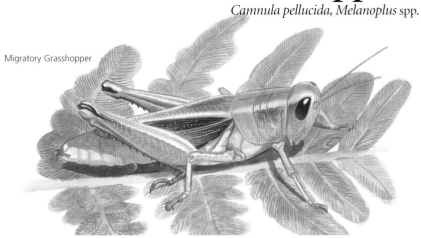

Migratory Grasshopper

All grasshoppers chew plant material and are capable of stripping plants bare. Common British Columbia grasshoppers include the Clear-winged Grasshopper *(C. pellucida)*, which is mainly a grass feeder, preferring Kentucky bluegrass; the Two-striped Grasshopper *(M. bivittatus)*, which feeds on grasses and broad-leaved plants including trees and shrubs; and Packard's Grasshopper *(M. packardii)*, which prefers herbs over grasses. The Migratory Grasshopper *(M. sanguinipes)* is one of our most successful species and is found throughout our region. It feeds on a variety of things and favours weedy fields, cropland, pastures and gardens—basically anywhere that has grass and weeds growing together.

Grasshoppers produce one generation per year. The eggs are laid in the soil beginning in late July and continuing into autumn. They overwinter in the soil and hatch from late April to late June. Hatching correlates with soil temperature and occurs after the soil containing the eggs accumulates 200 hours of 15 to 16° C temperatures. The young progress through five to six nymphal instars in 35 to 55 days (depending on species and temperature) before becoming adults. They are capable of dispersing great distances, even up to 1000 kilometres!

ID: *Adult:* dark brown to green or light yellow; biting/chewing mouthparts; enlarged hind legs adapted for jumping. *Nymph:* miniature representatives of the adult but lacks developed wings.

Size: *Adult:* up to 4 cm. *Nymph:* 5 mm.

Habitat and Range: found throughout the province in ditches, pastures and crop fields.

Scouting: Grasshopper populations increase through spring and peak in July and August, declining until the killing frosts of autumn. They are particularly abundant in dry years.

Cultural/Physical Control: Drenching early season rains during the time of egg hatch have the most damaging effect on grasshopper populations. Turn over soil in autumn to expose deeply buried eggs.

Biological Control: Beetles, small mammals and birds prey on grasshoppers, and velvet mites, ground beetles, rove beetles, bee flies and immature blister beetles eat grasshopper eggs. Nymphs are susceptible to parasitism by a tachinid fly and to several natural fungal diseases.

Field Crickets

Gryllus spp.

Spring Field Cricket

The Spring Field Cricket (*G. veletis*) and the Fall Field Cricket (*G. pennsylvanicus*) can occasionally become problems in the garden, feeding on a variety of plants including tomato foliage and fruit. Feeding is restricted to nighttime; field crickets seek shelter under vegetation and debris during the day. They may move in from weedy areas in August and September and occasionally enter people's homes to feed on natural fibres such as cotton or wool and synthetics.

Field crickets produce one generation per year. The eggs are laid in damp soil in autumn, where they overwinter and hatch in May. The nymphs mature through July and August, moulting eight or nine times.

Field crickets are considered to be "right-handed" because they fold their right wing on top of the left wing.

ID: *Adult:* predominantly shiny black, but may have brown at wing base; antennae as long or longer than body; 2 sensory appendages (cerci) arise from posterior abdomen; female has long ovipositor. *Nymph:* similar to adult but smaller

Size: *Adult:* 2 cm. *Nymph:* 0.5–2 cm.

Habitat and Range: can be found over most of southern BC in wild grassy or weedy areas.

Scouting: Field crickets are nocturnal, so catching sight of these elusive creatures is difficult. Instead, listen for the males' alluring mating call as they chirp for females by rubbing their forewings together.

Cultural/Physical Control: Field crickets are considered beneficial insects because they feed on grasshopper eggs and moth and fly pupae. However, should you feel the need to control cricket populations, remove debris that they can seek refuge under during the day. To prevent them from entering into your house, ensure weather stripping under doors and screens of windows is intact.

Biological Control: A variety of predators prey on crickets, including many species of birds.

Ambush Bug

Phymata erosa

These small bugs are ferocious hunters. They lie in wait in the flowers of weeds and garden vegetation for passing insects, which they grasp with their large, pincer-like front legs. They pierce their prey with their mouthparts and inject a fluid that paralyses it and liquefies its insides, then suck out the contents. Although they prey on some insect pests, they can do harm by consuming pollinators such as honey bees, bumble bees, butterflies, flies and wasps. Beekeepers consider them a damaging pest.

Ambush Bugs are true bugs, members of the family Phymatidae. Adults are commonly seen feeding and mating in late summer and early fall, often on goldenrod, daisies or sunflowers. Eggs overwinter and hatch in early spring. Nymphs go through five instars and hunt and feed like the adults. There is one generation per year.

ID: *Adult:* small, flat bug with large, pincer-like front legs; triangular-shaped abdomen with a wide, yellowish flare on either side; brown markings on head, thoracic shield and abdomen. *Nymph:* oval, almost triangular abdomen; colourless to yellowish green.

Size: *Adult:* 10–12 mm. *Nymph:* 1–6 mm.

Habitat and Range: throughout southern BC in gardens, meadows and weedy areas.

Scouting: Adults can be found in flowers in late summer and early fall. They are well camouflaged and lie quite still, so can be hard to spot unless they're feeding on prey.

Cultural/Physical Control: Controls are not usually necessary in a garden or landscape unless populations are very high. If there is one flower they really go for, consider growing something else to reduce the impact on pollinating bees.

Biological Control: None warranted.

Damsel Bugs

Nabicula spp., *Nabis* spp.

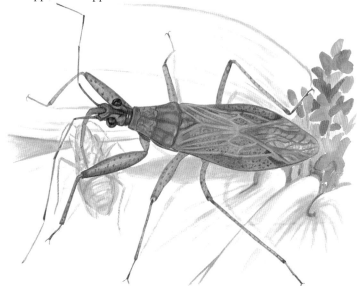

Damsel bugs are beneficial predators that feed on meadow spittlebugs, tarnished plant bugs, leaf beetle eggs and larvae, caterpillar eggs and larvae, leafhoppers, aphids, spider mites and sawflies. The most common damsel bugs found in BC are in the genera *Nabis* and *Nabicula*.

Adult damsel bugs overwinter in leaf litter or anywhere they can find protection from the elements. In spring, they emerge to mate and lay eggs in plant tissue. There are five nymphal instars lasting approximately 8 to 12 days each. There is usually only one generation per year with peak abundance later in the summer, around July and August. They are among the last predators to colonize pest infestations. However, evidence suggests that these beneficial bugs have a major impact on aphids and other crop pests.

Although primarily a predator, damsel bugs will feed on plant tissue if no other food source is available, though the damage is negligible. If they are really starved, they will eat each other!

ID: *Adult:* has raptorial forelegs adapted to grasping prey. *Nabis* spp.: slender, elongate, light brown to yellowish bug with protruding eyes. *Nabicula* spp.: shiny black body is more bulbous toward rear than *Nabis* spp. and wings are smaller. *Nymph:* resembles adult but lacks wings.

Size: Adult: 5–11 mm. Nymph: 3–7 mm.

Habitat and Range: widespread across the province; common in field crops, orchards, urban landscapes and gardens.

Scouting: You can often find these bugs in the lawn or garden and actively stalking prey in shrubs and trees.

Cultural/Physical Control: Reduce or eliminate the use of insecticides to protect this beneficial insect. Maintain a garden of diverse plantings to encourage colonization by damsel bugs.

How To Attract: Don't use insecticides and maintain a garden of diverse plantings.

Plant Bugs

Lygus spp.

L ygus ssp. bugs pierce and suck plant fluids from leaves, fruit and stems. Common British Columbia lygus bugs include *L. shulli* and *L. elisus*, the Western Tarnished Plant Bug *(L. hesperus)* and the Tarnished Plant Bug *(L. lineolaris)*. There are many other plant bugs, but these are the most commonly encountered and the most damaging.

Tarnished Plant Bug

L. hesperus and *L. lineolaris* feed on conifers in nurseries, especially pines and Douglas-fir. They suck plant juices from the terminal shoot (leader) causing the tree to have a shepherd's crook at the top, or a "bushy top" with multiple leaders. They also feed on new buds, causing them to drop. Other species feed on many different vegetables and flowers, including greenhouse crops.

Lygus bugs overwinter as adults in leaf litter and other protected habitats. The adults emerge in spring to feed on weeds or alfalfa, mate and then move into crops and emerging garden plants. Once in the new food, the females lay their eggs into plant tissue. There are five nymphal instars that develop over the course of the summer with adults active in August. Most species have only one generation per year.

Also Known As: Lygus Bugs

ID: *Adult:* Tarnished Plant Bug: characterized by overall bronze appearance; white triangle just behind pronotum or shoulders, white markings on elytra and white wing tips showing on back. Western Tarnished Plant Bug: similar but greenish or reddish brown overall; white triangle behind pronotum but few or no other white markings. *Nymph:* green overall; wingless early, with developing wingbuds in later instars; about the size and shape of an aphid but moves very rapidly.

Size: *Adult:* 3–5 mm. *Nymph:* 1–3 mm.

Habitat and Range: found everywhere on trees, shrubs, flowers and vegetables. Tarnished Plant Bug: primarily in the Interior.

Western Tarnished Plant Bug and other *Lygus* species: primarily coastal.

Scouting: Common symptoms of plant bug feeding include yellowing of leaves; "cat-facing" in strawberries; small, sunken feeding wounds or stippling on vegetables and fruit; blossom, bud or fruit drop; twisting and distortion of conifer leaders and needles.

Cultural/Physical Control: Remove weeds early in the season to deprive plant bugs of food. Remove plant bugs with repeated applications of a strong jet of water.

Biological Control: There are many generalist predators that attack plant bugs. Therefore, maintaining a diverse landscape will conserve and possibly attract beneficial insects to your yard to suppress plant bugs.

Stink Bugs

Acrosternum hilare, Brochymena spp., *Chlorochroa* spp., *Elasmucha lateralis*

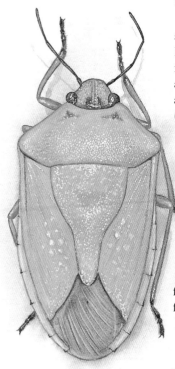

Say's Stink Bug

The Green Stink Bug (*A. hilare*) is common on leaves, fruit and flowers of trees and shrubs across British Columbia. The Say's Stink Bug (*C. sayi*) is the largest stink bug in BC and feeds on many different trees and shrubs as an adult, but nymphs will also feed on tomatoes and other vegetables. The Uhler's Stink Bug (*C. uhleri*) feeds on juniper. The Shield Bug (*E. lateralis*) feeds mainly on birch and willow. The Rough Plant Bug (*Brochymena* spp.) is one of the most common stink bugs in BC, but its dark brown colour makes it less noticeable than the green bugs.

Stink bugs overwinter as adults in sheltered areas, emerging in spring to lay barrel-shaped eggs in neat rows on the underside of leaves of weeds, trees and shrubs. The Rough Plant Bug can often be found under the bark of dead trees. Adult female stink bugs tend over the eggs until they hatch, ensuring maximal survival of their broods. The nymphs typically feed on weeds during their five nymphal instars before moving on to feed on leaves of shrubs and trees as adults. There is only one generation of stink bugs per year.

ID: *Adult:* Green, Say's and Uhler's stink bugs: green with broad shoulders and large triangular scutellum. Shield Bug: yellowish brown body. Rough Plant Bug: dark brown, mottled body. *Nymph:* Green, Say's and Uhler's stink bugs: light-coloured with black markings, becoming increasingly green in later instars. *E. lateralis:* newly emerged nymphs are bright red, becoming increasingly green in later instars. *Brochymena* spp.: mottled brown with red markings on back and legs.

Size: *Adult:* 8–12 mm. *Nymph:* 3–8 mm.

Habitat and Range: wooded areas and treed landscapes; occasionally in vegetable or flower gardens.

Scouting: The piercing/sucking feeding behaviour results in yellowing or mottling of leaves, sometimes resulting in uneven bumpiness. Fruit and flower buds are also attacked. Tomatoes can look like they were stabbed, leaving a dark pinprick surrounded by a yellow or light green halo (lygus bug nymphs cause identical injury).

Cultural/Physical Control: These insects rarely have high enough population densities to cause excessive damage. Overall plant health and elimination of weeds helps to reduce their impact. Pressure sprays of water are effective for dislodging adults from trees.

Biological Control: Generalist predators, including birds, will feed on the nymphs and adults. There are parasitoids that attack stink bug eggs. Look for infested eggs, which tend to be black instead of their natural green.

Lace Bugs

Corythucha spp., *Stephantitis* spp., *Gargaphia solani*

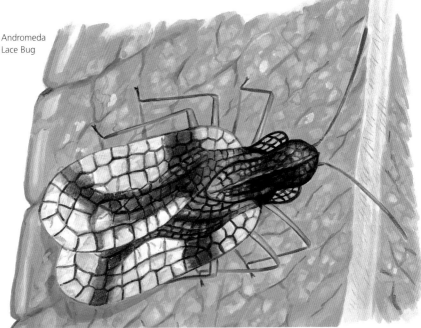

Andromeda
Lace Bug

Lace bugs are so called because of their broad, lacy wing covers. British Columbia has several species of lace bug, but some of the most common are the Rhododendron Lace Bug (*S. rhododendri*) and the Azalea Lace Bug (*S. pyrioides*), both of which feed on rhododendron, azalea and mountain laurel, and the Andromeda Lace Bug (*S. takeyai*), a recent introduction, which feeds on *Pieris* (andromeda). The Western Willow Lace Bug (*C. salicata*) and other *Corythucha* species feed on a wide range of broadleaf trees and woody ornamentals including sycamore, chokecherry, alder, poplar and birch as well as willow. The Eggplant Lace Bug (*Gargaphia solani*) has also been found in BC and feeds on eggplant, tomato, potato, sunflower and horsenettle.

Lace bugs are members of the family Tingidae. Like all true bugs, they have

Identification: *Adult:* small, flat bug with lace-like wing covers. *Nymph:* small, spiny, black or dark-coloured bug; often feeds in groups.

Size: *Adult:* 3–3.5 mm. *Nymph:* 1–2 mm.

Habitat and Range: throughout BC.

Scouting: Numerous small, white or yellow flecks on leaves are usually the first sign of lace bugs. Cast skins and dark, shiny, varnish-like excrement can be seen on the underside of the leaves, especially along the veins. Adults and nymphs can be found on the underside of leaves from April to early September. On evergreen hosts, leaf feeding is often apparent on older leaves long after the bugs are gone. Eggplant Lace Bugs are similar, but produce larger brown spots on leaves.

Cultural/Physical Control: Hose nymphs off leaves with a strong jet of water in spring.

Lace Bugs (continued)

The female Eggplant Lace Bug is the "soccer mom" of the bug world. She guards her eggs and nymphs, herding the whole colony around the leaf to feed until they become adults, which usually takes about 10 days.

sucking mouthparts. Both adults and nymphs puncture the underside of leaves and suck plant juice. These feeding wounds appear as numerous, light-coloured flecks on the upper leaf surface. The damage is generally cosmetic, but high populations can cause leaves to dry, curl, yellow and drop. Severe infestations over a few years can lead to decline of shrubs and trees.

Lace bugs that attack evergreen broadleaf shrubs overwinter as eggs on leaves. Lace bugs that attack deciduous trees overwinter as adults under the bark. Most female lace bugs insert their eggs along a leaf vein and seal the hole with shiny, dark excrement, but the Eggplant Lace Bug deposits a circular mass of 100 to 200 eggs on the underside of the leaf. Eggs hatch in April or May, and the nymphs go through five instars (four for the Rhododendron Lace Bug). Adult populations generally peak in July. Most lace bugs have two generations per year and sometimes a third in late summer or early fall; the Eggplant Lace Bug has up to eight generations per year.

Biological Control: Lacewings as well as predatory mites and bugs attack lace bugs, but not usually in large enough numbers to prevent damage. Insecticidal soap will kill lace bugs if sprayed on the underside of leaves to contact them, and it is not damaging to beneficial predators and parasites. More than one application is usually needed.

Boxelder Bug
Boisea trivittatus, B. rubrolineata

The Boxelder Bug (*B. trivittatus*) is a piercing/sucking bug that causes lesions to leaves and seeds of box elder (also known as Manitoba maple). The Boxelder Bug is also known as the Eastern Boxelder Bug and occurs across North America. The Western Boxelder Bug (*B. rubrolineata*), which is very similar, occurs from British Columbia south to California and east to Texas, and feeds primarily on maples.

The Boxelder Bug overwinters as an adult, often aggregating in large numbers in houses. This behaviour may be why some people dislike this insect. It can be unnerving to have tens or hundreds of these bugs appear in your home in the middle of winter. Normally, the adult overwinters in a sheltered area outside, emerging in spring, when the female lays her rusty red eggs on leaves of the Manitoba maple. The nymph undergoes five instars, feeding on the underside of leaves and on developing seeds. The adult is present from July onward. There may be one or two generations per year, depending on temperature.

Although related to plant bugs and stink bugs, this species does not have any scent glands and therefore does not use an offensive odour as a defensive mechanism.

ID: *Adult:* predominantly black with red outlining pronotum and basal half of wings; both species are very similar in appearance. *Nymph:* bright red with increasing amounts of black in later instars.

Size: *Adult:* 8–12 mm. *Nymph:* 3–8 mm.

Habitat and Range: Eastern Boxelder Bug: across Canada on Manitoba maple, occasionally on big-leaf maple or ash. Western Boxelder Bug: in British Columbia, primarily on maples.

Scouting: Nymphs and adults can be found on the underside of leaves or on seeds. Adults will often bask in sun-drenched areas, such as south-facing walls and fences.

Cultural/Physical Control: Damage to trees is negligible, but if it bothers you to have these bugs soaking up some sun in your garden, a jet of water will flush them from their reverie. If large numbers are entering your home to overwinter, ensure your house is "bug-tight" by sealing gaps and holes in window frames and screens, weather stripping around doors and any place utilities enter through the outer wall.

Biological Control: As with plant bugs, there are many generalist predators that attack the Boxelder Bug.

Minute Pirate Bug

Anthocoris spp., *Orius* spp.

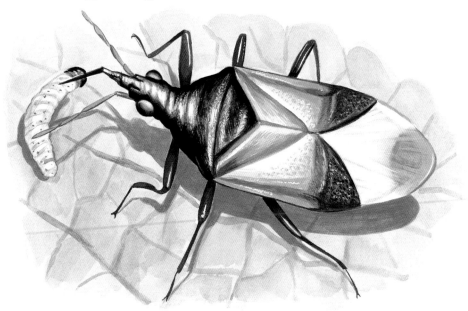

The Minute Pirate Bugs' family name, Anthocoridae, means "flower bug." These generalist predators have piercing/sucking mouthparts, but unlike damsel bugs, they do not have raptorial forelegs for grasping their prey. The most common pirate bugs in British Columbia belong to the genus *Orius*.

Adults overwinter in leaf litter, emerging in early spring to mate. Pirate bugs are among the earliest of the predators to emerge in spring. Eggs are laid in plant material but do not cause any lasting harm. Nymphs go through five instars in approximately 20 days under warm conditions. There can be as many as four generations in a season.

ID: *Adult:* predominantly black; moderately elongate with white markings at base and tips of wings. *Nymph:* reddish brown to yellowish; has more bulbous abdomen than adult, making it pear-shaped.

Size: *Adult:* 2–5 mm. *Nymph:* 1–2 mm.

Habitat and Range: widespread across the province in grasses, flowers, vegetables, trees and shrubs.

Scouting: In early spring, pirate bugs are abundant in weeds and early emerging plants. They venture into your yard and garden as the season progresses. In the absence of prey, pirate bugs will feed on foliage and pollen but are not considered a problem for doing so. Being able to sustain themselves through periods of low prey numbers ensures their presence when troubling numbers of pests do arise. In the absence of prey, pirate bugs will feed on foliage or pollen to sustain themselves, but they more than make up for this minor damage by feeding on plant pests.

How to Attract: These little fellows feed on spider mite eggs, nymphs and adults; aphids; leaf beetle eggs; moth eggs and young caterpillars; thrips; and psyllids. Diversify the flowers available throughout the season to sustain pirate bug numbers.

Aphids

Aphis gossypii, Cinara spp., *Pemphigus* spp. and others

Giant Conifer Aphid

Generally, aphids can be found sucking plant juices from the growing tips and undersides of leaves or on the stems and roots. Almost every plant has an aphid that will feed on it. Many species transmit plant viruses. The most common aphid you will encounter is the Green Peach Aphid (*Myzus persicae*). It feeds on more than 200 species of herbaceous plants. The Potato Aphid (*Macrosiphum euphorbiae*), Melon Aphid (*A. gossypii*) and Foxglove Aphid (*Aulacorthum solani*) feed on a wide range of flowers, vegetables and weeds as well. The Honeysuckle Aphid (*Hyadaphis tartaricae*), Giant Conifer Aphid (*Cinara* spp.), Green Spruce Aphid (*Elatobium abietinum*), Common

ID: *Adult:* soft-bodied and pear shaped; can be winged or wingless; usually green but can be yellow, white, bronze, dark brown, black or pink; bears a pair of clubs called cornicles on posterior end. *Nymph:* identical to adult except smaller; if adult is winged, you will see wingbuds on nymph.

Size: *Adult:* 2–4 mm. *Nymph:* 1–2 mm.

Habitat and Range: common in grassy areas, on shrubs and in trees province-wide.

Scouting: Aphids prefer warm, humid conditions. Because of their preference for actively growing plant parts, they do the most damage to growing tips and new shoots in spring. The high level of nutrient drain caused by aphid feeding often distorts plant tissue, making it become curled, puckered or discoloured. Heavy infestations can cause a plant to lose vigour. Aphids excrete "honeydew," a sticky fluid that favours sooty mould development and may attract ants,

Aphids (continued)

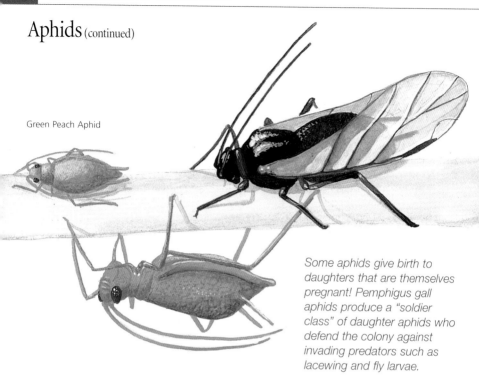

Green Peach Aphid

Some aphids give birth to daughters that are themselves pregnant! Pemphigus gall aphids produce a "soldier class" of daughter aphids who defend the colony against invading predators such as lacewing and fly larvae.

Blueberry Aphid (*Ericaphis fimbriata*) and Smoky-winged Poplar Aphid (*Chaitophorus populicola*) are all named for their food preference.

Some aphids have very complex life cycles, which involve more than one host plant species, migratory winged and stationary wingless forms, and summer asexual and autumn sexual generations. In summer, all aphids give birth to live young without mating. Some aphids, such as the Green Peach Aphid, reproduce asexually all summer long on

herbaceous hosts but produce males in autumn for sexual mating, resulting in an egg that overwinters on a woody host.

Pemphigus species form galls that persist all season long on the leaves and stems of poplar. During summer, the aphids leave the gall to feed on the roots of herbaceous plants such as wild mustard.

One common feature of aphids is their ability to rapidly increase in population, in extreme cases up to 12-fold within one week.

wasps and flies. Look at the underside of leaves, growing points and stem tips for aphid nymphs and the white, cast skins. Yellow sticky traps can be used to monitor winged adults.

Cultural/Physical Control: Because of the enormous potential for population growth, action should be taken upon first detection. Limit weeds that often serve as alternate hosts. Heavy rainfall or high winds dislodge aphids, so try using a hard spray of water

to wash aphids off. Soapy water acts like an insecticide. Hand pick or prune infested leaves or galls. Use sticky bands on the tree trunks to prevent ants from tending to aphids.

Biological Control: Many invertebrates feed on aphids, including ladybird beetles, hover fly larvae, lacewing larvae and midge larvae. Parasitic wasps can have a huge impact on aphid populations; if these wasps are active in your yard, you will see swollen, silvery, grey-brown parchment-like remains of aphids.

Cooley Spruce Gall Adelgid

Adelges cooleyi

The Cooley Spruce Gall Adelgid is one of a few woolly aphids and adelgids that feed on conifers. It resembles an aphid and feeds by piercing the plant and sucking out phloem sap. On white spruce, a gall results at the tip of new growth. The gall usually kills the new shoot and can persist for several years. Damage is rarely serious, but the galls can be unsightly, and persistent infestations can stunt growth.

A related species, the Balsam Woolly Adelgid (*A. piceae*), attacks balsam fir and other true fir (*Abies* spp.). It has been found in south-coastal BC. As a result, all *Abies* species must be inspected and grown under permit, and movement of plants is restricted.

Some woolly aphids may live on only one host; other species require two hosts to complete their life cycle. The Cooley Spruce Gall Adelgid alternates between white spruce and Douglas-fir, or it can survive on either host alone. A free-living stage that feeds on the lower surface of Douglas-fir needles in tufts of white wool begins the cycle. Winged and wingless forms develop, with the wingless form producing long strands of wax, referred to as flocculence. Winged forms migrate in summer to white spruce to lay eggs that develop into wingless males and females. These aphids mate and lay eggs at the base of old bud scales. Once the eggs hatch, the nymphs feed for a while and then move to the stem below a bud to overwinter. In spring, the awakening nymphs feed, which spurs the plant to produce a gall. The overwintered females lay a new batch of eggs and the hatching nymphs enter the developing gall to feed in relative safety. Winged females emerge from the galls later in summer to fly back to Douglas-fir to lay eggs, the nymphs of which hatch out to overwinter and begin the cycle again

ID: *Adult:* soft-bodied; winged or wingless; black overall; wingless adult is covered in white waxy material. *Nymph:* also soft-bodied, but bluish purple overall.

Size: *Adult:* 2–4 mm. *Nymph:* 1–2 mm.

Habitat and Range: across Canada but more abundant on Prairies and west coast; alternates between spruce and Douglas-fir.

Scouting: In early summer, look for white, waxy material on needles near the branch tips. In mid-summer, look for swollen branch tips that progress from light green to brown. Galls only form on spruce, whereas flocculence can be seen on both spruce and Douglas-fir.

Cultural/Physical Control: Prune galls while they are still green or purple to prevent adult emergence. A strong jet of water in spring will wash off nymphs that are feeding on the needles.

Biological Control: Many insects prey on adelgids, including lady beetles, minute pirate bugs and lacewings.

Mealybugs

Planococcus citri, Pseudococcus longispinus

Mealybugs suck out plant juices, and the saliva of the Citrus Mealybug (*Planococcus citri*) has a toxic effect on some plants. While they feed, mealybugs produce liquid waste, which may contribute to growth of black, sooty mould. Mealybug infestations are unappealing, and the fluid drain can stunt the plant.

Mealybugs are pests of houseplants and greenhouses. The Citrus Mealybug feeds on African violet, begonia, cacti, citrus, coleus, fuchsia, gardenia, geranium, impatiens, oleander and poinsettia.

The Longtailed Mealybug (*Pseudococcus longispinus*) prefers dracaena but can be found wherever the Citrus Mealybug feeds. Most mealybugs undergo gradual metamorphosis, with the females laying up to 600 eggs in wax-covered clusters. The Longtailed Mealybug gives birth to live young, and Citrus Mealybug eggs hatch into mobile first instar "crawlers" that are the primary stage for dispersal. Older nymphs and adults slowly disperse among plants. Nymphal instars last two to three weeks, and several generations occur each year.

ID: *Adult:* small, flattened, bluish and wax-covered. Longtailed Mealybug: 2 or more long, waxy filaments arise from the rear. *Nymph:* identical to adult, only smaller.

Size: *Adult:* 2–5mm. *Nymph:* 1–3 mm.

Habitat and Range: eggs, all three nymphal instars and the adults live on the undersides of leaves, along veins or in leaf axils.

Scouting: Look for waxy build-up and sooty mould in dense infestations, and for browning of leaf midribs in coleus.

Cultural/Physical Control: For light infestations, hand wash or treat with cotton swabs dipped in rubbing alcohol. For heavy infestations, remove the leaf.

Biological Control: A small ladybeetle (the Mealybug Destroyer, *Cryptolaemus montrouzieri*) and a parasitic wasp (effective only against the Citrus Mealybug) are available. However, the lady beetle is not as effective against the Longtailed Mealybug.

Scale Insects

Chionaspis spp., *Lepidosaphes ulmi, Parthenolecanium corni* and others

Oystershell Scale

Armoured scale insects pierce and suck plant cell contents, whereas soft scale insects feed on plant fluids. Injury to the plant resulting from scale insect activity includes reduced host plant vigour, defoliation, dieback and the unsightly presence of the scales themselves. Soft scales produce honeydew, which may result in sooty mould.

Armoured scales produce a hard protective covering. Armoured scales are flattened and may be elongate, whereas soft scales are hemispherical. All life stages can be present on the host plant at the same time. Some armoured scale species have winged males, whereas others are parthenogenic. Immature male armoured scales are usually smaller and more elongate than the females. Adult armoured male scale insects do not feed.

In both groups of scale insects, the eggs are laid beneath the female, who serves as a protective cover. All of the scales mentioned below overwinter in the egg stage with the exception of the European Fruit Lecanium (*P. corni*), which overwinters as a nymph. The first stage crawlers emerge and move about for several days before settling down to feed. This is the only dispersal stage. There is typically only one generation per year.

ID: *Adult:* Pine Needle, Scurfy and Oystershell Scale: elongate; white to grey overall. San Jose Scale: circular with white centre. European Fruit Lecanium: brown to black rounded hump. *Nymph:* identical to adult, only smaller.

Size: *Adult:* 1–8 mm. *Nymph:* 1–5 mm.

Habitat and Range: common species of armoured scales in British Columbia: Pine Needle Scale (*C. pinifoliae*): on pine, Douglas-fir and cedar but most often on white and Colorado spruce. Scurfy Scale (*C. furfura*): on ash, aspen, dogwood, elm and willow. Oystershell Scale (*L. ulmi*): on ash, birch, cotoneaster, elm, fruit trees, lilac and poplar. San Jose Scale (*Quadraspidiotus perniciosus*): on ornamentals and mountain ash. Common species of soft scale in British Columbia: European Fruit Lecanium: on ash, birch, dogwood, elm, fruit trees and rose.

Scouting: Crawlers are very small and often overlooked. Scales tend to cluster together and, at first glance, resemble rough bark.

Cultural/Physical Control: Inspect plant material before planting out. Prune infested limbs or treat with horticultural oil in early spring to suffocate eggs.

Biological Control: Scale insects have several predators including lacewings and lady beetles.

Oak Leaf Phylloxera

Phylloxera spp.

The Oak Leaf Phylloxera (or Phylloxeran) is believed to have been introduced to the city of Victoria from Europe in 1961. It now occurs in native Garry oak stands throughout southern Vancouver Island and the Gulf Islands and, on the mainland, throughout south-coastal BC and the Fraser Valley and in the Okanagan Valley. Along with the Jumping Oak Gall Wasp, this pest poses a serious threat to the unique native Garry oak

ID: *Adult:* small, yellowish orange, shiny, pear-shaped bug. *Nymph:* similar to adult but smaller.

Size: *Adult:* 1.5 mm. *Nymph:* up to 1 mm.

Habitat and Range: southern Vancouver Island and Gulf Islands, south-coastal BC and the Okanagan Valley.

Scouting: Look for yellowing oak leaves and nymphs feeding on the underside of leaves. On English oak, look for eggs laid in a concentric ring pattern on the underside of leaves.

Cultural/Physical Control: Prune off, bag and dispose of infested leaves and branches, as much as possible. Rake up and dispose of fallen leaves under infested trees. Inspect small trees and remove leaves with egg masses in spring.

grove and meadow ecosystem of the southwestern BC coast.

The Oak Leaf Phylloxera is a serious pest of Garry oak in nurseries. Non-native ornamental species such as bur oak, English oak, valley oak, oriental white oak and blue oak are attacked also, but usually don't suffer serious damage. A related species called the Vein-Feeding Oak Leaf Phylloxera (*Phylloxera* spp.) attacks Garry, valley and blue oaks.

Phylloxerans are small, sucking insects and are related to aphids, lace bugs, psyllids and whiteflies. Both nymphs and adults feed on oak leaves by piercing the leaf and sucking the plant juices. From May to July, oak leaves appear mottled with circular, yellow spots from nymph and adult feeding. These spots coalesce into large, brown blotches and leaves often turn completely yellow or brown and drop. Damage is often misdiagnosed as anthracnose or other fungal disease.

The Oak Leaf Phylloxera has a complex life cycle including both sexual and asexual reproduction and several generations per year. It overwinters as an egg or first-instar nymph in bark crevices. At bud break, nymphs feed on newly developing buds and leaves. The first adult mothers, called "stem mothers" feed on the lower surface of new leaves, causing them to curl, and lay their eggs inside the curled leaves. The newly hatched nymphs feed on the undersurface of the leaves, causing the typical yellow leaf spots. The next generation of adult females lays eggs asexually on the undersurface of leaves in early June. On Garry oak, the eggs are laid singly because the leaves are very hairy; on English oak, the yellow, shiny, cylindrical eggs are laid in a precise pattern of radiating, concentric circles. In late July, when feeding damage is at its peak, the next generation of winged females, which resemble small, black gnats, lay eggs. These eggs hatch to produce non-feeding nymphs, which then develop into sexual males and females in September. Each mated female lays one egg, which overwinters.

By late July, the yellow, infested leaves turn brown and drop, and trees may appear to be scorched. Some trees may be severely defoliated by the end of summer. Infested trees often produce a second flush of leaves in August, and lightly infested trees usually survive. However, about one out of 10 trees suffers a repeated, severe infestation every year and eventually dies. It is not known why one tree of the same species is more susceptible than another. Presumably, there is some genetic difference that makes these trees more attractive to the insect.

Biological Control: Provide habitat for natural predators such as parasitic wasps, lacewings and hover flies. Lady beetles, especially the voracious, introduced Asian Lady Beetle *(Harmonia axyridis)*, feed on phylloxera too.

Psyllids

Cacopsylla buxi, C. pyricola, Paratrioza cockerelli

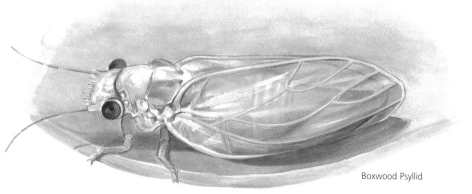

Boxwood Psyllid

Psyllids, or "jumping plant lice," are small, sucking insects in the Family Psyllidae. They are related to aphids, lace bugs and whiteflies. The nymphs are covered with a white, waxy substance that looks like white wool or sugary deposits on the leaves. There are over 3000 known species of psyllids worldwide. The Boxwood Psyllid (C. *buxi*) and the Pear Psylla (C. *pyricola*) are two common species seen in gardens in British Columbia. Some references refer to these species by the older genus name, *Psylla*.

The Pear Psylla is one of the destructive pests of pear trees in North America. Introduced to Connecticut from Europe in 1832, it has since spread throughout the continent. It feeds and reproduces only on pear trees and has become a serious pest of pear in the Okanagan and southern Interior valleys.

The Potato Psyllid, or "Tomato Psyllid" (*P. cockerelli*), feeds on hydroponic greenhouse tomatoes and peppers. The nymph of this species injects a toxin into the leaves while it feeds, resulting in a condition known as "psyllid yellows." It feeds on eggplant and many common weeds including field bindweed, lamb's-quarters, mallow, pigweed and nightshade but has not been found outdoors in BC. Several generations per year can occur in commercial greenhouses.

ID: *Adult:* Boxwood Psyllid: small, greyish green, winged insect. Pear Psylla: Summer: light orange to reddish brown body with 4 dark stripes on back and clear wings with a black spot; winter: dark reddish brown to black body with very dark veins and a conspicuous black spot on wings. Potato Psyllid: small, dark brown body with clear wings. *Nymph:* Boxwood Psyllid: small, flat, grey insect covered with white, cottony "wool." Pear Psylla: pale yellow when young; older nymph is brown and looks like a flattened aphid. Potato Psyllid: small, flat, scale-like, brown to yellowish green body; short spines in a fringe around the outer edges; looks like a flattened aphid.

Size: *Adult:* Boxwood Psyllid: 3 mm. Pear Psylla: Summer: 2–3 mm; winter: 3–4 mm. Potato Psyllid: 2–2.5 mm. *Nymph:* 1–2 mm.

Habitat and Range: throughout the southern regions of BC; Potato Psyllid is known to occur only in commercial vegetable greenhouses.

Scouting: Look for leaf curling and white, woolly tufts on boxwood leaves in spring and early summer; leaves often appear dirty.

Pear Psylla

Both adults and nymphs suck plant sap from new shoots and leaves. Leaves often become curled or cupped and covered with honeydew and black, sooty mould. Boxwood Psyllids overwinter as eggs in protected areas on the plant. In the Fraser Valley, nymphs appear in white, woolly tufts on boxwood leaves in late June or early July but may appear earlier in other areas. Nymphs go through five instars; winged adults emerge in late July or early August. There is one generation per year. Pear Psyllas overwinter as adults in or near pear trees. In spring, adults fly to pear trees and lay eggs on fruit spurs and young leaves. Pear Psyllas have three generations per year. Summer adults lay up to 300 white to yellowish orange, football-shaped eggs, each on a short stalk, mostly along leaf veins. Fruit becomes scarred and covered with a black, sticky, sooty mould. Bartlett and Anjou pears are highly susceptible; Asian pears are less affected. Potato Psyllid eggs resemble those of the Pear Psylla but are usually laid on the outer edge of leaves.

Examine growth scars on leaves and twigs in early spring for Pear Psylla eggs. In summer, hold a piece of paper under a twig and beat the twig a few times. Pear Psylla nymphs will drop down onto the paper. On Bartlett and Anjou pears, as few as 3 nymphs per 10 leaves in spring can indicate a high risk of fruit damage from summer populations. Potato Psyllids create a white, powdery deposit on the upper leaf surface; leaves curl and yellow; nymphs are usually seen on the underside of leaves.

Cultural/Physical Control: Keep boxwood hedges and pear trees healthy, pruned and vigorous. Boxwood can sustain psyllid feeding without permanent damage. These psyllids generally disappear in August. The Pear Psylla continues all summer.

Biological Control: Some naturally occurring predatory bugs such as *Dicyphus* and *Orius* (available for greenhouse use) and parasitic wasps attack psyllids but have not been evaluated for control on outdoor plants. Insecticidal soap will control psyllids if sprayed on the underside of leaves to contact them. Usually, more than one application is needed. A spray with dormant oil and lime sulphur before bud break will kill eggs and helps reduce populations. After bloom, apply summer oil (horticultural oil) to pear trees at half the concentration of dormant oil.

Whiteflies

Bremisia tabaci, Trialeurodes vaporariorum and others

Greenhouse
Whitefly

Whitefly
(*Dialeurodes
chittendeni*) and
the Azalea
Whitefly (*Pealius
azaleae*) are the
most common
species here.

Whiteflies look like very tiny white moths, but they are sucking insects in the Order Homoptera, family Aleyrodidae. Both adults and nymphs suck plant juices. Heavy feeding causes stunting and yellowing, and severely affected plants may die. Leaves, flowers and fruit become covered with sticky honeydew and black, sooty mould. Species in the genus *Bremisia* transmit plant viruses.

Indoors, the most common species are the Sweet Potato Whitefly (*B. tabaci*) and the Greenhouse Whitefly (*T. vaporariorum*). Outdoors, the Rhododendron

The time from egg to adult varies between species, but all have four nymphal stages. Eggs are laid on the underside of leaves. The young nymphs, called crawlers, emerge from the eggs and soon settle down to suck sap from a leaf vein. The next two instars are scale-like and sedentary. The fourth instar is called a pupa, although it is not a true pupa like those of moths. The instar forms a shell from which the adult emerges via a tiny, T-shaped slit. If a parasitoid wasp has consumed the pupa, there will be a circular hole in the shell, instead of a slit.

ID: *Adult:* tiny, moth-like insect with snow white wings and body; wings are held horizontal or flat when at rest. *Larva:* crawlers are greenish yellow; sedentary stages are oval with a yellow or black, scale-like covering, often with a fringe of waxy filaments.

Size: *Adult:* 2–3 mm. *Larva:* 1–2 mm.

Habitat and Range: throughout southern BC in gardens, landscapes, greenhouses and on houseplants.

Scouting: Plants appear mottled and yellow. Look for tiny, white, moth-like insects or scale-like nymphs on the underside of leaves and black, sooty mould from feeding. Whiteflies flit away quickly when disturbed.

Cultural/Physical Control: Yellow sticky cards or pie plates painted yellow, filled with soapy water and placed on the ground will trap adult whiteflies. Heavily infested plants may have to be discarded.

Biological Control: Encourage natural predators such as lacewings, lady bugs and pirate bugs by leaving refuges for them and not applying broad-spectrum insecticides. In greenhouses, the parasitoid wasps *Encarsia formosa* and *Eretmocerus* are available commercially and should be released when whiteflies are first seen. The Whitefly Predatory Beetle (*Delphastus pusillus*) kills eggs and larvae and can be released in combination with the wasps.

Leafhoppers

Edwarsiana rosae, Empoasca spp., *Macrosteles fascifrons* and others

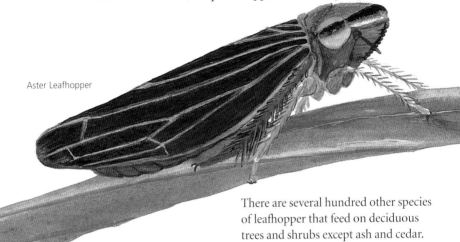

Aster Leafhopper

Leafhoppers pierce and suck fluids from leaves. Their feeding can cause the leaves to curl, wrinkle or wilt. In some cases, the leaves turn brown, giving them a scorched appearance—hence the term "hopperburn." The Aster Leafhopper (*M. fascifrons*) transmits a phytoplasma disease called Aster Yellows. Common British Columbia leafhoppers include the Virginia Creeper Leafhopper (*Erythoneura ziczac*) on Virginia creeper, grapes, elm and hops; the Aster Leafhopper on grasses, lettuce and carrots; Potato Leafhoppers (*Empoasca* spp.) on potato and beans; and the Rose Leafhopper (*Edwarsiana rosae*) on roses.

There are several hundred other species of leafhopper that feed on deciduous trees and shrubs except ash and cedar.

Leafhoppers produce one to four generations per year. Some species, such as the Rose Leafhopper and many that feed on trees, overwinter as an egg inserted into the host plant. Other species, such as the Aster Leafhopper, overwinter in the Great Plains or Gulf of Mexico and arrive in the north as adults in late spring. These migrants lay eggs in the host plant, and the hatching and development of the nymphs progresses as for the resident species. Nymphs are wingless initially but develop wingbuds as they moult from instar to instar. Leafhoppers are very agile and spring away at the slightest disturbance.

ID: *Adult:* can range from pale white to black with vivid red stripes; bluntly rounded head tapers towards posterior, with wings folded tent-like over body. *Nymph:* pale overall.

Size: *Adult:* 4–8 mm. *Nymph:* 1–4 mm.

Habitat and Range: Many species are blown in from the south with weather systems in spring, while others successfully overwinter in British Columbia.

Scouting: Look for leaf curling or hopperburn. On a disturbed plant, you are not likely to miss the leafhoppers living up to their name...hopping away.

Cultural/Physical Control: A strong water stream will knock these insects off your plant. Eliminating grasses that serve as alternate hosts will suppress leafhopper numbers. Control measures are rarely needed in British Columbia, except on wine grapes.

Biological Control: Any generalist predator will feed on leafhoppers.

Cicadas
Okanagana spp.

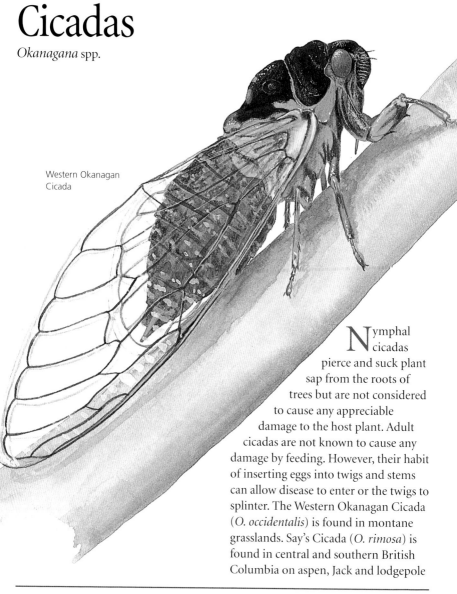

Western Okanagan
Cicada

Nymphal cicadas pierce and suck plant sap from the roots of trees but are not considered to cause any appreciable damage to the host plant. Adult cicadas are not known to cause any damage by feeding. However, their habit of inserting eggs into twigs and stems can allow disease to enter or the twigs to splinter. The Western Okanagan Cicada (*O. occidentalis*) is found in montane grasslands. Say's Cicada (*O. rimosa*) is found in central and southern British Columbia on aspen, Jack and lodgepole

ID: *Adult:* blunt-headed; stout body with large, thick-veined clear wings. Canadian Cicada: black with yellowish tan markings. Western Okanagan Cicada: shiny black with orange markings. Say's Cicada: black with yellowish orange markings and relatively narrow wings compared to other species. *Nymph:* similar to adult but wingless and tan in colour.

Size: *Adult:* 30–55 mm. *Nymph:* 20–30 mm.
Habitat and Range: Western Okanagan Cicada: montane. *O. fratercula* and *O. synodica*: southern grassland. Canadian Cicada: boreal forest. Say's Cicada: mixed-wood forests.
Scouting: Listen for the male "song" and look for splintered twigs and branches caused by egg laying.

pine. The Canadian Cicada (*O. canadensis*) feeds on pine in the boreal forest. It is the northern-most cicada in North America. Two other species, *O. fratercula* and *O. synodica,* can be found in the grasslands of central and south-eastern British Columbia.

Eggs are laid in twigs and stems of host plants. The nymphs hatch in summer and drop to the ground, where they burrow into the soil to feed on roots. The nymphs can take up to four years to mature. Adults crawl to the soil surface and fly to host plants to mate and lay eggs. Often, you can hear the long, sustained buzzing song of the male as he calls for the female. Although a nymph may take from two to five years to mature, there are overlapping generations; therefore, you will see cicadas every year.

*In the eastern United States, the Periodical Cicada (*Magicicada septendecim*) has a synchronized emergence every 17 years! The next ear-splitting racket is expected in 2021.*

Cultural/Physical Control: No effort need be expended, because neither the nymph nor the adult causes noticeable damage.

Biological Control: Adult cicadas make a fine meal for many birds and insectivorous rodents.

Spittlebugs

Aphrophora gelida, Lepyronia quadrangularis, Philaenus spumarius

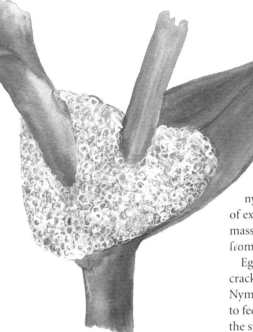

Spittlebugs are piercing/sucking insects that feed on xylem fluids. Many species occur in British Columbia and can be found feeding primarily on woody plants. However, the Meadow Spittlebug (*P. spumarius*) feeds on a wide variety of decorative flowering plants as well as strawberries and peas. The adult Boreal Spittlebug (*A. gelida*) feeds on pine, spruce and Douglas-fir while the nymphs feed on goldenrod, fireweed and other forbs. The Diamondbacked Spittlebug (*L. quadrangularis*) feeds on hardwood trees and shrubs in the aspen parkland ecozone. All spittlebugs produce a spittle mass in the nymphal stage. It is a combination of excess plant sap, air and mucus. The mass is thought to protect the nymph from predators and from drying out.

Eggs are laid in small masses in cracks and crevices on the host plant. Nymphs hatch out in spring and move to feed on stems, where they produce the spittle mass. Adults fly to new hosts in late spring or early summer and continue feeding throughout summer. Overwintering eggs are laid on host plants in autumn. The Diamondbacked Spittlebug overwinters in the adult stage in leaf litter.

The spittlebug's prominent Klingon-esque face houses the many muscles needed for the strong sucking pump it uses to draw in plant sap.

ID: broad, pointed head; wings taper to a point. *Adult:* Meadow Spittlebug: tan to brownish. Boreal Spittlebug: mottled, with pale patch on wings. Diamondbacked Spittlebug: blackish brown diamond shape on wings. *Nymph:* light green to yellowish overall. **Size:** *Adult:* 7–15 mm. *Nymph:* 1–8 mm.

Habitat and Range: widespread in British Columbia.

Scouting: Look for the spittle mass of the nymphs on stems. Adults are difficult to spot.
Cultural/Physical Control: Hose off spittle masses in spring and eliminate or suppress weedy alternate hosts.
Biological Control: Birds and yellow jacket wasps prey on spittlebugs.

Pacific Dampwood Termite

Zootermopsis angusticollis

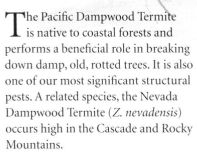

The Pacific Dampwood Termite is native to coastal forests and performs a beneficial role in breaking down damp, old, rotted trees. It is also one of our most significant structural pests. A related species, the Nevada Dampwood Termite (*Z. nevadensis*) occurs high in the Cascade and Rocky Mountains.

The Pacific Dampwood Termite eats damp or rotting wood, often when it is in contact with soil, but will occasionally feed on sound, dry wood adjoining a damp area. Unlike the Western Subterranean Termite (*Reticulitermes hesperus*), which, in BC, is found only in the southern Interior, the Pacific Dampwood Termite deposits only fecal pellets in its feeding tunnels.

Adult termites fly and swarm on warm evenings in late summer. They are relatively poor fliers and often drop their wings when caught. Both males and females excavate a chamber in rotted wood, enter it and seal it behind them. They mate, and about two weeks later, the queen lays about 12 eggs. The queen overwinters and lays a second batch of eggs the following spring. Larvae (soldiers and nymphs) hatch and burrow into the wood. Soldiers resemble adults but are wingless and have a large, black head with long mandibles. There are no "workers": this function is performed by the nymphs.

ID: *Adult:* shiny, reddish brown body with 4 light brown to grey, finely netted wings. *Soldier:* long, black-tipped mandibles; reddish brown body shading to black near head; golden-tan thorax and abdomen. *Nymph:* white to cream overall.

Size: *Adult:* wingspan 2–3 cm; body length 1.5 cm. *Soldier:* 1.3–2 cm. *Nymph:* 1.3 cm.

Habitat and Range: damp and rotted wood in south-coastal BC, Vancouver Island and Gulf Islands.

Scouting: Look for piles of sawdust or dead termites near damp and rotted wood or wood that sounds hollow when tapped. Pry into suspect areas with a screwdriver or short pick and look for long, cream to white nymphs and small, brown, box-shaped fecal pellets about 1 mm long in tunnels.

Cultural/Physical Control: Remove infested, rotted wood and repair moisture leaks. Contact a structural pest management specialist to treat and eradicate all remaining termite colonies before reconstruction.

Biological Control: None known.

European Earwig
Forficula auricularia

The European Earwig was first reported in Newfoundland in 1827–35 and in Rhode Island in 1911. It spread to California during the Gold Rush and north to Canada and has since spread across North America.

The European Earwig is a beneficial insect that feeds on many pests, such as slugs and aphids, and decaying organic matter. However, it also feeds on young leaves, fruit, vegetables and flowers, usually in moist environments or when fruit and vegetables are ripe or flowers are senescing. It seems to prefer flowers such as marigolds, asters, zinnias, dahlias and chrysanthemums, but will feed on gladiolas, roses and carnations too. Its favourite vegetables include lettuce, celery, potatoes, beans, carrots, sweet corn and cabbage.

Earwigs feed at night. During the day, they stay hidden in dark, moist cracks and crevices. Adults overwinter in damp, protected areas, often along house foundations, fences or decks. In June and July, they may crawl into dark, damp places in bathrooms and even under bed covers.

ID: *Adult:* shiny, brown, flat, elongated bug with small, leathery wings; prominent pair of pincers, like forceps. Male: pincers are larger and curved. Female: pincers are shorter and straight. *Larva:* similar to adult but lacking wings.

Size: *Adult:* 1.5–2 cm. *Larva:* 0.5–1.5 cm.

Habitat and Range: throughout southern BC.

Scouting: Earwigs are most often seen in damp, protected areas in the evening or at night. Evidence of feeding can resemble that caused by slugs or snails, but earwigs don't leave a slime trail.

Cultural/Physical Control: Harvest fruit and vegetables before they become overripe.

Minimize standing moisture on leaves. Place rolled corrugated cardboard, crumpled newspaper or commercial earwig baits on the soil to trap earwigs. In vegetable gardens, place plastic containers with tissue paper in the bottom, upside down on the soil, to trap earwigs. Pick up traps in the morning, drop the tissue paper into a bucket of soapy water or freeze before disposal, and replace the traps. On fruit trees, a band of sticky Tanglefoot®, corrugated cardboard or burlap wrapped around the trunk will prevent them from crawling up the tree.

Biological Control: The European Earwig has few natural enemies.

Thrips

Echinothrips americanus, Frankliniella spp., *Thrips* spp.

Western Flower Thrips

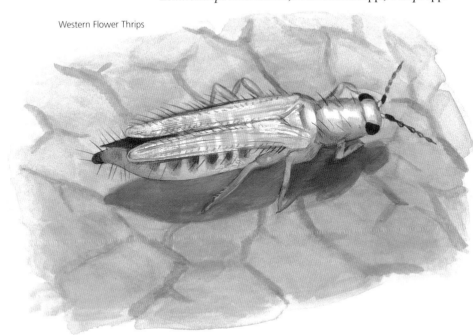

Thrips are unusual in that they have asymmetrical mouthparts—they lack one mandible. This asymmetry results in a form of feeding called "punch and suck," in which thrips use their sole mandible to punch a hole in a plant cell and then form a mouth cone with the remaining mouthparts to suck out the cell contents, leaving a void in the tissue. There are many thrips in British Columbia but the most damaging and commonly encountered thrips are the Western Flower Thrips (*F. occidentalis*), the European Flower Thrips (*F. intonsa*), the Onion Thrips (*T. tabaci*), the Rose Thrips (*T. fucipennis*) and a species with no common name, *Echinothrips americanus*.

Thrips are capable of having many generations per year. Most thrips can reproduce asexually by parthenogenesis.

ID: general body form is elongate with short legs and slightly protruding antennae. *Adult:* delicate wings with long fringe of hairs on trailing edge. Western and European Flower Thrips: yellow overall. Onion and Rose Thrips: small (< 1 mm); variable (yellow to dark brown); thorax may be a lighter colour than abdomen. *E. americanus*: dark with white band across thorax at base of wings. *Nymph:* light yellow overall.

Size: *Adult:* 0.8–3 mm. *Nymph:* 1–2 mm.

Habitat and Range: widespread across the province; can be found in vegetables, flowers, shrubs and trees; prefers warm, dry habitats such as greenhouses; often found in association with spider mites and feeds on their eggs; larvae usually on found on leaves, and adults can be on leaves or in flowers.

Scouting: Look in flowers, under leaves and on stems of plants in drier or exposed

Thrips (continued)

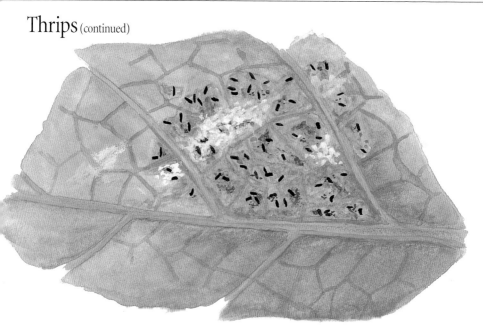

In this form of reproduction, there are no males and the female clones herself. The Onion Thrips reproduces in this manner. The Western Flower Thrips will produce females if mated and males if unmated in a form of reproduction called haplodiploidy. If no males are around, she makes some—how handy is that?

Adult thrips lay eggs into a slit in the host plant. First and second instar thrips punch and suck, feeding on surface tissues, commonly on the undersides of leaves. Non-feeding prepupal and pupal stages are usually spent in the soil, though some species, such as *E. americanus*, pupate on the plant. Adults can fly but prefer to walk or hop around on the plant surface. Adult Western Flower Thrips and European Flower Thrips prefer to feed on pollen within the protective confines of a flower. The life cycle from egg to adult can take as little as three weeks in warm weather.

"Thrips" is both plural and singular, just like "moose." If you walk through a grassy field, you will commonly get thrips on you, and they will bite. Fear not. They cannot draw blood; they are just taking a little taste.

areas. Some species of thrips form abnormal growths called galls, whereas others feed on the surface tissues, causing irregular patches of dead cells or streaks (owing to cell death and subsequent growth of surrounding tissue). Thrips can cause deformed leaves and flowers by feeding at the bud stage.

Cultural/Physical Control: Encourage vigorous plant growth. Larvae can be dislodged with a jet of water. Remove weeds because they serve as an alternate food source.

Biological Control: While thrips will feed on spider mite eggs, which is beneficial, thrips cause more harm than good. Fortunately, there are many generalist predators that feed on thrips, including lady beetles, pirate bugs, damsel bugs and some predatory mites.

Lacewings & Snakeflies

Common Green
Lacewing

Chrysoperla spp., *Chrysopa* spp., *Hemerobius* spp., *Agulla* spp.

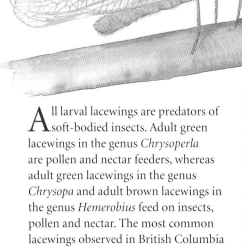

All larval lacewings are predators of soft-bodied insects. Adult green lacewings in the genus *Chrysoperla* are pollen and nectar feeders, whereas adult green lacewings in the genus *Chrysopa* and adult brown lacewings in the genus *Hemerobius* feed on insects, pollen and nectar. The most common lacewings observed in British Columbia are the green lacewings in the genus *Chrysoperla*, and the Common Green Lacewing (*Chrysoperla carnea*) and the Goldeneyed Lacewing (*Chrysopa oculata*), which are widespread across Canada. Brown lacewings are found mostly in wooded areas, with *H. humulinus* distributed across Canada. A related insect, the Snakefly (*Agulla* spp.), occurs only west of the Rocky Mountains. Snakeflies are predators of many small bugs and are often seen on flowers and other vegetation in southern British Columbia.

Adults overwinter in leaf litter. They emerge in spring to lay several hundred eggs on leaf and stem surfaces. Green lacewing eggs are supported on a long silken stalk, whereas brown lacewing eggs are laid directly on the plant surface. The larvae (nymphs) hatch in four to seven days, undergo three larval moults and pupate in a silken cocoon in the open on the plant surface (green lacewing) or in protected places (brown lacewing). There may be several generations per year, depending on temperature.

ID: *Adult:* Green lacewing: delicate light green with lacy, green-veined wings. Brown lacewing: similar to green lacewing but smaller and brown. Snakefly: dark brown with an elongated head and thorax and lacy, brown-veined wings. *Nymph:* flat, elongate nymph bulging in middle; pair of long, curved, pointed mandibles on head used to skewer prey; often mottled white and brown or white and green.

Size: *Adult:* 10–12 mm. *Nymph:* from <1 to 8 mm.

Habitat and Range: Green lacewing: open areas throughout the province. Brown lacewing: limited to wooded areas. Snakefly: open areas in southern BC.

Scouting: adults rest during the day but will fly if disturbed (they are clumsy fliers and are quite comical to watch); larvae are voracious predators that can be found patrolling leaves, fruit and stems for prey.

How to Attract: Flowering plants will attract lacewings into your yard. Lacewing larvae are known as aphid-lions for their prowess at feasting on aphids. However, they also feed on eggs and soft-bodied insects such as caterpillars and psyllids, spider mites, thrips and leafhoppers.

Blister Beetles

Epicauta oregona, Meloe montanus

A dult blister beetles chew on the leaves and flowers of plants. There are many species, but the most common in British Columbia are *E. oregona* and *M. montanus*. The name "blister beetle" is not an idle label; the beetles produce a chemical called cantharidin that causes blistering when it comes in contact with moist skin. Males produce the chemical and pass it to the female during mating.

The adult blister beetle emerges in June and July to feed on foliage, mate and lay eggs. The female lays her eggs in soil near a source of food, such as grasshopper eggs or ground-nesting bumble bee nests. The first instar larva is an active crawler that searches out leafcutter bee and bumblebee nests or grasshopper and cricket eggs, upon which subsequent larval instars feed. The larva overwinters, pupating the following spring.

A European species of blister beetle, Lytta vesicatoria, *is ground up and sold as a cure-all and aphrodisiac known as Spanish Fly. It isn't just snakes (and their oil) that are flogged as a panacea for your ills.*

ID: *Adult: Epicauta* spp.: long-legged, elongate and colourful with soft, often iridescent or metallic green, purple or blue elytra; rounded pronotum is usually narrower than head or abdomen. *Meloe* spp.: dark blue to black and elongate; bulbous abdomen gives appearance of greatly shortened wing covers. *Larva:* brownish to whitish grub.

Size: *Adult:* 12–25 mm. *Larva:* 5–13 mm.

Habitat and Range: widespread across Canada; naturally occurs on wild legumes such as vetches; in British Columbia is predominantly a pest of vegetable crops such as beans, peas, potatoes, squash and tomatoes.

Scouting: The adults will colonize your yard and garden, chewing on younger leaves

and flowers. They cling tenaciously to the foliage when you shake the plant. They are most abundant one to two years after a grasshopper infestation. The larvae are soil dwellers that do not affect plant material.

Cultural/Physical Control: In high numbers, these beetles can occasionally defoliate a plant.

Biological Control: Here we witness the Jekyll-and-Hyde nature of this beetle. The adult is a nuisance in the garden, but the larva feeds on grasshopper and cricket eggs. Unfortunately the larva also attacks eggs and larvae of leafcutter bees and bumblebees.

Flea Beetles

Epitrix spp., *Phyllotreta* spp.

Adult flea beetles feed on foliage, whereas larvae feed on roots and tubers. Common flea beetles in British Columbia include the Western Potato Flea Beetle (*E. subcrinita*), the Tuber Flea Beetle (*E. tuberis*), the Crucifer Flea Beetle (*P. cruciferae*), the Horseradish Flea Beetle a.k.a. Cabbage Flea Beetle (*P. albionica*) and the Striped Flea Beetle (*P. striolata*).

Flea beetles typically overwinter as adults in sheltered areas or leaf litter and emerge in spring, feeding on weeds and emerging crops. Females lay eggs in the soil near food plants and die soon after. One to two weeks later, the larvae hatch and feed on roots and tubers. The larvae pass through four instars and then pupate in the soil. Adults emerge and feed through until autumn. There may be up to three generations of Tuber Flea Beetle per year, whereas most other species have only one or two generations.

ID: *Adult:* shiny, metallic beetle with jumping hind legs; most are blue to black. Striped Flea Beetle: 2 wavy yellow stripes along elytra. *Larva:* elongated, brown to whitish body with 3 pairs of legs near head; head capsule is usually distinct.

Size: *Adult:* 2–3 mm. *Larva:* 1–2 mm.

Habitat and Range: throughout the province. Cabbage Flea Beetles attack crops in the cabbage family, and Crucifer and Striped Flea Beetles, introduced from Europe, attack canola in the Peace River district. The Tuber Flea Beetle, a fairly recent introduction, is one of the most damaging pests of potatoes in British Columbia.

Scouting: Adult flea beetles feed on newly emerging host plants in spring, especially the cotyledons, where severe damage can occur. In July and August, they feed mostly on the upper but also the lower surface of leaves. Feeding is characterized by pitting or a shot-hole appearance. The Tuber Flea Beetle adult feeds on leaves in a similar manner to the other flea beetles. Leaf feeding is not much of a concern, but larvae burrow into and feed on the potato tuber, resulting in tunnels, channels and pimples that are much more destructive and provide an entry for tuber-rotting fungi and bacteria.

Cultural/Physical Control: Keep weeds at bay because they serve as alternate food hosts for flea beetles. Flea beetles overwinter in litter near food plants, so rotate or move your plantings of crucifers and potatoes around the yard to escape the beetles. You can also plant early emerging crops such as radish, daikon or Indian mustard to serve as "trap crops," thereby limiting the need to spray your cabbage, broccoli or other food crop. Flea beetle adults prefer to feed in open, sunny, warm areas, so try to shade your plants wherever possible.

Biological Control: Natural enemies abound but do not have a substantial impact on large populations of flea beetles.

Ground Beetles

Calosoma spp., *Harpalus* spp., *Scaphinotus* spp., and others

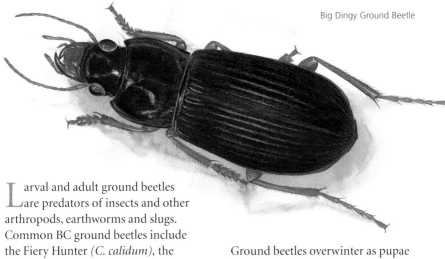

Big Dingy Ground Beetle

Larval and adult ground beetles are predators of insects and other arthropods, earthworms and slugs. Common BC ground beetles include the Fiery Hunter *(C. calidum)*, the European Carabid *(Pterostichus melanarius)*, the Snail-killer Carabid *(S. angusticollis)* and the Big Dingy Ground Beetle *(H. pennsylvanicus)*. There are many others including *Elaphrus* spp. found around bogs, *Bembidion* spp. located along shorelines, *Agonum* spp. near bodies of water and *Patrobus* spp. in forested areas and cultivated lands, to name only a few.

Ground beetles overwinter as pupae or adults, with adults often living two or three years. Eggs are laid in soil or, with some species, in mud cells attached to plants. Larvae go through four instars in shallow soil or on the soil's surface. Pupation occurs in the soil. Adults emerge in June and July and are active until autumn. Adults are typically nocturnal, though, if disturbed, they will scurry around during the day.

ID: *Adult:* Big Dingy Ground Beetle: black with protruding head, flared pronotum and broadly oval abdomen that tapers to a point. Fiery Hunter: similarly shaped but with red spots on elytra. European Carabid: not as curvy and is uniformly shiny black. Snail-killer Carabid: elongated head and thorax; large, oval, brown body. *Larva:* yellowish brown; elongate, tapering towards posterior.

Size: *Adult:* 12–22 mm. *Larva:* 5–15 mm.

Habitat and Range: Big Dingy Ground Beetle and Fiery Hunter: widespread in urban areas throughout southern BC. European Carabid: originally from Europe but is now widespread in urban areas and is slowly spreading out to rural habitats. Snail-killer Carabid: moist coastal forests and Vancouver Island.

Scouting: The Fiery Hunter is arboreal, feasting on caterpillars in trees. Although most active at night (you can often hear them rustling through leaves after sundown), they can sometimes be seen during the day. The Big Dingy, European and Snail-killer Carabids are more earthbound. During the day, look for them under logs or leaf litter or in other dark hiding places.

How to Attract: Despite their conspicuously large size, these insects are beneficial; they are not to be feared and should not be harmed. Ground beetles are among the most abundant predators in the landscape. They are diligent and seemingly inexhaustible in their pursuit of prey. These beetles thrive in undisturbed areas; therefore, try to leave some earth undisturbed so that they can help you maintain a healthy and happy garden.

Leaf-feeding Beetles

Chrysomela spp., *Crioceris* spp., *Entomoscelis americana*, *Pyrrhalta viburni* and others

Spotted Asparagus Beetle

Common Asparagus Beetle

Adult and larval leaf beetles chew leaf material and, in extreme cases, are capable of stripping a tree bare. There are many leaf beetles in British Columbia but some of the most commonly encountered species are the Cottonwood Leaf Beetle (*Chrysomela scripta*), Aspen Leaf Beetle (*Chrysomela crotchi*) and Willow Leaf Beetle (*Calligrapha multipunctata multipunctata*). The Viburnum Leaf Beetle (*P. viburni*), an introduced species from Europe, feeds on leaves of *Viburnum* species, especially *V. opulus*, and severe infestations can kill a shrub over a few years. The same family, Chrysomelidae, includes the Red Turnip Beetle (*E. americana*), which feeds on canola and other cruciferous plants in the Peace River district and southwestern Interior, and the Common and Spotted Asparagus Beetles. The Common Asparagus Beetle (*Crioceris asparagi*) feeds on young asparagus spears, causing them to develop crookedly, but the Spotted Asparagus Beetle (*Crioceris duodecimpunctata*) only feeds on asparagus berries and does little damage.

ID: *Adult:* head and pronotum roughly equal in width, with wider elytra that is often brightly coloured or marked with lines or spots. Willow Leaf Beetle: white with black spots. Cottonwood Leaf Beetle: yellowish or white with black stripes. Common Asparagus Beetle: bluish brown with 6 cream-coloured spots on elytra. Spotted Asparagus Beetle: reddish orange with black spots on elytra. Viburnum Leaf Beetle: small, brown beetle. Red Turnip Beetle: red overall. *Larvae:* black to yellowish or reddish; elongate, clearly segmented and rough looking, almost like little alligators. Viburnum Leaf Beetle: dark coloured when small; older instars are yellowish green.

Size: *Adult:* 10–12 mm. Viburnum Leaf Beetle: 4.5–6.5 mm. *Larva:* 3–10 mm.

Habitat and Range: widespread across the province on broadleaved trees and shrubs; most leaf beetles are named for their preferred host plant. Cottonwood Leaf Beetle: feeds on willow and poplars other than trembling aspen. Aspen Leaf Beetle: feeds on trembling

Leaf-feeding Beetles (continued)

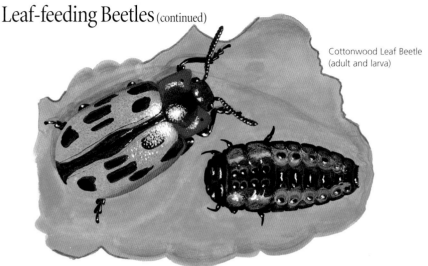

Cottonwood Leaf Beetle
(adult and larva)

In general, leaf beetles overwinter as adults in leaf litter near host trees, although Viburnum Leaf Beetles overwinter as eggs inserted into young branches. The beetles emerge in spring to feed on flushing leaves and tender bark. Females of most other species lay eggs in clusters on the underside of leaves. Larvae feed in groups in the early instars and spread out to feed singly in later instars. After two to three weeks, they pupate on the underside of leaves, on the stem of the tree, at the base of grasses or host plants, or in the soil, depending on the species. The Viburnum Leaf Beetle has one generation per year; other species may have two or more generations per year depending on species, temperature and food availability.

aspen but will also feed on other poplars. Red Turnip Beetle: most common on canola in the Peace River district. Common and Spotted Asparagus Beetles: in the southern Interior and south coastal BC wherever asparagus is grown. Viburnum Leaf Beetle: southern Vancouver Island and the Fraser Valley.

Scouting: Leaf-feeding beetles typically scrape away the tissue on the under and upper surfaces of leaves. Later instars chew small holes in the leaves. Adults skeletonize the leaves but cause much less damage than do the larvae. The Red Turnip Beetle prefers cole crops, such as canola, but will also feed on potato, lettuce and beans. The adults and larvae feed on seedlings, leaves, stems and flowers. Mass immigration from canola fields of non-flying adults in June can rapidly defoliate a garden. The adults disappear into the litter during the hottest part of summer, re-emerging in August to resume feeding. Crooked spears of asparagus indicate that the Common Asparagus Beetle is present. Look for egg-laying sites of the Viburnum

Leaf Beetle in late fall or early spring on small twigs from the previous year. These appear as small holes in a straight line on the underside of the twig. Each hole contains several eggs and is capped by the female with a mixture of chewed wood and excrement. In spring, the holes swell, the eggs hatch, the caps fall off and the larvae emerge to feed on leaves.

Cultural/Physical Control: Pruning of egg masses and pressure sprays of water are effective means of reducing the impact of tree-feeding species. Prune out Viburnum Leaf Beetle eggs in early spring, before they hatch. The Cottonwood Leaf Beetle prefers to attack saplings, and controlling the beetle on these plants will greatly reduce pressure on older trees. Rotating crops or planting in various areas will limit the damage done by the Red Turnip Beetle. In gardens, Common Asparagus Beetle adults can be hand picked from plants, but chemical control may be required in larger plantings.

Biological Control: Generalist predators will attack the eggs and early instar larvae.

Sap Beetles

Family Nitidulidae

These little beetles are strongly attracted to rotting, fermenting fruit, alcohol and fresh paint. There are over 60 species of sap beetles in BC. Most feed on fruit or fungi, but some feed on and breed in carrion, and some in flowers, where they consume petals and pollen. One of the most common species, *Glischrochilus quadrisignatus*, has four yellow spots on elytra and is often called the Picnic Beetle, Beer Beetle or Four-spotted Sap Beetle.

Adults or larvae overwinter in plant debris. Females emerge in late spring and lay eggs in rotting fruit or another food source. Larvae feed through four or five instars before pupating in the soil. There are two to four generations per year, depending on the species, and numbers generally peak in late June or July. Every few years there is a high population of these beetles, which then crashes because they are attractive to predatory insects and birds. A few larvae are predators of other insects.

Sap beetles love ripe BC-grown berries, and their feeding on corn silks can seriously reduce the quality of sweet corn. When they chew on the silk, the cob develops with missing kernels. Sap beetles also bore into ripe tomatoes, apples and pears, and they can be a nuisance around garbage cans.

ID: *Adult:* black with yellow or reddish orange spots on elytra. *Larva:* small, white worm with a dark brown head.

Size: *Adult:* 3–12 mm. *Larva:* 2–10 mm.

Habitat and Range: widespread in BC.

Scouting: Look for sap beetles in June or July on ripe berries, fruit or sweet corn silks. A few species live in flowers and feed on petals and pollen.

Cultural/Physical Control: Pick fruit before it rots. Keep cull piles far away from producing crops. Bury and turn compost piles regularly. There is no effective control for sap beetles on corn silks or berry crops, but they can sometimes be trapped using banana peels or muskmelon rinds. Check traps every 3 or 4 days and replace frequently. Adding pineapple scraps, or a bait made from stale beer, yeast, vinegar, molasses and water may help attract them.

Biological Control: Many natural predators feed on sap beetles.

Elm Bark Beetles

Hylurgopinus rufipes, Scolytus multistriatus

European Elm
Bark Beetle

Elm Bark Beetles are the vectors of one of the most destructive diseases in North America, Dutch Elm Disease (DED). The beetles themselves are relatively harmless to elms and can live in trees without killing them, but they are deadly when combined with the DED fungus. When DED arrived in North America and began infecting and weakening elms, it created the perfect conditions for these opportunistic beetles.

Bark beetles and their larvae spend most of their lives feeding on plant tissues under the bark, creating a series of tunnels known as galleries. Adults emerge in early to mid-spring and move to the crowns of healthy elms to feed. Healthy trees often make life difficult for bark beetles, which bore through the bark and are flushed out by sap. In early to mid-summer, the beetles seek unhealthy, weakened or dead trees or firewood, where they lay eggs and build galleries under the bark.

Almost every American elm infected with DED dies within two years.

ID: *Adult:* dark, ovate beetle. Native Elm Bark Beetle (*H. rufipes*): dark brown to black. European Elm Bark Beetle (*S. multistriatus*); dark red to brown; smaller overall. *Larva:* white, legless grub.

Size: *Adult:* 2–3 mm. *Larva:* similar to adult.

Habitat and Range: European Elm Bark Beetle: occurs throughout the province where elm trees are found. Native Elm Bark Beetle: occurs on the Prairies but not in BC.

Scouting: Trees infected with DED have wilting, yellowing foliage on some branches (called "flagging") and a brown ring or streaks in the infected area underneath the bark. DED is currently absent from Alberta and British Columbia. Contact your municipal or provincial authorities if you suspect a tree has

this disease or if you would like to know more about the status of the disease in the region. Do not transport firewood to or from other provinces and report anyone who does.

Cultural/Physical Control: Prevention is the best control. Keep elms healthy and vigorous. Water the trees in years of drought. Prune off any dead or dying branches annually in late winter. Remove and destroy infected trees. Replace with another species or with a DED-resistant elm variety such as *Ulmus davidiana* var. *japonica* 'Jacan' or the 'Liberty' elms. Ensure you purchase a variety that is hardy for your area.

Biological Control: Unknown.

Carrion Beetles

Nicrophorus spp., *Aclypea bituberosa*

Spinach Carrion
Beetle larva

Carrion beetles (*Nicrophorus* spp.), also called burying beetles, aid in decomposition of dead animals. These beetles feed at night and, if disturbed, will drop to the ground and rapidly seek cover under clumps of soil. Although most feed on carrion, the Spinach Carrion Beetle (*A. bituberosa*) feeds on spinach, cabbage, radish, lettuce, strawberry and other leafy vegetables.

Adults overwinter in leaf litter and protected areas. They emerge in early May and mate. Females then lay eggs in the soil or in a dead animal. Larvae emerge a week later and start to feed on the dead carcass, or, in the case of the Spinach Carrion Beetle, on the leaves of young garden plants. In a few weeks, the last instar larvae tunnel 2 to 5 centimetres into the soil to pupate, with adults emerging two to four weeks later. There is only one generation of Spinach Carrion Beetles per year but other species may have two to three generations.

Carrion beetles are necessary to reduce dead animals to a state where bacteria and fungi can finish off the decomposition process. Crime scene investigators may use the instars of carrion beetle larvae, along with those of fly maggots, to estimate time of death.

ID: *Adult:* Carrion Beetle: shiny black with four orange spots on elytra. Spinach Carrion Beetle: dull black with raised edges on elytra. *Larva:* elongate, flattened, shiny black and tapered toward posterior end.

Size: *Adult:* 10–12 mm. *Larva:* 3–10 mm.

Habitat and Range: widespread in British Columbia.

Scouting: Feeding damage results in ragged edges and holes. Adult feeding is not usually overly damaging and does not have a substantial impact on yield.

Cultural/Physical Control: Weeds are a good source of food early in May, so removing them will prevent beetle numbers from climbing. Hand picking when they are active at night might prove to be impractical but is effective.

Biological Control: Generalist predators consume the larvae.

Click Beetles/Wireworms

Agriotes spp., *Alaus* spp.

Western Eyed
Click Beetle

These species feed on germinating corn seeds, potato tubers, and roots and crowns of ornamental plants and strawberries. Some native wireworm species also attack crops but rarely reach a density that warrants concern. Other native species, such as the Western Eyed Click Beetle (*Alaus melanops*) and other *Alaus* species, are beneficial predators of wood-boring beetles in pines, and adults and larvae are often seen in downed, rotting trees and firewood.

Adults generally emerge from pupation in April and May. Females lay eggs in loose, moist soil in grassy areas or pasture. Eggs hatch in three to seven weeks, and the larvae persist for three to six years before pupating (4 to 11 years for *Alaus* spp.). Pupae overwinter and adults emerge the following spring. Adults expire the season they emerged.

You can bury a potato in the soil and dig it up in a few weeks to see how many wireworms are in your garden. Newly hatched larvae feed near the surface when it is cool and moist and move down in the soil to find moisture when it is hot and dry.

Click beetle larvae, called wireworms, shred roots and burrow into and feed on crowns of plants. Of several species of click beetles in British Columbia, the most damaging are two introduced species from Europe, *Agriotes obscurus* and *Agriotes lineatus*.

ID: *Adult: Agriotes:* elongated and dark brown overall; characterized by having pronotum pointed towards rear on either side of posterior margin. Western Eyed Click Beetle: large, dull black with small, oval eye-like spots on elytra. *Larva:* colour progresses from white to yellow to golden or dark brown as it matures; elongate, cylindrical and hardened.

Size: *Adult:* 8–12 mm. Western Eyed Click Beetle: 35 mm. *Larva:* 5–20 mm.

Habitat and Range: Native click beetles are provincewide; European *Agriotes* species occur primarily in south coastal BC and the Fraser Valley.

Scouting: Adults rest on trees and shrubs. Larvae (wireworms) live in the soil. They form tunnels when feeding in potato tubers and strawberry crowns and "shred" plant material instead of biting and chewing. The inner leaves wilt and die first.

Cultural/Physical Control: Most wireworm larvae die shortly after emerging from the egg. Consistently moist soils favour the larvae. Remove grasses near vegetables or refrain from early seeding and encouraging rapid germination. Do not seed potatoes or strawberries directly after grass or pasture. Plant trap crops of wheat seed treated with insecticide in early spring between crop rows.

Biological Control: Larvae are eaten by ground and rove beetles.

Bark Beetles

Dendroctonus spp., *Ips pini*

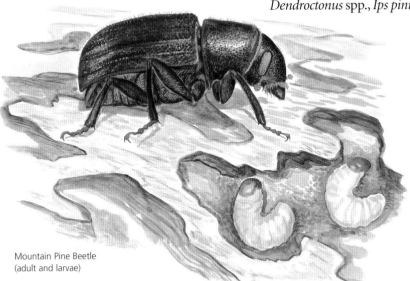

Mountain Pine Beetle
(adult and larvae)

These beetles are the miners of the beetle world. Their primary hosts are conifers, and they live in galleries under the bark. They attack stressed trees and can lead to the trees' demise. These beetles are quite difficult to fight: consider removing an infested tree.

Bark beetles common here are the Spruce Beetle (*D. rufipennis*), the Eastern Larch Beetle (*D. simplex*), the Lodgepole Pine Beetle (*D. murrayanae*), the Red Turpentine Beetle (*D. valens*) and the Pine Engraver (*I. pini*). The Mountain Pine Beetle (*D. ponderosae*) occurs in pines, especially lodgepole pine, near the Interior mountains. Gardeners in these areas must take immediate action if they suspect the Mountain Pine Beetle is present. If you are in a high-risk area, contact your local municipal or forestry office for more information.

Also Known As: Mountain Pine Beetle

ID: *Adult:* dark ovate beetle. *Larva:* legless white grub.

Size: *Adult:* 4–7 mm. *Larva:* similar in size to adult but earlier stages are smaller.

Habitat and Range: found in the boreal forest and mountains of BC in stressed and decaying conifers. Many bark beetles are carriers of fungi that spread throughout their galleries. In some cases it is the fungus that kills the tree and not the beetle (e.g., the blue stain fungus carried by the infamous Mountain Pine Beetle).

Scouting: Watch for a sappy paste oozing from tiny holes (pitch tubes) on the trunk or branches, wood dust at the base of tree and signs of beetle galleries underneath bark. In later stages of infestation, the bark peels easily away.

Cultural/Physical Control: Keep trees healthy and stress free. Prune off dead or dying branches before beetles start looking for new homes in spring. Remove and dispose of infested trees. If a tree only has a few beetles, about 10 or fewer, dig them out carefully with a knife.

Biological Control: Hang synthetic, anti-aggregation Mountain Pine Beetle hormone can from trees to deter beetles. There is little that can be done when the Mountain Pine Beetle reaches epidemic proportions.

Rove Beetles

Aleochara spp., *Atheta* spp., *Creophilus maxillosus*

Hairy Rove Beetle

Most rove beetles, family Staphylinidae, are beneficial predators of soil-dwelling arthropods. This very important group of predators is most active in carrion, dung and decaying vegetation. There are more than 4000 species of rove beetles in North America. A rather imposing species is the Hairy Rove Beetle (*C. maxillosus*), commonly found on carrion. Members of the genera *Aleochara* and *Atheta* have been the most studied as potential species to be introduced or mass-produced as biocontrol agents.

Members of the genus *Aleochara* are not so much predators as they are parasitoids. The female lays her eggs on or near root maggot larvae, and the rove beetle larvae enter into the maggot, ultimately killing it. Other species, such as *Atheta coriaria*, are more like a traditional predator, feasting from the outside in. The larvae are short lived because of the temporary nature of the substrate in which they hunt. Adults are relatively longer lived, a necessary adaptation to seek out egg-laying sites. Larvae pupate in the soil or substrate that they have colonized. Rove beetles are active throughout spring, summer and autumn.

ID: *Adult:* elongate, parallel-sided and often hairy; distinct among beetles for having shortened elytra, often exposing majority of abdomen. *Larva:* tan or brown; elongate with strongly armoured head sporting large pair of curved mandibles; body tapers towards rear.

Size: *Adult:* 3–20 mm. *Larva:* 5–20 mm.

Habitat and Range: widely abundant throughout the province; many hunt for prey in soil or on carrion, dung or decaying vegetation; some are forest specialists, whereas others prefer grasslands.

Scouting: The larvae tend to remain in the soil, carrion or dung. Adults hunt with the larvae or can crawl up plants to find other sources of prey, such as aphids. Larvae and adults can be found in the soil and crawling around on plants at night.

How to Attract: Rove beetles lay their eggs near where they expect the larvae to feed, such as in soil, manure, carrion or decaying vegetation. Avoid applying pesticide to the soil because it is harmful to these insects.

June Beetles & European Chafer

Phyllophaga spp., *Polyphylla decemlineata, Rhizotrogus majalis*

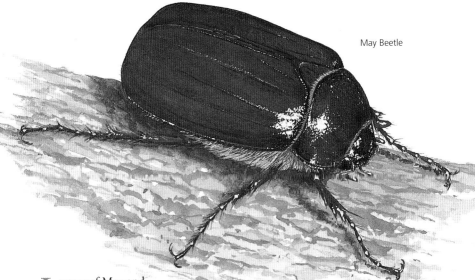

May Beetle

Larvae of May and June beetles and the European Chafer are white grubs that feed on roots of grasses and other plants; the adults do not feed. There are several *Phyllophaga* species of May beetles in British Columbia. The distinctive Ten-lined June Beetle (*Polyphylla decemlineata*) is the largest scarab beetle in BC. The European Chafer (*R. majalis*), a serious pest of lawns and turf in eastern Canada, was found in New Westminster in 2001 and has since been found in several locations in Vancouver.

May beetle adults emerge from the soil in late May and June in British Columbia, except the Ten-lined June Beetle, which emerges in July. Females lay their eggs in soil below turf that is near a light. May and June Beetle larvae develop in the soil over three

---

ID: *Adult:* May and June beetle: brownish, robust beetle with antennae resembling a stack of long, thin pancakes impaled at one end on a stick. Ten-Lined June Beetle: similar but with white stripes on elytra; the male antennae are large and resemble moose antlers when spread. European Chafer: resembles a small June beetle. *Larva:* large, C-shaped grub with well-developed head and thoracic legs; May and June Beetles: underside of rear end has characteristic elongate V-shaped pattern of hairs. European Chafer: a Y-shaped anal slit and parallel rows of spines on rear end.

Size: *Adult:* 15–25 mm. *Larva:* 5–30 mm.

Habitat and Range: May and June beetles: occur throughout the province. Ten-lined June Beetle: primarily in the southern Interior. European Chafer: Vancouver area only. Larvae of all species feed on native, lawn and sod grasses.

June Beetles & European Chafer (continued)

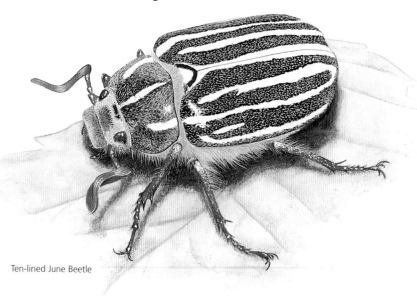

Ten-lined June Beetle

years. First instar larvae hatch in June, feed until September, moult to second instar and burrow down to overwinter. The following spring, the larvae return to the root zone to feed until autumn, when they again burrow deep for winter. In spring of the third year, the third instar larvae return to the root zone to feed for a short while and then burrow down to pupate. The adults develop in autumn and stay in the soil until the following spring. There can be overlapping generations, with adults and all three instars present in one season. The European Chafer completes its life cycle in one year. Eggs hatch in mid-July, and grubs feed throughout the summer and autumn and overwinter in the soil. The larger autumn and spring larvae do most of the feeding damage. Adults emerge in late May.

Scouting: The larvae inhabit the soil or sub-surface layer of turf beneath the thatch in open fields, meadows, lawns, grasslands, pastures, tree and shrub nurseries and cultivated fields. Larval damage occurs throughout summer. Damage consists of irregularly shaped patches of dead turf. The larvae cut the roots, loosening the sod, which can be rolled up like a carpet. Adults readily come to lights, and it is common to find stunned adults buzzing and flailing about on their backs below street and porch lights.

Cultural/Physical Control: The best defence is a well-maintained lawn. Weekly deep watering will help turf tolerate low levels of infestation. Excessive thatch should be removed. Control of adult beetles is not practical.

Biological Control: Ground beetles, birds and small mammals will feed on the grubs. If crows, raccoons or skunks are tearing up your lawn, it is a good sign you have white grubs. Manage the white grubs and you should not have any problems with the vertebrates. Predatory nematodes (*Steinernema* and *Heterorhabditis* spp.) are available commercially and can be used to treat the grubs when soil temperatures are above 10° C and there is adequate moisture.

Dung Beetles

Aphodius granarius, Ataenius spretulus and others

Aphodius Beetle

Aphodius and *Ataenius* beetle larvae feed on dung, decaying organic matter or grass roots. Adults generally do not feed. There are several species of these little scarab beetles in British Columbia. *Ataenius spretulus* grubs occasionally damage turfgrass in the south coastal region. *Aphodius granarius,* another turf-feeding species has recently been reported in the south Okanagan.

Adults emerge from overwintering from April through July, depending on the species and temperature. Females lay their eggs in dung, thatch or soil. The larvae go through three instars and pupate in the soil. The beetles typically overwinter in the adult stage. There can be one or more generations per year, depending on temperature.

ID: *Adult:* stout with broad head equal in width to pronotum and abdomen; legs sport backward-projecting spines to aid in digging; most are black or black with reddish or brown elytra. *Larva:* small, whitish, C-shaped grub with well-developed thoracic legs.

Size: *Adult:* 3–7 mm. *Larva:* 1–5 mm.

Habitat and Range: found across the province in open pastureland; many are specific to one kind of dung, whether cow or deer, while others prefer decaying vegetable matter, including thatch in lawns; a few species feed on turfgrass roots.

Scouting: Adults can be seen crawling through turfgrass from early April until autumn. Adults prefer turf warmed by the sun and are especially prevalent on sun-drenched golf course greens. The larvae feed on decaying organic matter in the thatch layer of lawns. Rarely do these insects become a pest. In cases where populations are very high, crows may tear up the turf in search of the tasty little grubs. *A. granarius* or *A. spretulus* may, in rare instances, pose a threat to lawns.

Cultural/Physical Control: Maintain a healthy lawn because healthy turf can withstand feeding by these beetles, and de-thatching will reduce available food sources, keeping beetle numbers low.

Biological Control: Soil-dwelling predators such as ground beetles and rove beetles feed upon the larvae.

Lady Beetles

Adalia bipunctata, Coccinella spp., *Hippodamia* spp. and others

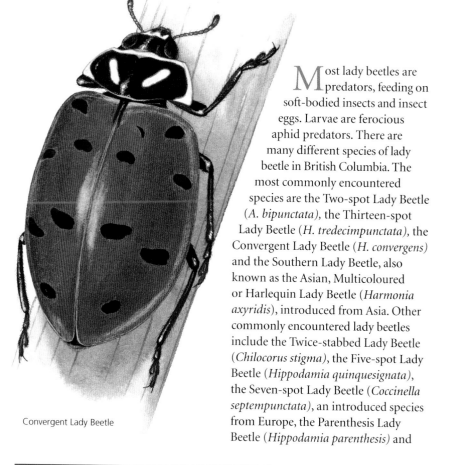

Convergent Lady Beetle

Most lady beetles are predators, feeding on soft-bodied insects and insect eggs. Larvae are ferocious aphid predators. There are many different species of lady beetle in British Columbia. The most commonly encountered species are the Two-spot Lady Beetle (*A. bipunctata*), the Thirteen-spot Lady Beetle (*H. tredecimpunctata),* the Convergent Lady Beetle (*H. convergens)* and the Southern Lady Beetle, also known as the Asian, Multicoloured or Harlequin Lady Beetle (*Harmonia axyridis*), introduced from Asia. Other commonly encountered lady beetles include the Twice-stabbed Lady Beetle (*Chilocorus stigma*), the Five-spot Lady Beetle (*Hippodamia quinquesignata*), the Seven-spot Lady Beetle (*Coccinella septempunctata*), an introduced species from Europe, the Parenthesis Lady Beetle (*Hippodamia parenthesis)* and

Also Known As: Ladybugs, Lady Bird Beetles

ID: *Adult:* round bodied; variously coloured, but predominantly black head and thorax (some have white markings on pronotum), orange-red elytra and 1 or more black spots or stripes. Two-spot Lady Beetle: 2 black spots on red background. Convergent Lady Beetle: 13 black spots and 2 converging white spots on pronotum. Thirteen-spot Lady Beetle: 13 black spots on orange, somewhat elongated body. Southern (Harlequin) Lady Beetle: 20 or more spots on round, red to orange body. *Larva:* looks like a rough little alligator, usually blue or black with white, orange or pale markings and tapering towards rear.

Size: *Adult:* 4–8 mm. *Larva:* 3–10 mm.

Habitat and Range: found throughout the province in vegetable and flower gardens, sandy dune areas, grasslands, forested areas, near wetlands, alongside streams and rivers, virtually everywhere. Some species are herb, vegetable, flower or shrub specialists, whereas others are better adapted to hunting in trees: birch, spruce, Manitoba maple, mountain ash and alder are likely places to find lady beetles.

the Transverse Lady Beetle (*Coccinella transversoguttata*).

Adults lay up to several hundred eggs in spring and throughout summer. Not all eggs are destined to hatch; some, called trophic eggs, serve as the first meal for the newly emerged larvae. There are four larval instars and one pupal stage. Development from egg to adult can be as quick as two weeks or as long as seven weeks. There may be more than one generation per year. Adults may live from a few months up to two or three years. Some species aggregate in dense masses under leaf litter or in homes when overwintering.

Lady Beetle larva (above), Lady Beetle adults (below)

Thirteen-spot Lady Beetle

Lady beetles are coloured so distinctively as a warning to predators that they taste bad. Some lady beetles contain alkaloids that they can excrete in a behaviour called "reflex bleeding," hence the smelly liquid left on your fingers after you handle a lady beetle.

Scouting: Eggs are laid singly on the leaf surface. Larvae can be readily seen on the upper and lower surface of the leaf, particularly in the vicinity of aphids. Adult lady beetles roam the leaves and stems in search of suitable prey. Lady beetle adults are also capable fliers and will be seen "on the wing."

How to Attract: The lady beetle has long been considered the "gardener's friend" because of its penchant for feasting on aphids. While most aphid populations will be reduced more or less by lady beetles, some aphids, such as the foxglove and potato aphids, can become more of a problem if lady beetles are about. Store-bought lady beetles are inclined to disperse away from your yard shortly after release. You would do better to encourage natural colonization by lady beetles by providing many different plants in your yard (lady beetles will feed on nectar and pollen in the absence of aphid prey). Southern (Harlequin) Lady Beetles will attack other lady beetles, lacewings, hoverflies and even butterflies, if aphids are scarce. This species was introduced to Washington State in the 1920s as an aphid predator and is now the most common species in south coastal British Columbia. As a result of competition, several native lady beetle species are in decline or have become extinct in many habitats. This species is the most common invader of homes in autumn.

Tiger Beetles

Cicindela spp., *Omus* spp.

Pacific Tiger Beetle

Tiger beetles are in Family Cicindelidae. Few bugs can outrun the long-legged Pacific Tiger Beetle (*C. oregona*) across open ground. It has powerful jaws for crushing and devouring prey. The Parowana Tiger Beetle (*C. parowana*) is rare, and the Purple Tiger Beetle (*C. purpurea*), is an endangered species in North America.

The Primitive Tiger Beetle (*Omus* spp.) doesn't fly, and its wings are reduced to vestigial stubs under small elytra.

Tiger beetles lay eggs singly in soil, and the larva lives in a perpendicular burrow in the soil. The head of the larva is near the surface and it ambushes small insects passing by. The third instar larva builds a pupal chamber to the side of the burrow and the adult emerges 18 to 24 days later. In some species, the pupa overwinters.

ID: *Adult:* Pacific Tiger Beetle: dark beetle with white spots on elytra, long legs and antennae and large eyes. Parowana Tiger Beetle: bright yellow with black or orange-red head and markings. Purple Tiger Beetle: usually iridescent green, but occasionally greenish purple or even black, with 2 white marks on the elytra. Primitive Tiger Beetle: black with a large, oval abdomen, narrow waist, large heart-shaped thoracic shield and small eyes; resembles a ground beetle. *Larva:* elongate, cylindrical grub with powerful mandibles that curve upwards.

Size: *Adult:* Pacific, Parowana and Purple tiger beetles: about 12 mm. Primitive Tiger Beetle: about 15 mm. *Larva:* about 10 mm long.

Habitat and Range: Pacific Tiger Beetle: on sand and gravel along Okanagan & Similkameen Valley riverbanks and lakes. Primitive Tiger Beetle: in forest clearings in the southwest and Vancouver Island. Parowana and Purple tiger beetles: salt flats in the Okanagan.

Scouting: Look for adult Pacific Tiger Beetles on sunny days along waterways. Primitive Tiger Beetles are nocturnal; during the day look for them under debris in wooded areas; Parowana and Purple Tiger Beetles can be found in muddy salt flats on sunny days.

Biological Control: The beetles' main enemies are humans who destroy their habitat.

Root Weevils

Otiorhynchus sulcatus and *O. ovatus*

Black Vine Weevil

Adult root weevils chew foliage, and larval stages feed on plant roots. The Black Vine Weevil (*O. sulcatus*) is the most common species in British Columbia. Both the Black Vine Weevil and Strawberry Root Weevil (*O. ovatus*) were introduced from Europe and have found great success across North America.

Adults and larvae or pupae overwinter in debris or soil beneath host plants. Adults hide during the day and emerge to feed at night. They also have the annoying habit of entering homes to overwinter and can sometimes be found trundling about in autumn and late spring, looking for a host plant on which to lay eggs. Eggs are laid near food hosts. Larvae from spring eggs burrow down to feed on roots and pupate in the soil. Larvae from autumn-laid eggs will overwinter. Adults are incapable of flight, instead relying on determination to walk everywhere, and they certainly can walk!

ID: *Adult:* Black Vine Weevil: stout, black beetle with rounded sides and yellow spots on elytra; mouthparts positioned at end of sharp, narrow muzzle. Strawberry Root Weevil: small, brown weevils with sharp, narrow muzzle. *Larva:* C-shaped white grub with light brown head.

Size: *Adult:* 3–6 mm. *Larva:* 3–12 mm.

Habitat and Range: thrives throughout the province. Adults feed at night on the foliage of strawberry, raspberry, blueberry, rhododendron, clover, grasses and various ornamental plants and weeds. Larvae feed on the roots of strawberry, raspberry, blueberry, rhododendron, containerized evergreens such as cedars and junipers, euonymus, roses and many other plants including grasses and weeds.

Scouting: As they feed, adults notch the edge of leaves. They puncture strawberry fruit, but this feeding usually does not cause serious damage. Larval feeding on roots stunts plants, resulting in death in severe infestations.

Cultural/Physical Control: Reduce the weevil's impact on your strawberry plants by moving your strawberries to different patches or by rotating them with another plant species every 2 to 3 years. Adult weevils in your home are harmless and only need be vacuumed up.

Biological Control: Ground beetles and rove beetles, among others, will feed on the larvae. Predatory nematodes, *Heterorhabditis* spp., are very effective at killing the soil-borne larvae when soil temperatures are above 10° C. The best time to apply them is the last week of August or early September, but they also can be applied in spring after soils warm up.

Terminal Weevils

Pissodes spp.

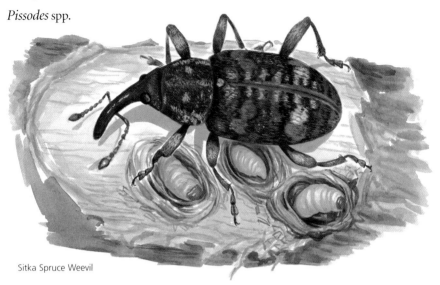

Sitka Spruce Weevil

The two species observed in our region are the Sitka Spruce Weevil, also known as the White Pine Weevil (*P. strobi*), which affects eastern white pine and Sitka, Engelmann and white spruce; and the Terminal Weevil (*P. terminalis*), which prefers lodgepole pine. It is easy to tell if a spruce or pine has these fellows attacking it because the tree leader (the top or 'terminal' shoot) is either dead or swollen and wilting. This causes the tree to become disfigured.

Adults overwinter in the duff beneath infested trees. They emerge in early spring and either walk or fly to a nearby host to begin feeding and laying eggs in last year's leader. Young trees in full sun are most susceptible. The larvae feed and pupate inside the stem, emerging as adults in late summer.

Damage is often observed in late spring and early summer and can be diagnosed by a wilting leader that has a series of tiny holes at its base. Pitch (conifer sap) may be flowing from the holes. If you dig into this area, you will often observe white grubs as well. Don't panic if you have to remove the tree's leader, as frustrating as this may be; a new leader can be easily trained, and after a couple of years, the tree will be back to normal.

ID: *Adult:* small, dark, elephant-like beetle with long snout. *Larva:* white, "legless" grub.

Size: *Adult:* 4–7 mm. *Larva:* similar in size to adult but earlier stages are smaller.

Habitat and Range: throughout the province on white, Engelmann and Sitka spruce as well as lodgepole pine in open sunny locations.

Scouting: Look for dead or wilting leaders on conifers. Adults may be present near the tree's terminal buds in early spring.

Cultural/Physical Control: To deal with attacks on yard trees, prune off the infested leader, and bag and dispose of it. Keep the ground under infested trees free of duff.

Biological Control: Provide plenty of habitat for natural predators such as parasitic wasps and flies.

Bronze Birch Borer
& Jewel Beetles

Agrilus anxius, Buprestis spp.

The metallic wood-boring beetles of the family Buprestidae are some of the world's most attractive beetles and have earned the title of "Jewel Beetle." Unfortunately they are destructive, as is the case with the Bronze Birch Borer (*A. anxius*), the Golden Jewel Beetle *(B. aurulenta)*, the Pink-faced Jewel Beetle *(B. lyrata)* and other species in BC.

In August, adult females lay an egg or small cluster of eggs in a crevice in sunny areas on south-facing branches of stressed trees. Eggs hatch about two weeks later, and larvae tunnel into the inner sapwood where they mine and feed against the wood grain. It generally takes two years to complete their life cycle, but in particularly warm years, the life cycle can be one year. In the two-year cycle, young larvae overwinter in their galleries and continue feeding through the following year. In autumn, the mature instars excavate a cell just under the bark where they pupate. The following summer, adults chew a D-shaped hole through the bark and feed on the foliage.

ID: *Adult:* Bronze Birch Borer: slender, cylindrical body, olive green to black with a metallic bronze sheen. Golden Jewel Beetle: bright metallic green with orange trim around wing covers. Pink-faced Jewel Beetle: bright pink or yellowish to orange markings on face. *Larva:* white, distinctly segmented, flattened grub with a deeply embedded brown head in a slightly swollen prothorax.

Size: *Adult:* 6–11 mm. *Larva:* similar in size to adult but earlier stages are smaller.

Habitat and Range: Bronze Birch Borer: weakened birch trees, including native and ornamental species; occurs over a wide range. Pink-faced Jewel Beetle: pine and fir. Golden Jewel Beetle: conifer species.

Scouting: Look for dead or dying treetops, wilting and flagging branches and D-shaped holes in bark. The larval galleries are filled with new tissue and create a bumpy ridge in the bark. These ridges and holes are often used to diagnose whether wood borers are attacking trees.

Cultural/Physical Control: Plant resistant species, and do not plant birch trees in full sun. Keep trees healthy and vigorous. Water, especially during drought. Remove dead and dying branches annually. Cut and burn infested branches before adults emerge.

Biological Control: Woodpeckers and wasp parasitoids are natural controls of larvae.

Poplar Borer

Saperda calcarata

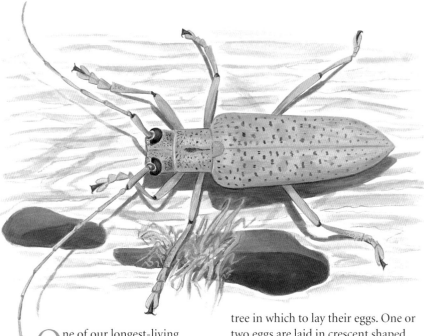

One of our longest-living beetles, the Poplar Borer can take up to five years to fully develop. It is in the family Cerambycidae, which is commonly known as the long-horned beetles.

Adults emerge in late June, when they feed on foliage for about one week. Females mate and seek out a stressed tree in which to lay their eggs. One or two eggs are laid in crescent shaped notches that the females chew into the trunk in the upper crown and exposed areas. Once the eggs hatch, the larvae bore into the inner bark. Larvae feed, grow and hibernate each autumn until maturity. Mature larvae hibernate one last time in a prepupal stage and pupate the following spring.

ID: *Adult:* large, pale, colourfully flecked beetle with antennae as long as its body. *Larva:* white, legless grub with brown head and thoracic shield.

Size: *Adult:* 20–30 mm. *Larva:* 20–35 mm but other stages may be smaller.

Habitat and Range: primary hosts are native aspen and black poplar but sometimes attack ornamental species such as hybrid poplar; occur throughout aspen parkland and boreal forest regions of the province.

Scouting: Watch for copious, bark-staining, amber-coloured sap flow and emergence holes. Sawdust is present at the base of the trunk and in sap. In young trees, borers are found either at the trunk base or in the root collar region.

Cultural/Physical Control: Keep trees healthy and vigorous to reduce tree susceptibility. You can mimic a woodpecker by using a piece of wire thrust into gallery entrances on the trunk to injure and kill the larvae.

Biological Control: A number of natural predators exist for this species, including parasitic insects such as wasps. Woodpeckers can reduce populations by up to 75 percent.

Banded Alder Borer

Rosalia funebris

This large, striking, black and white-striped beetle bores into dead and dying alder trees. Thus, while some people call it a "borer" and others a "beetle," either name is correct. The Banded Alder Borer is native to western North America, occurring west of the Rocky Mountains from Alaska to California and New Mexico. It is a member of the Cerambycidae family.

Banded Alder Borers do not harm healthy trees. Adults feed on leaves and larvae bore into tree trunks and large branches. They are also known to feed on Oregon ash, New Mexico willow and California laurel and are sometimes called California Laurel Borers.

The larvae are typical white borers: their large heads are well adapted for tunneling through wood. Larvae bore into the tree and feed and pupate inside; then the adults burrow out again. Females lay eggs on bark. There are one or two generations per year, which often overlap.

The Banded Alder Borer is often mistaken for the Asian Longhorned Beetle (*Anoplophora glabripennis*). This foreign relative has large, white spots on its elytra, not bands. In Asia, it is called the "Starry Sky Beetle" because the white spots look like stars in the night sky. It attacks healthy trees of many hardwood species. Since 1996, Asian Longhorned Beetles have been found in New York, Chicago and Toronto and have been intercepted at the Port of Vancouver. The beetles are believed to have been imported from China in shipping crates and packing materials. The Canadian Food Inspection Agency and the United States Department of Agriculture have acted to eradicate the beetle wherever it has been found. Asian exporters are legally required to treat all wood used for packing and shipping, to kill these beetles.

Also Known As: Banded Laurel Beetle

ID: *Adult:* elongated, flat, shiny, black beetle; white bands across elytra; white around head; long, black and white-banded antennae. *Larva:* long, white worm with rings around its body; large head.

Size: *Adult:* body length 2.5–3 cm. *Larva:* 2–3 cm.

Habitat and Range: throughout the province wherever alder is found.

Scouting: Look for circular holes and small mounds of sawdust on dead or dying alder trunks and branches.

Cultural/Physical Control: These controls are not required because these beetles don't damage healthy trees.

Biological Control: Woodpeckers and sapsuckers feed on borer larvae.

Poplar & Willow Borer

Cryptorhynchus lapathi

The Poplar and Willow Borer is an introduced weevil from Europe, and is probably the most prevalent species encountered in landscape willows and poplars. The damage it causes can setback, weaken, disfigure and kill trees.

The life cycle takes two years to complete. Adult beetles emerge from late June until late July, depending on the year, and feed heavily on new shoots. After mating, the female lays eggs in small holes chewed in the lower part of the stem. Once the eggs hatch, the first instar larvae burrow under bark and hibernate for the winter. In spring, the larvae become active and bore into the wood, forming tunnels that meander around and into the stem. Larval feeding causes quite extensive damage. The larvae continue to feed and grow, eventually pupating at the end of the tunnel. Adults then mine their way back through the tunnel, making their way to the outside world.

ID: *Adult:* black, elephant-shaped beetle with dark erect hairs and light-coloured rump patch. *Larva:* white, legless grub with brown head.

Size: *Adult:* 8–10 mm. *Larva:* 13 mm but other stages may be smaller.

Habitat and Range: throughout the province.

Scouting: Look for dead, wilting or discoloured stems and branches, irregular splits and holes in the tree bark that exude shavings-laden sap, and shavings at the bottom of the stem. Tunnels may be seen in split stems.

Cultural/Physical Control: Remove infested branches and burn or bury them deep in the ground. A piece of wire can be slid into tunnels and jammed into boring larvae. Squishing and pruning doesn't hurt the beneficial insects, other than removing a potential food supply.

Biological Control: Chickadees and nuthatches pick larvae off leaves and out of bark crevices. Other predators include predacious beetles and parasitic wasps and flies. Letting nature take its course is often the cheapest, easiest and simplest method of control.

Swallowtails & Tiger Swallowtails

Papilio spp.

Western Tiger Swallowtail

B ritish Columbians are fortunate to have several species of these large, beautifully coloured butterflies in our province. They are strong fliers and are often observed swiftly darting through gardens, parks and woods. Adults are valuable pollinators and can often be observed feeding on nectar from flowers in gardens, especially lilacs, or in sunny areas along woodland streams. Large groups may be seen drinking at puddles after a rain shower or feeding on fresh scat. There have been a number of sightings of groups feeding on coyote dung.

The Anise Swallowtail (*P. zelicaon*) is one of the most common swallowtails in southern BC. The Old World Swallowtail (*P. machaon*) occurs in the southern Interior, with sub-populations in the north and Peace River regions. The Indra Swallowtail (*P. indra*) occurs only in Manning Provincial Park. Among the tiger swallowtails, so-called because of the black stripes on their wings, the Western

ID; *Adult:* Swallowtails: yellow and black butterflies with dark body and blue and red or orange markings on hindwing. Tiger Swallowtails: yellow (or white) wings striped with black except the Pale Swallowtail, which is black and white; hindwing has black tail. *Larva:* Swallowtails: black, orange, yellow or pink stripes. Tiger Swallowtails: large and dark green, resembling a snake; thin yellow stripe separates thorax and abdomen; swollen head region has 2 black, yellow and blue eyespots; immature larva resembles bird droppings and is brown and white.

Size: *Adult:* Swallowtails: wingspan 60–100 mm. Tiger Swallowtails: wingspan 70–120 mm. *Larva:* up to 50 mm.

Habitat and Range: throughout the province in sunny, open areas, along woodland streams and river valleys, on hilltops with nectar flowers, and in gardens and parks.

Swallowtails & Tiger Swallowtails (continued)

Two-tailed Swallowtail

Tiger Swallowtail (*P. rutulus*) and the Pale Swallowtail (*P. eurymedon*) are the most common species in the south-coastal region. The Canadian Tiger Swallowtail (*P. canadensis*) is rarely seen at the coast but is common elsewhere throughout the province. Hybrids can occur between the Western and Canadian Tigers. The largest swallowtail in the province, the Two-tailed Swallowtail (*P. multicaudata*)—which actually has three tails—occurs only in the southern Interior.

Adults fly from spring to early summer and often congregate on hilltops to mate. Females lay eggs on host plant leaves and may mate more than once. The eggs hatch in a week or so, and larvae spend the summer feeding. In late summer, mature larvae seek out a suitable pupation site, often in the leaf litter beneath the host tree, and can sometimes be found crawling through the garden. They pupate and overwinter as chrysalids, emerging as adults the following spring.

Tiger Swallowtail: caterpillar feeds on aspen and poplar, willow, birch, cherry, ash and crab apple. Two-Tailed Swallowtail: also feeds on saskatoon. Anise and Indra swallowtails: caterpillar feeds on plants in the carrot family. Old World Swallowtail: caterpillar feeds only on wild tarragon.

Scouting: Watch for adults from May to August cruising through openings in wooded areas. Larvae may be found in curled leaves of host trees.

How to Attract: A few garden flowers attract this species, but their favourite ornamental seems to be lilac shrubs. When lilacs are in full bloom, they can have a number of swallowtails feeding at them. Leave some natural groves of swallowtails' host trees, such as aspen, poplar and willow, undisturbed.

Cabbage Butterfly

Pieris rapae

The Cabbage Butterfly can be one of the most unwanted garden pests and is a common site in gardens. It was introduced to Quebec in 1860 from Europe and is now found all over the continent. This average-sized butterfly is sometimes called a cabbage moth or cabbage worm.

This species can have up to three generations per year in our region, with adults emerging from overwintering chrysalids in spring. A female lays eggs on the host. Larvae hatch, feed and mature within three to four weeks.

Planting repellant plants such as mint (above) will help control the Cabbage Butterfly.

Cabbage Butterfly larvae have very successful defensive capabilities. A series of glandular hairs arranged in rows on their back flanks excretes oil that repels insect predators such as ants. In experiments where ants were allowed to interact with larvae, the ants immediately became irritated and began cleaning themselves, eventually leaving the larvae alone. Even birds leave Cabbage Butterfly larvae alone.

ID: *Adult:* white with black forewing tips; female has 2 black forewing spots. *Larva:* velvety, green caterpillar with faint yellow dorsal line.

Size: *Adult:* 30–50 mm. *Larva:* up to 30 mm.

Habitat and Range: throughout the province, especially common in gardens; host plants include cabbage, cauliflower, broccoli, canola and other domestic and wild mustard family plants.

Scouting: Watch gardens for feeding damage such as holes in leaves and for frass on leaves.

Cultural/Physical Control: Handpick larvae off plants. Deter ovipositing females by covering plants with a row cover or lightweight netting as a barrier. Interplant repellent plants such as mint, sage, rosemary, catnip, nasturtium, tomatoes and celery.

Biological Control: Many beneficial insects parasitize and feed on the larvae, including an array of parasitoid wasps, and predators such as ground beetles, hornets and birds. Leave or develop some natural areas in the yard to encourage these beneficial animals.

Admirals

Limenitis lorquini, Limenitis arthemis, Vanessa atalanta

Red Admiral

The only two true admiral butterflies in British Columbia are Lorquin's Admiral (*L. lorquini*) and the White Admiral (*L. arthemis*). Another butterfly commonly known as the Red Admiral (*V. atalanta)* is, in fact, part of the group of butterflies known as painted ladies; thus, some lepidopterists prefer to call it by its older name, the "Red Admirable." These butterflies are in the family Nymphalidae.

Admirals are large, dark brownish purple butterflies with a band of white spots across their wings. Lorquin's Admiral is sometimes called the "Orangetip Admiral" because it has

ID: *Adult:* Lorquin's Admiral: dark brownish purple butterfly; band of white spots on wings and orange wing tips. White Admiral: dark brownish purple butterfly; numerous blue and red markings on wing margins. Red Admiral: brown to black wings with a red band across them and white spots on the tips. *Larva:* Lorquin's and White admirals: grey and brown caterpillar with white, saddle-shaped mark on mid-dorsal surface; large head with 2 horn-like protrusions; body covered with short spines

and oval swellings. Red Admiral: black, spiny caterpillar with lateral white markings.

Size: *Adult:* Lorquin's and White admirals: wingspan 50–70 mm. Red Admiral: wingspan 50–60 mm. *Larva:* up to 30 mm.

Habitat and Range: Lorquin's Admiral: southern BC and Vancouver Island. White Admiral: east of the Cascades from US border north to Yukon. Red Admiral: throughout the province.

orange wing tips; the White Admiral lacks these orange tips but has red and blue markings along the edges of its wings. Hybrids of these two butterflies may be found in areas where their ranges overlap. In eastern North America, a sub-species of the White Admiral is called the Red-spotted Purple. The Viceroy (*L. archippus*) is in the same sub-family. The Red Admiral is a dark brown to black butterfly with a red band across its wings.

Lorquin's Admiral

Unlike Painted Ladies (including the Red Admiral), true admirals do not migrate. They overwinter in BC as larvae in leaves curled up and tied with silk. The caterpillars, which look like bird droppings, feed briefly in spring and pupate. Adults are usually seen in June and July, often perched high in trees. Eggs are laid on willow and poplar and either birch (White Admiral) or chokecherry and other *Prunus* species (Lorquin's Admiral). There is one generation and a partial second generation each year. Second generation adults fly in August and September. The Red Admiral can be seen from May to September before it migrates to California for winter. Its caterpillar feeds on nettles.

Male admirals are highly territorial. Each one surveys his territory from his high perch and will swoop down to fight and drive off any other male who wanders in.

Scouting: Lorquin's and White admirals perch high up in trees. Their caterpillars can be found in spring and again in late July or early August, feeding or pupating in rolled-up leaves. The Red Admiral can be found in many habitats.

Cultural/Physical Control: Larvae rarely do enough feeding damage to landscape trees to require control. Caterpillars can be hand picked from leaves if necessary.

Biological Control: B.t.k. (*Bacillus thuringiensis kurstaki*) will kill young caterpillars.

Mourning Cloak Butterfly

Nymphalis antiopa

This holarctic species is known as the Camberwell Beauty, Grand Surprise or White Petticoat in Europe and Asia. The holarctic region encompasses the northern and arctic ecoregions of the planet.

The appearance of Mourning Cloaks is often a sign that seasons are changing. Adults emerge in August, indicating that autumn is just around the corner. On a warm day in March, they are one of the first out of hibernation and indicate that spring is coming. Adults feed on sap, decaying fruit, nectar and scat into autumn. They hibernate in nest boxes, woodpiles and a number of other spots in the garden or yard. If you are burning wood in the house and bringing logs in from outside, watch for these guys—there may be a few sitting on a log you intend to burn. These amazing butterflies increase the levels of antifreeze chemicals in their bodies in autumn so that they don't freeze in winter.

Once spring settles in, adult females lay clusters of eggs on tree branches. Larvae hatch and feed colonially, often defoliating one entire branch before moving to another. Mature larvae then pupate, emerging as adults in late July or early August.

ID: *Adult:* large, dark brown butterfly with yellow to white banding on rims of wings; forewings have row of blue spots along inside of band; resembles dead leaf when sitting. *Larva:* black caterpillar covered in branchy spines and tiny white dots, with distinct row of red spots along dorsal area.

Size: *Adult:* 60–80 mm. *Larva:* 50 mm.

Habitat and Range: common throughout the province; larvae feed on willow, American white elm and aspen.

Scouting: Adults lay clusters of eggs, so the branch they hatch on is usually defoliated. Watch for defoliation on host plants and for the presence of dark, spiny caterpillars.

Cultural/Physical Control: These caterpillars really aren't much of a pest but can have good years where they are quite common. Colonies of larvae can be hand picked.

Biological Control: There are many parasitic wasps that attack this species, as well as a wide range of other predators, such as birds.

Azures & Blues

Celastrina ladon, Glaucopsyche lygdamus, Everes amyntula

Spring Azure

These butterflies are the gems of gardens as they flutter from flower to flower. Spring Azures (*C. ladon*) emerge in late April and flutter among the flushing trees. Once the leaves flush, the Silvery Blues (*G. lygdamus*) appear, and a week or two later the Western Tailed Blues (*E. amyntula*) arrive. Blues are nectar feeders so they love having a garden full of nectar-producing flowers. On hot, dry days, large groups of blues can be observed drinking at puddles.

Spring Azure adults emerge in spring, mate and lay eggs. Small, slug-like larvae

ID: *Adult:* male is more colourful than female. Spring Azure: purplish blue dorsal wings; grey ventrally with black spotting. Silvery Blue: bright blue dorsally and grey ventrally with numerous round black spots. Western Tailed Blue: easily separated from all others by its little hindwing tail. *Larva:* slug-shaped caterpillar. Spring Azure: green overall. Silvery Blue and Western Tailed Blue: vary in colour from green to purplish, with darker dorsal stripe and lighter diagonal stripes.

Size: *Adult:* wingspan 20–32 mm. *Larva:* body length 15–20 mm.

Habitat and Range: all species are found throughout southern British Columbia, especially in areas near native bush, ravines or riparian areas. Spring Azure: prefers sheltered woodland in the boreal forest or aspen parkland; host plants for larvae include dogwoods, cranberries, bunchberries, blueberries and other low shrubs. Silvery

Azures & Blues (continued)

Western Tailed Blue

produce a sticky secretion that attracts ants. In return, the ants protect them. Larvae feed throughout summer on flowers and flower buds and overwinter as pupae. The other species' life cycles are similar, but occur slightly later. The larvae eat the flowers, leaves and seeds of their hosts. Silvery Blues overwinter as pupae and Western Tailed Blues overwinter as mature caterpillars.

Planting small shrubs such as dogwood (above) will help attract Spring Azures to your garden.

Blues and Western Tailed Blues: prefer open forests and wildflower meadows, and legumes such as vetch, clover, pea vines, locoweed and lupines as hosts.

Scouting: Look from early spring to early summer for adults feeding at flowers and for males perched on plants, especially in gardens bordering woodlands.

How to Attract: All species thrive where natural and wild areas have been maintained, so the preservation of these habitats, especially those with host plants, is essential. To attract these butterflies into the garden, plant flowers that produce nectar and flower early in the year.

Monarch

Danaus plexippus

If you spot a Monarch butterfly soaring through the garden, consider yourself lucky—this species is uncommon in BC. The Monarch is most likely to be encountered in the southern Interior and is more rarely seen at the coast. This amazing butterfly is one of our province's largest and showiest species. It is a huge orange and black butterfly and is unmistakable when you see it. East of the Rockies, Monarchs migrate from their summer homes in Canada to forests west of Mexico City. West of the Rockies,

---

ID: *Adult:* large, bright orange butterfly with heavy black wing veins and white spots on wing margins and tips. *Larva:* caterpillar has black, white and yellow bands; 2 pairs of fleshy filaments, 1 pair just behind its head and the other near the rear.

Size: *Adult:* wingspan 90–105 mm. *Larva:* body length 50 mm.

Habitat and Range: open habitats including fields, wildflower meadows and ditches in southern parts of the province.

Scouting: Look for adults in gardens and yards, often gliding but sometimes feeding at host plants.

How to Attract: To attract this butterfly to your garden, it is best to have a thriving patch of milkweed. One of the Monarch's favourite nectar sources is a species of milkweed called butterfly weed, but all plants in the *Asclepias* genus will attract these butterflies.

Monarch (continued)

Monarchs from BC migrate to overwintering sites in California, and possibly to Mexico.

Adults mate in spring before they migrate north. Monarchs arrive in June in BC and lay eggs on milkweed. These hatch into caterpillars, which begin to feed. If the climactic conditions are favourable and temperatures are warm enough, the larvae will pupate in a cocoon and complete their development, with the adults then heading south to overwinter in California.

Milkweed plants in the genus *Asclepias,* the primary food of Monarchs, contain cardiac glycosides that the Monarch larvae and adults retain in their bodies, making them toxic and distasteful to predators. Birds have learned to avoid them. Another species of butterfly, the Viceroy (*Limenitis archippus*), even mimics them. The Viceroy is almost identical in appearance, but it has a black line through its hindwing and is much smaller. The Viceroy is believed to have been extirpated from British Columbia.

Try planting butterfly weed (*Asclepias tuberosa)* in your garden to help attract Monarch butterflies.

Painted Lady

Vanessa cardui

When Painted Ladies arrive in BC, they capture everyone's attention because they seem to be everywhere. It all starts in the southwestern deserts of the US and Mexico, where populations slowly build up until the butterflies eat themselves out of house and home and then migrate north looking for food. Although a few arrive every year, large migrations happen once every 10 years or so, most recently in 2005, when the butterflies made the news several times. The larvae are not hardy enough to survive our winters, so the huge populations disappear in autumn and the following year. Two similar species can be found in southern BC, the West Coast Lady (*V. annabella*) and the rarer American Lady (*V. virginialis*).

Migrants arrive in May. Though they are all called "ladies," the population includes both males and females. Larvae appear shortly after the migrants have arrived and laid eggs. The spiny larvae build silken structures on the leaves of host plants. In years of heavy infestation, larvae can entirely defoliate hosts. The larvae pupate, and adults fly from July to autumn.

ID: *Adult:* Painted Lady: brown with a hairy thorax and abdomen; orange wings with white-spotted, black wing tips; 4 eyespots on underside of hindwings. West Coast Lady: more orange-coloured wings. American Lady: 2 eyespots on hindwings. *Larva:* dark-coloured head; pale body has yellowish dorsal and lateral stripes and is covered with light-coloured hairs; each body segment has 6 spines known as scoli.

Size: *Adult:* Painted Lady wingspan 50–70 mm. West Coast Lady: 40–55 mm. American Lady: 40–60 mm. *Larva:* body length 45 mm.

Habitat and Range: migrants. Painted Lady: throughout the province during northern migrations; caterpillar feeds on a variety of plants, especially thistles. West Coast Lady: only in the south; caterpillar feeds on stinging nettle and hollyhock. American Lady: only in south; caterpillar feeds on plants in the Asteraceae family.

Scouting: Painted Ladies often arrive in huge numbers. They love nectaring at flowers, so look for them in your garden.

How to Attract: Plant nectar-producing flowers.

Crescents

Phyciodes pulchella (P. campestris), P. cocyta

Field Crescent

Crescents are common orange and brown butterflies in the family Nymphalidae. The Field Crescent (*P. pulchella*) and the Northern Crescent (*P. cocyta*) are two of the most common butterflies in British Columbia. They are found throughout the province in many different habitats, but the Field Crescent is more common in south-coastal BC.

Crescents get their name from a single, crescent-shaped spot on their hind wings. Although the Field and Northern crescents have very different wing markings, there are other, closely related crescent species in BC with which they may hybridize. Crescents somewhat resemble fritillaries checkerspot butterflies.

Crescent caterpillars feed only on plants in the Asteraceae family. Field and Northern crescent larvae feed only on wild asters. There is usually only one generation in the north, but in southern regions there is often a second generation which flies in early fall.

ID: *Adult:* Male: orange and brown butterfly with irregular orange and brown wing markings and a crescent-shaped spot on hind wings. Female: yellow butterfly with orange and brown wing markings; crescent-shaped wing spot is cream to white. *Larva:* reddish brown caterpillar with rows of reddish brown spines, sometimes tipped with white.

Size: *Adult:* wingspan 35–40 mm. *Larva:* up to 25 mm.

Habitat and Range: open areas such as fields, meadows and roadsides; poplar forests. Field Crescent: southern Vancouver Island and Lower Mainland; throughout the interior of the province from US border to Yukon. Northern Crescent: south-central Interior and Peace River district.

Scouting: Adults can be present from May to early fall. Look for caterpillars on wild asters or thistles.

How to Attract: Wild and cultivated asters will attract crescent butterflies.

Fritillaries

Boloria epithore, Speyeria cybele and others

Great Spangled
Fritillary

Fritillaries are members of the Nymphalidae family, the brush-footed butterflies, a family that includes the admirals, alpines, arctics, commas, crescents, monarchs, mourning cloaks, wood-nymphs and satyrs, painted ladies and tortoiseshells. Like crescents, fritillaries have orange wings with brown markings on the upper surface. However, on fritillary wings, these markings tend to be smaller and more regular in pattern than those of the crescents, and, unlike almost all the fritillaries, crescents don't have silver spots on the underside of their wings, visible when the butterflies are at rest.

ID: *Adult:* orange butterfly with black spots and bars across upper wing surface; silver spots on underside of hind wings. *Larva:* brown or reddish brown caterpillar with black spines and rows of white spots or bars on lateral and dorsal surface.

Size: *Adult:* Western Meadow Fritillary: wingspan 35–40 mm. Great Spangled Fritillary: wingspan 65–90 mm. *Larva:* up to 30 mm.

Habitat and Range: open, sunny areas in coniferous forests, meadows and marshes. Western Meadow Fritillary: coastal BC and the southern Interior. Great Spangled Fritillary: the southern Interior. Other fritillary species: throughout the south-central areas of the interior and northern regions of the province.

Fritillaries (continued)

Western Meadow
(Pacific) Fritillary

In British Columbia, fritillaries are represented by several species found primarily in the southern Interior, central and northern mountain regions of the province. One of the few species that occurs in coastal BC is the Western Meadow Fritillary (*B. epithore*), also called the "Pacific Fritillary." The Great Spangled Fritillary (*S. cybele*), perhaps the most well-known butterfly in this group, occurs in the southern Interior. The Zerene Fritillary (*S. zerene*) can be found in the Lower Mainland and on Vancouver Island as well as in the southern Interior. Adults of the Variegated Fritillary (*Euptoeita claudia*) migrate into southeastern BC (Cranbrook) and southern Alberta from the US each summer. Their caterpillars feed on a variety of plants including violets, but they are not known to overwinter in BC.

All fritillary caterpillars feed on wild and cultivated violets (*Viola* spp.). However, some northern species are believed to feed on wild huckleberry (*Vaccinium* spp.) or other plants. The half-grown caterpillars overwinter and then start feeding and pupate in spring. There is one generation per year. Adults can be found from May to August but usually peak in June and July.

The brush-footed butterflies are so called because their two front legs are very short with brush-like appendages that function as chemo-receptors, like a second pair of antennae. Thus, these butterflies appear to have only four legs instead of six.

Scouting: Look on wild violets for caterpillars with black spines. Adults can often be seen in sunny openings in meadows, fields and forests.

How to Attract: Wild and cultivated violets will attract fritillary butterflies.

Coppers

Lycaena helloides, L. mariposa

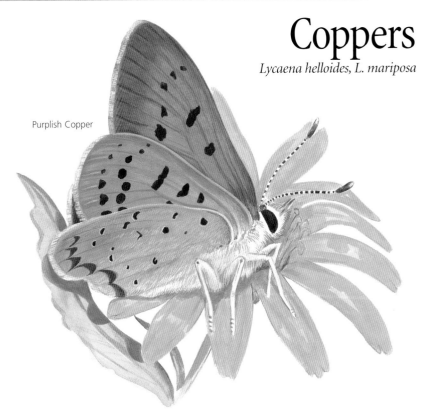

Purplish Copper

The Purplish Copper (*L. helloides*) is one of the most common butterflies encountered in meadows, roadsides and urban areas across southern British Columbia. The male's wings are coppery-brown with a purplish sheen. A related species, the Mariposa Copper (*L. mariposa*), is found in forested areas throughout the province. The male Mariposa Copper's wings are dark purplish brown.

Coppers are members of the Lycaenidae or gossamer-winged family of butterflies. Gossamer-wings are relatively small butterflies with large, black eyes surrounded by a white fringe, like a beard, that often extends along their body.

The Purplish Copper has two generations per year. The first adult flight occurs mainly in June and the second in September, although adults

ID: *Adult:* Purplish Copper: Male: copper-coloured wings with brown spots; gold-coloured band on margin of hind wings. Female: yellowish orange wings with a coppery bronze sheen. Mariposa Copper: Male: dark purplish brown wings; black and white, checkered fringe on forewings; hind wings are mottled grey on underside. Female: yellowish brown wings with checkered fringe on forewings. *Larva:* green with white and red spots.

Size: *Adult:* Purplish Copper: wingspan 25–35 mm. Mariposa Copper: wingspan 25–30 mm. *Larva:* up to 30 mm.

Habitat and Range: Purplish Copper: weedy fields, meadows, roadsides and urban areas across southern BC, the Peace River district and southern Vancouver Island. Mariposa Copper: forested sites throughout the province.

Coppers (continued)

Blueberries (above), huckleberry (below)

can be found in May and October in warm sites. Caterpillars feed on leaves of weeds in the Polygonaceae family such as sheep sorrel, dock, smartweed and knotweed. Caterpillars of the Mariposa Copper feed on blueberry and huckleberry (*Vaccinium* spp.) and bog rosemary leaves but don't damage commercial blueberry crops because they prefer wooded sites. Adults fly from June to September. Caterpillars of both species overwinter and pupate at the base of their food plants.

Scouting: Look for the Purplish Copper in open, weedy and moist areas, including vacant lots, gravelly sites and roadsides. It is sometimes seen flitting across urban lawns. Look for the Mariposa Copper in forest clearings, often along streams. Newly hatched caterpillars feed on the surface of leaves without perforating the tissue; third and later instars cause feeding holes in leaves.

How to Attract: If you have a wooded area on your property, plant wild Vaccinium species as an understory plant to attract the Mariposa Copper. Weeds in the Polygonaceae family will attract the Purplish Copper and are present naturally in most environments.

Clouded Sulphur
Colias philodice

The Clouded Sulphur has to be one of our most common butterflies, often seen from spring to autumn in our yards and gardens. This bright yellow butterfly is often observed nectaring at garden flowers or drinking at puddles on the driveway. A few similar-looking species also appear in our gardens. The Alfalfa Butterfly (*C. eurytheme*) looks almost identical to the Clouded Sulphur but tends to have orange forewings. The two species hybridize, and the resulting adults have characteristics of both species.

This species has two to three generations in our southern regions but only one in the northern regions. Eggs are laid in spring on various herbaceous legumes. Larvae later hatch and feed on legume foliage and, once mature, pupate. The first big adult population appears in June, the second occurs in July and a third small population appears in autumn. Adults of this final generation can survive into October and are able to survive a few frosty days. Either the pupae or the larvae overwinter—research is uncertain on the subject.

ID: *Adult:* forewing has somewhat centrally placed black dot; dorsal hindwing has central orange spot; ventral hindwing has row of spots behind single larger white dot lined with red; male is yellow with broad, black marginal forewing bands; female is either yellow or white with yellow spots within black borders. *Larva:* green with white stripe along side; stripe is lined with dark green and has faint orange to red line within.

Size: *Adult:* wingspan 32–54 mm. *Larva:* body length 35 mm.

Habitat and Range: throughout British Columbia wherever alfalfa, clover, sweet clover, vetch and many other legumes are found.

Scouting: If you see a yellow butterfly flitting in the garden, it is likely a Clouded Sulphur.

How to Attract: Host plants are common throughout BC. Plant various nectar-producing flowers that bloom from spring to autumn.

Gypsy Moth
Lymantria dispar

Gypsy Moth (larva)

Gypsy Moth caterpillars are known to feed on at least 500 species of deciduous and evergreen trees and shrubs, including conifers. It's been estimated that a single Gypsy Moth caterpillar eats about 1 square metre of foliage during its lifetime.

The Gypsy Moth is native to Europe and North Africa. There is a European and an Asian strain. The European strain became established in the northeastern United States in the 1870s, in Ontario and Quebec in the 1960s and was found in Nova Scotia and New Brunswick in the 1980s. Throughout the 1970s and 80s, a few adults and eggs were found in the Fraser Valley, Vancouver Island and Kelowna, but the insect did not become widespread. However, in 1991, thousands of Asian Gypsy Moth egg masses were found on Russian grain ships in the Port of Vancouver and adults were trapped

ID: *Adult:* Male: small, brown moth. Female: white with a dark brown, zigzag band across the mid-wings. *Larva:* tan (young) to dark grey (older) with a double row of five blue dots and six red spots on its back and tufts of short spines.

Size: *Adult:* wingspan 30 mm. *Mature larva:* 6–7.5 cm. *Pupa:* Male: about 2.0 cm long. Female: about 3.5 cm long.

Habitat and Range: deciduous and coniferous trees and shrubs; present only in isolated areas on Vancouver Island and Salt Spring Island and is under eradication.

Scouting: Keep a lookout for gypsy moths in your area. Watch for tan, "chamois-like" egg masses on tree trunks, leaves and even on fences, sheds and decks, vehicles and lawn furniture. Look for the tiny caterpillars of the European Gypsy Moth on tree trunks at bud break, or leaf feeding by both European and Asian Gypsy Moth larvae. Destroy egg masses and caterpillars before they develop

onshore. In addition, there was an increasing number of European Gypsy Moth finds on Vancouver Island and in the Lower Mainland.

Since then, the British Columbia Ministry of Forests, the Canadian Food Inspection Agency and other provincial, federal and municipal agencies have intensified their efforts to eradicate the Gypsy Moth in British Columbia and prevent further introductions. Ships are inspected, traps containing mating pheromones are used to trap male moths, and government inspectors, homeowners, landscapers, and nursery and park staff check trees for egg masses every spring. Egg masses are removed by hand and, where necessary, trees are sprayed with B.t.k., an insecticide derived from a naturally occurring bacterium. In 2007, the Gypsy Moth was found only at a few sites on Vancouver Island and Salt Spring Island.

European females don't fly, and they lay eggs close to the ground at the base of trees. Asian females fly, so can spread over greater distances and lay eggs on foliage at the tops of trees. The Gypsy Moth overwinters as an egg on bark or in a sheltered area. Egg masses are chamois-like and cream to tan in colour. They are the diameter of about a dime to a dollar coin and contain 100 to 1000 eggs each. Asian Gypsy Moth caterpillars begin feeding as soon as they hatch; European caterpillars must first crawl up the tree trunks. Caterpillars feed for about seven weeks and then pupate for 10 to 14 days in late June and July in protected areas on the tree. Pupae are brown, tear-dropped shaped and covered with tiny hairs. Moths fly in July and August, and there is one generation per year.

The European Gypsy Moth was introduced to Massachusetts in 1869 by a French scientist who hoped to breed them with the Asian silk moth and create a silk industry in the United States. He was unsuccessful and eventually returned to France, but the Gypsy Moths escaped and soon established themselves in the New World.

into adults in July and August. Notify authorities in your area if you find Gypsy Moth eggs or caterpillars.

Cultural and Physical Control: Kill egg masses with dormant oil in winter or with a spray of soap, bleach, household ammonia, or vegetable oil and water. For European Gypsy Moth, wrap tree trunks with burlap tied with string and folded over to trap caterpillars in early spring. Pick off and destroy pupae and caterpillars. Be sure to wear gloves because the hairs can cause allergic reactions. Cut, crush or freeze pupae solid before disposal.

Biological Control: Home garden insecticides containing B.t.k., a crystal produced by the naturally occurring bacterium *Bacillus thuringiensis kurstaki* will kill young caterpillars. Spray on leaves when young caterpillars are first seen.

Northern Pitch Moth

Retinia albicapitana

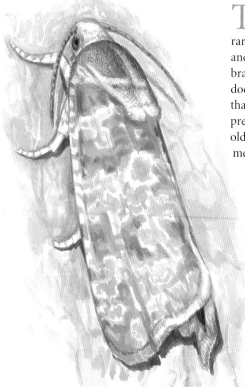

This moth gets its name from the sappy nodule its larva forms. It rarely does extensive damage to trees and often does not girdle or kill branches. The most common damage it does is to weaken twigs and branches so that they break in the wind. This moth prefers young trees that are 8 to 12 years old and range in height from 0.5 to 5 metres.

This species has a two-year life cycle. Adults appear in late June to July and eggs are laid at the base of needle buds. Larvae later hatch and burrow into tissue to begin feeding. Over time, a protective nodule is constructed from frass, silk and sap. Young larvae overwinter within the nodule, continuing to feed the following spring. Once June arrives, the larvae migrate to new feeding sites, forming nodules up to 30 millimetres in diameter. Mature larvae overwinter in the new nodules and pupate the following spring.

ID: *Adult:* reddish wings with dark speckling and black banding. *Larva:* variable from yellow to orangey brown body; reddish brown head.

Size: *Adult:* wingspan 16–23 mm. *Larva:* body length 15–17 mm.

Habitat and Range: found in regions that border forests with wild pines, including mountains and boreal forest regions; larvae feed on lodgepole, Jack and ornamental pines, such as Scots pine, in nurseries and landscapes.

Scouting: Look for red needles, needles losing colour, broken twigs and branches, and blister-like growths at the nodes of branches and twigs. Fresh nodules appear red while older ones are encrusted with white. Active nodules are often a combination of these colours and possess a larva.

Cultural/Physical Control: Dig out and dispose of larvae. Prune off broken twigs and branches. Catching the larvae early is best—older larvae weaken braches more extensively. Grow resistant pines or conifers such as spruce in areas that encounter repeated outbreaks. Develop a natural style of garden and limit insecticide use.

Biological Control: Many parasites and natural predators, including chickadees, keep pitch moth populations low. Parasitoid wasps can control up to 10 percent of the population.

Gallium Sphinx

Hyles spp., *Hemaris* spp., others

Gallium Sphinx adult
(*Hyles galli*)

If you see a hornworm, you are likely looking at the larva of a sphinx or hawk moth from the Sphingidae family. The Gallium Sphinx is likely our most widespread species of sphinx moth. It is a large, fast moth sometimes observed nectaring at flowers like a hummingbird.

This species has one generation per year. Adults appear in June and are primarily nocturnal, commonly observed coming to lights at night. After mating, pregnant females cruise around and lay eggs on host plants. Larvae feed on the hosts and mature in August, when they begin a march to find a pupation site. At this time of year it is common to observe them, and they may be seen marching up your sidewalk. When they find a suitable location, they submerge themselves in the soil and pupate in an underground pupation chamber.

ID: *Adult:* brown to black forewings have wide, light stripe; dark hindwings have central pink to red band. *Larva:* variable, from green to brown or black, with red horn on posterior; body lined with light spots.

Size: *Adult:* wingspan 60–90 mm. *Larva:* body length 70 mm.

Habitat and Range: throughout the province; larvae feed on bedstraw, fireweed and other plants in evening primrose family

(Onagraceae) and madder family (Rubiaceae).

Scouting: In summer, adults are commonly seen nectaring at dusk or at night (and sometimes during the day) on flowers such as lilacs, phlox, lungworts and evening primroses.

How to Attract: Plant a variety of nectar-producing plants such as lilacs. Also leave some wild areas intact—especially those that possess host plants such as fireweed and bedstraw.

Gallium Sphinx (continued)

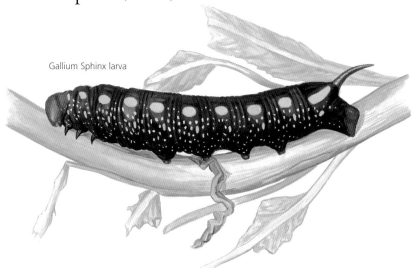

Gallium Sphinx larva

Other similar species may be encountered. The Spurge Hawk Moth (*Hyles euphorbiae*) was introduced from Europe as a biological control for leafy spurge. Its forewing is much lighter and is freckled with light spots,

Plant nectar-producing plants such as lilacs; *Syringa* x *hyacinthiflora* 'Pocahontas' (below).

and its larvae have a prominent red dorsal stripe. The Snowberry Clearwing (*Hemaris diffinis*), also known as the Hummingbird Moth, is a sphinx with "see-though" wings that feeds on flower nectar during the day. Less common are the Great Ash Sphinx (*Sphinx chercis*) and the Big Poplar Sphinx (*Pachysphinx occidentalis*), two of the largest moths in Canada. Tomato growers in the Thompson, Okanagan and Similkameen valleys will be familiar with the Tomato Hornworm (*Manduca quinquemaculata*).

Sphinx moths are likely named for the posture their larvae assume when resting. When they are not feeding, larvae sit with their head and front legs lifted off the branch while the rear prolegs remain secure. Their head is also tucked in, much like that of the Sphinx statues of Egypt.

Satin Moth

Leucoma salicis

Satin moths arrived in southwestern BC in 1920 from Europe and soon became established residents, feeding on native and non-native poplar, aspen and cottonwood trees. Native and introduced predators and parasites have since reduced populations and feeding damage to small areas.

Adults emerge in the middle of July and are quite obvious. They are attracted to lights, and large numbers are sometimes seen in the morning sitting on the wall around a light. Females tend to be poor fliers because they are often heavy with eggs. Females lay shiny whitish egg masses, which contain about 150 to 200 eggs, on the leaves, trunk or branches of a host. About two weeks later, the caterpillars hatch and move to the foliage to begin feeding. The larvae are skeletonizers. In late summer and autumn, the larvae find a hibernation site in the bark and construct a silken chamber to overwinter. Once leaves flush in May, the larvae climb out of hiding and begin to feed again, consuming entire leaves except the main veins. By June, maturing colonies become quite obvious because they can defoliate entire trees. By July, mature larvae spin cocoons to pupate. Adults emerge about 10 days later.

ID: *Adult:* medium-sized, silver-white moth; dark body covered in glossy white hairs. *Larva:* dark, hairy body with yellow lateral lines and large pale yellow to white dorsal spots rimmed by subdorsal orange bumps with brownish hairs.

Size: *Adult:* wingspan 24–47 mm. *Larva:* body length 35 mm.

Habitat and Range: southern BC; feeds on *Populus* species, especially trembling aspen, black cottonwood and ornamental poplars such as Lombardy poplar and silver poplar.

Scouting: Watch for defoliation in May and June, skeletonized foliage in late summer, and the presence of caterpillars; pupae may be found in rolled leaves.

Cultural/Physical Control: For a few trees and small populations, pick larvae off by hand and dispose of them. Keep trees healthy, watering them when they are dry. A shot of fertilizer in spring often helps trees recover from defoliation.

Biological Control: Predators include birds, lacewing larvae and other beneficial insects. Parasitoid wasps such as *Meteorus versicolor* (a member of the Braconidae family) and tachinid flies can greatly suppress these pests. A nuclear polyhedrosis virus (NPV) can significantly reduce numbers. Allow nature to do its job by promoting biological controls and natural processes.

Underwing Moths

Catocala spp.

White Underwing

moths. He fell in love with them as a child and has been infatuated with them ever since. "Cats," as many lepidopterists refer to them, are some of the most attractive moths we have and rival the giant silk, tiger and sphinx moths in popularity. They are an elusive nocturnal species but are common in our gardens. Three commonly encountered species are the White Underwing (*C. relicta*), the Briseis Underwing (*C. briseis*) and the Aholibah Underwing (*C. aholibah*). Larvae hatch from eggs in spring and move up the tree to feed. Mature larvae descend to the ground to pupate. The adults emerge in August, mate and lay eggs on the bark of host trees.

In his famous book, *Legion of Night: The Underwing Moths,* Theodore Sargent wrote of his love for underwing

---

ID: *Adult:* White Underwing: white birch bark patterned forewings and black and white hindwings. Briseis Underwing: greyish black forewings with a few central whitish patches; red-orange hindwings with broad outer black bands and central black bands. Aholibah Underwing: similar to the Briseis but larger with lighter grey forewing that has one whitish patch and hind wings patterned in red and black. *Larva:* large and grey, generally resembling stick or lump on tree bark.

Size: *Adult:* wingspan 59–80 mm. *Larva:* body length 55–75 mm.

Habitat and Range: throughout the boreal and parkland regions and along river valleys in British Columbia; host plants include poplar, birch, oak and willow.

Scouting: Larvae and adults are well camouflaged and nocturnal.

How to Attract: Heat a magnificent brew of beer, molasses and rotten fruit in a pot and mix until smooth. At dusk, take a pail of your brew outside and paint it onto a few tree trunks or fence posts. Wait until it gets pretty dark. With flashlight in hand, go check out the sugary masses. On a good night, there will be a flurry of moths. The mixture will attract a variety of moth species, but look for large moths with brilliant red hindwings. If you find one, approach it quietly, maintaining a comfortable distance. Active Yellow-Bellied Sapsucker galleries on birch are also an excellent attractant for these moths, especially on warm August nights.

Large Aspen Tortrix

Choristoneura conflictana

These moths belong to the Tortricidae family and can defoliate trees, especially aspen, in gardens or farms during an outbreak. Outbreaks of Large Aspen Tortrix often precede outbreaks of the Forest Tent Caterpillar. Tortrix adults emerge in July and are active both day and night. They can travel remarkable distances, and you may even see adults laying on snow packs on the tops of mountain ridges.

Eggs are laid in July in clusters on leaves and hatch about two weeks later. The larvae hatch, immediately web a couple of leaves together and begin feeding and skeletonizing the leaves. In mid-August, the second instar larvae stop feeding and find a place, such as a crevice in the tree bark on the lower parts of the trunk, where they spin silken hibernacula in which to overwinter. In early spring, larvae emerge and mine into flushing leaf buds to feed and moult. As the leaves emerge, the larvae roll the leaves together and continue feeding. Larvae mature in late June, pupating within their silken den. Adults emerge 10 days later.

ID: *Adult:* grey-brown forewings have dark grey medial band with basal and outer patches; hindwings are smoky grey with fringe of hairs. *Larva:* yellow to green body with black head.

Size: *Adult:* wingspan 25–37 mm. *Larva:* body length 15–21 mm.

Habitat and Range: throughout the boreal and parkland regions of British Columbia; larvae feed primarily on aspen but also on willows and other poplars.

Scouting: In spring, look for delayed bud break, silk webbing on foliage and sometimes on surrounding vegetation, rolled foliage and tree defoliation. Many of the webbed leaves will have a larvae or pupae inside.

Cultural/Physical Control: Tree mortality rarely occurs, as many trees are adapted to defoliation by insects. Trees can be wrapped with a sticky strip around the trunk about a metre off the ground to trap larvae that are migrating to and from the hibernacula. If there are only a few larvae, it is likely okay to let them be, but large populations may need spraying.

Biological Control: Predators include vireos, woodpeckers, warblers, predacious and parasitic wasps, parasitic tachinid flies, ants and other predatory insects. Disease and inclement weather also reduce large populations.

Cherry Bark Tortrix
Enarmonia formosana

The Cherry Bark Tortrix is a small, mottled, brown moth whose larvae bore into the bark of ornamental and fruit trees in the Rosaceae family, including cherry, apple, crab-apple, plum, apricot, almond, peach, laurel, quince, firethorn, photinia and hawthorn. Oriental cherry, weeping cherry and sweet cherry are highly susceptible. Tunnelling causes branches to wilt and die back and provides entry to bacteria and fungal pathogens. After

ID: *Adult:* small, mottled, light and dark brown moth with coppery spots on wings; forewings have purple, orange and silver markings on the margin. *Larva:* small, transparent caterpillar with a pink gut.

Size: *Adult:* wingspan 2–2.5 cm. *Larva:* body length 1–2.5 cm.

Habitat and Range: Lower Mainland and southern Vancouver Island.

Scouting: Watch for wilting and dieback. Inspect tree trunks for entry holes and the orange or brown tubes made of insect frass

and silk, about 1 cm long, extending outward from each hole. Infested tree trunks and branches will be often covered with these tiny tubes sticking out from the bark.

Cultural/Physical Control: Do not plant highly susceptible ornamental cherry species in areas where this pest occurs. On ornamental flowering cherry trees, do not prune living branches, only dead wood. Prune fruiting trees with good, close, clean cuts to allow the wounds to heal quickly. Be careful not to wound trees with weed-eaters and

repeated attacks, severely infested trees may weaken and die.

The Cherry Bark Tortrix is a Eurasian species first seen on ornamental cherry trees in the BC Lower Mainland in 1990. Since then, it has been found in the Fraser Valley and southern Vancouver Island and in Washington and Oregon as far south as Portland.

Adult moths fly from April to September and lay eggs on bark in cracks, crevices, wounds or lenticels, often in the crotch between a branch and the main trunk. The larvae (tiny, transparent caterpillars) hatch about two weeks later and crawl around on the bark for a few days until they find an entry point. Then they tunnel through the bark down into the cambium of the tree (the layer of actively dividing cells between the wood and the soft, green tissue under the bark that transmits nutrients from leaves). A gummy exudate may appear around entrance holes.

The larvae create narrow, winding tunnels under the bark as they feed. These tunnels cut the flow of nutrients in the tree, resulting in wilt and dieback of leaves and branches. While burrowing into the tree, the larvae construct an orange-coloured, cylindrical mass of frass and silk, which extrudes from their entrance hole. Larvae overwinter in the tree and pupate in spring. There is one generation per year.

It is thought that the orange frass tubes seal the entrance to the tunnels and help to protect the larvae from predators, allowing them to overwinter in safety. In late September and early October, larvae emerge from their tunnels to tend and repair their frass tubes before returning to their bark tunnels to pupate.

mowers. Control weeds and other vegetation around the base of trees—the Cherry Bark Tortrix will lay eggs in protected areas at the base of trees if other egg-laying sites are not available. Some people recommend painting pruning wounds and bark cracks with grafting wax or pruning emulsion; others say it has no effect. Cut down old, dying or non-productive ornamental or fruiting trees to remove breeding sites. Provide flowering plants throughout the growing season to encourage natural populations of Trichogramma wasps and other beneficial insects that attack Cherry Bark Tortrix eggs and larvae.

Biological Control: In its native habitat in Europe, natural predators and parasites keep the Cherry Bark Tortrix below damaging levels. A native Trichogramma wasp parasitizes eggs in the Pacific Northwest. Trichogramma wasps can be purchased commercially for release and some people have reported success in reducing Cherry Bark Tortrix infestations with release of these wasps in April or May when egg-laying commences.

Snowberry Clearwing

Hemaris diffinis

"Is it a bumble bee, hummingbird or moth?" This question often runs through the mind of a gardener who sees a Snowberry Clearwing for the first time. This moth is swift and agile, as are all members of the Sphingidae family. The adult is a day flier and is commonly observed hovering at flowers such as lilacs. It often looks like a miniature hummingbird as it zips from flower to flower. If you watch closely, you will see it hovering as it extends its long proboscis into a flower.

The adult emerges in spring and is on the wing starting in late May and continuing into early June. Larvae hatch and feed throughout summer and pupate in the soil. There are two other species of clearwing moths. The Hummingbird Moth (*H. thysbe*) and the much less common Slender Clearwing (*H. gracilis*) are found in our boreal regions and also may be observed nectaring in gardens.

The long proboscis of Sphingidae moths is an adaptation for reaching nectar deep inside trumpet-shaped flowers such as honeysuckles.

ID: *Adult:* resembles bumble bee; yellow with dark abdominal band covered in hairs; clear wings have brown edges and dark veins. *Larva:* blue-green or brown with dark lateral spots along abdomen; horn at end of abdomen is black with yellow base.

Size: *Adult:* wingspan 40–50 mm. *Larva:* body length 45 mm.

Habitat and Range: open areas throughout the province from the Peace River district south; tends to be most common in gardens in the aspen parkland and prairie habitats; larvae feed on snowberry, honeysuckle and dogbane.

Scouting: The best way to find these guys is to grab a lawn chair and a cold drink on a sunny day and sit in front of your lilacs. These moths seem to enjoy the purple lilacs the best. It may take a while, but if your weather and timing are right, the moths will be there.

How to Attract: These moths enjoy brightly coloured flowers such as honeysuckles, phlox and lilacs, as well as wild snowberries and dogbane that are in flower. Flowering cherry, saskatoon and hawthorn trees also attract this species. If any of these flowering plants are planted in the garden, this species will likely appear.

Garden Tiger Moth

Arctia caja

The name Garden Tiger Moth suggests that this species is a common sight in gardens. However, it is this species' larval stage, the woolly bear caterpillar, which is most frequently encountered. The Garden Tiger Moth is a holarctic species and is sometimes called the Great Tiger Moth. It is the largest and most attractive species of the tiger moth family, Arctiidae, in our region.

Adults appear in August and eggs are laid shortly after. Eggs hatch in late August and caterpillars overwinter. In spring, the polyphagus caterpillars begin looking for food. In late June to early July, they spin a cocoon made of silk and their own body hair. The naked caterpillars pupate inside, and adults emerge about four weeks later.

A similar species, the Isabella Tiger Moth (*Pyrrharctica isabella*) is more common in some parts of south-coastal BC (its caterpillar is a woolly bear, too). The St. Lawrence Tiger Moth (*Platarctia parthenos*) occurs in the boreal region. It has a two-year life cycle. Adults are similar in size and have brown forewings with some white spotting. The hindwings are orange with interconnected black banding. The abdomen is black with an orange tip versus the solid orange abdomen of the Garden Tiger Moth.

ID: *Adult:* chocolate brown forewings have white patches and banding; orange hindwings with large black to blue spots; orange abdomen. *Larva:* woolly caterpillar covered with short, dense, black hair, with orange hair around head and long whitish hair on sub-ventral region of abdomen.

Size: *Adult:* wingspan 55 mm. *Larva:* body length 60 mm.

Habitat and Range: forest and prairie habitats throughout the province; larvae are generalists and feed on a variety of forbs and shrubs, including dandelions, common plantain, willow and alder.

Scouting: This species is most easily observed as woolly bear caterpillars that are marching through a garden, across a sidewalk or through the farmyard.

How to Attract: Leave some untouched and naturalized patches around the yard that contain this moth's host plants.

Cypress Tip Moth

Argyresthia cupressella

leaf damage

The small, silvery moths with white bands across their wings fly in June and July. They lay eggs on leaf scales, often in crevices or twig crotches. Larvae burrow into (mine) the scales to feed and overwinter. In spring, from about mid-April in coastal regions, the larvae burrow into shoots from the tip downward; one larva can hollow out four to six shoots. In May and June, they emerge to pupate in papery, white, spindle-shaped cocoons on the leaves. The tiny, round exit holes of the larvae can be seen on leaf scales with a hand-lens. There is one generation per year.

The Cypress Tip Moth, also called the Cypress Tip Miner, is a Tortricid moth. The larvae feed on cypress, cedar (especially eastern white cedar) and juniper. They burrow into leaf scales and shoot tips on one- and two-year-old branches, causing the foliage to turn yellow, then brown and drop. Infested trees, shrubs and hedges have a brown, scorched appearance in early and mid-summer, especially the new growth at the tips.

The browning caused by the Cypress Tip Moth can look similar to that caused by drought, frost damage, nutrient deficiency, spider mites or even root rot. Western red cedar is not affected by the Cypress Tip Moth but exhibits a browning and dieback of scattered branches called "cedar flagging" in late summer and fall. Cedar flagging is a natural phenomenon and does not damage the tree.

ID: *Adult:* small, inconspicuous, silvery tan, pale gold or silvery grey moth with white bands across its wings. *Larva:* greenish yellow to light green caterpillar with a brown head.

Size: *Adult:* wingspan 5–6 mm. *Larva:* body length 1.5–7 mm.

Habitat and Range: urban areas in south-coastal BC.

Scouting: Look for white cocoons and larval exit holes on leaf scales in April and May. On brown shoots, check for hollowed-out twigs that snap off easily.

Cultural/Physical Control: Shear hedges or prune out damaged shoots in spring and remove cocoons by hand, where practical. Consider replacing heavily damaged plants with resistant species or varieties such as western red cedar. Generally, larger landscape trees can sustain high populations of tip moths without severe damage.

Biological Control: A few wasp parasitoids, such as Trichogramma, attack eggs, and other predators attack the cocoons and larvae when they emerge from the scales and twigs.

Polyphemus Moth

Anthera polyphemus

This moth is one of the biggest and showiest moths in our region. It is a nocturnal species and is a member of the Giant Silkworm Moth family, Saturniidae. Other silk moths that you may encounter are the Columbia Silkmoth (*Hyalophora columbia*) and the Cecropia Moth (*H. cecropia*). These two moths have large dark to reddish wings with a central white band. The wings each have a centrally placed kidney-shaped eyespot. The Cecropia is generally larger and has a red band along side the white band.

Adults emerge from cocoons in late May into early July. Pregnant females cruise at night and lay eggs on hosts. Large caterpillars emerge in early summer and mature by late August. They spin elaborate silken cocoons among the leaves or on the ground. The cocoons are quite tough and protect the caterpillars from predators and the elements during winter. Adults have no mouthparts and basically hatch and breed.

ID: *Adult:* light brown wings with transparent eyespot on both wings; hindwing eyespot is rimmed with dark scaling; outer edges of wings are lined with purple and white bands. *Larva:* florescent green caterpillar with faint vertical lines on central part of body; segments have 8 central reddish spots and a series of red and silvery "warts" with a few clear hairs sticking out; orange-brown head often retracted into thorax slightly when resting.

Size: *Adult:* wingspan 110–125 mm. *Larva:* body length 75 mm.

Habitat and Range: throughout the province; larvae feed on birch, oak, elm, dogwood, apple, ash, hazel, hickory, maple, rose, willow and a number of other trees and shrubs.

Scouting: Adults and larvae are both tricky to find; however, the larvae are most often encountered. Watch branches of host for half-eaten leaves or small areas of defoliation. Scan for a large green lump sitting on a branch among the leaves. It may take awhile, but once you find one, you may be surprised at how many others you will find.

How to Attract: This species is seldom a pest but the caterpillars are large and have big appetites. If you wish to attract them to the garden, plant a variety of potential host trees and shrubs.

Plume Moths
Amblyptilia pica, Alucita spp.

Alucita spp.

These elegant moths are rarely observed but are always present around our homes, gardens and yards. Once you learn how to find them, you will likely see them everywhere.

Common Plume Moths (*Amblyptila pica*) are seen flitting about in spring, summer and autumn. They are micro-moths of the family Pterophoridae. This species has two generations per year, the first in early summer and the second in autumn and early spring. Their larvae mine leaves, flowers and seeds. Adults of the second generation overwinter and are often observed nectaring at pussy willows or coltsfoot in April.

Many Plumed Moths (*Alucita* spp.) are most commonly observed on the walls of houses in autumn and even into winter. They are members of the family Alucitidae and are easily separated from the Pterophoridae by their multi-lobed forewings. Adults overwinter and lay eggs in spring. Their larvae are fruit, flower, bud and stem borers. Three species occur in our region, *Alucita montana, A. adriendenisi* and *A. lalannei*, and you need to be an expert to separate them.

ID: *Adult:* Common Plume Moth: dark grey with non-lobed forewings and 3-lobed hindwings; grey-brown mottled forewings have dark central triangle-shaped patch; hindwing is smoky grey, and 3rd lobe has distinct dark triangle shaped spot called a "scale tooth." Many Plumed Moth: wings are feather-like plumes that spread apart fan-like when moth is at rest; 6 plumes on each wing. *Larva:* pale and tapered at both ends; has tiny hairs with swollen tips; prolegs are slender and stalk-like.

Size: *Adult:* wingspan 10–18 mm. *Larva:* body length 8–10 mm.

Habitat and Range: throughout our region. Common Plume Moth: host plants include Indian paintbrush, snapdragon and geraniums. Many Plumed Moth: host plants include honeysuckle and snowberry.

Scouting: Both species are sometimes seen around our porch lights. The Common Plume Moth is often observed flitting among snapdragons in summer, or nectaring at pussy willows in spring. Many Plumed Moths are commonly seen in autumn in our gardens and at our windows.

How to Attract: Plant larval host plants or adult nectar sources in the garden.

Codling Moth
Cydia pomonella

The Codling Moth, now common in southern BC, is a pest from Eurasia that was first recorded in Victoria in the 1890s. It soon spread to the Lower Mainland and up the Fraser. By 1922, this pest was causing serious damage to Okanagan fruit and pesticide spray programs were introduced.

In 1994, the BC government, with growers and municipal agencies, instituted SIR, "Sterile Insect Release," a program in which laboratory-reared, sterile male moths are released in commercial apple orchards to mate with females and reduce the number of eggs laid. Since then, over two million sterile males have been released in BC's apple orchards. The Codling Moth has been reduced to an insignificant pest in most orchards, without using insecticides.

Elsewhere in BC, Codling Moth caterpillars overwinter in cocoons in main tree crotches or bark crevices, and in litter under the trees. They pupate in spring, and adults emerge at bud-break and bloom. Eggs are laid on leaves and young fruit, often at the top of the tree. Larvae burrow into the core of the fruit, where they feed on seeds. Feeding holes are surrounded by frass. The second generation of adults appears in late July or August. There are two, sometimes three, generations per year.

ID: *Adult:* brownish grey body and forewings; forewings have lighter, net-like markings; hind wings are brown with a pale fringe. *Larva:* white to pinkish, grub-like caterpillar with a black or dark brown head.

Size: *Adult:* wingspan 15–22 mm. *Larva:* Young: 2–3 mm. Mature: 12–20 mm.

Habitat and Range: apple, crab apple, quince and pear trees throughout south-coastal BC and the southern Interior.

Scouting: On Fruits look for circular, reddish spots called "stings," feeding damage on the bottom (calyx) end and small holessurrounded by frass, in June and July.

Cultural/Physical Control: Prune trees. Wrap corrugated cardboard bands, 10–15 cm wide and corrugated side against tree, around base and main branches in mid-June. Larvae collect in and under the band. Replace the band in mid-July. Remove second band in fall or winter. Destroy old bands and kill the larvae.

Biological Control: B.t.k. will kill young caterpillars, and several natural predators and parasites attack larvae, but none of theses solutions provides sufficient control.

European Skipper

Thymelicus lineola

In late summer, this intruder can be the most abundant butterfly on the wing and is commonly observed in gardens, farmyards and fields. It arrived in North America from Europe in 1910 and began to spread west into our region, often as eggs in hay crops. The European Skipper was first discovered in southern British Columbia in 1960. Since then, this species has been observed all over Alberta, Colorado, Idaho, northern Montana and south and central British Columbia. This unwelcome guest is an excellent example of how quickly something can spread if conditions are favourable. The European Skipper is not considered a serious pest, but it can significantly defoliate hay crops. Areas with populations of 20 to 25 larvae per square metre can suffer significant crop damage.

Adults emerge and plague fields from July into mid-August. Females lay groups of up to 30 whitish eggs in parallel rows on the leaf sheath or grass seedheads. The eggs overwinter, and larvae hatch in April and May.

ID: *Adult:* orange wings with dark border and dark wing veins. *Larva:* green body has dark green dorsal stripe and 2 lateral and subdorsal stripes; head is pale green and has pair of black and white stripes on either side. *Pupa:* green chrysalid with 2 longitudinal white stripes, about 2 cm long; usually attached to a grass stem at ground level.

Size: *Adult:* wingspan 26 mm. *Larva:* body length 25 mm.

Habitat and Range: central and southern BC, especially in urban and surrounding areas, meadows, pasture and grassy fields; larvae feed on timothy, cocksfoot or orchard grass, quackgrass, bentgrass, and redtop and velvet grass. Adults nectar on hawkweed, milkweed and pea species such as cow vetch or birdsfoot trefoil, and in eastern North American have been found drowned in lady slipper orchids.

Scouting: In mid- to late summer, watch for orange skippers flitting among grassy fields or nectaring at flowers in your garden.

Cultural/Physical Control: Purchase hay locally and/or confirm with the people who produce your hay supply that this insect is not present in their field.

Biological Control: Predators include parasitic flies and wasps, predatory beetles and birds. Ensuring habitat for these beneficial predators will help reduce European Skipper populations. Infested fields may be treated with *Bacillus thuringiensis* to kill larvae.

Peach Tree Borer

Synanthedon exitiosa

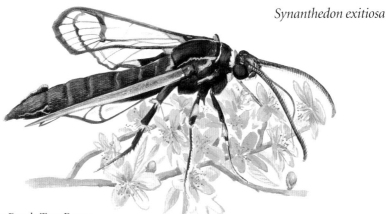

The Peach Tree Borer, sometimes called the "Peach Crown Borer," is a clear-winged moth that attacks peaches, plums, cherries, apricots and other wild and cultivated stone fruit trees. It is native to North America and occurs across the continent. Related species such as the Douglas-fir Pitch Moth (*S. novaroensis*) and the Sequoia Pitch Moth (*S. sequoiae*) attack Douglas-fir, pine and sequoia throughout the province.

Adults are active from July to September. Eggs are laid on the trunk of the tree and the larvae crawl down to soil level, where they burrow into the inner bark and cambium at the base of the tree and roots. The larvae feed and tunnel under the bark, where they overwinter. In spring, they pupate for 18 to 30 days in a silken cocoon that they cover with bits of chewed wood.

Boring girdles the trunk, causing young trees to wilt, yellow and die back. Older trees usually survive but are weakened. The tunnels provide entry to bacterial and fungal diseases.

ID: *Adult:* dark, steel-blue, clear-winged moth resembling a hornet. Male: narrow, yellow bands around abdomen. Female: 2 broad, orange bands. *Larva:* cream-coloured worm with a brown head.

Size: *Adult:* wingspan 2.5–3 cm. *Larva:* body length 1.5–3 cm

Habitat and Range: primarily in the Okanagan and southern Interior; throughout southern BC wherever stone fruit trees grow.

Scouting: Look for a reddish brown gum containing bits of sawdust oozing from holes at the base of the trunk. Trees yellow and wilt. Empty, brown pupal cases may be found at the base of the tree.

Cultural/Physical Control: In fall, cut out the larvae with a sharp knife or by pushing a piece of stiff wire into their tunnels. Carefully remove the soil about 10–15 cm deep around the base of the tree to be sure of finding all the larvae, without cutting or damaging the tree. Protect trees from new boring by wrapping the base of the trunk up to about 45 cm with a cone-shaped collar made from aluminum, tar paper, plastic sheeting or polyester batting, sealed as tight as possible at the top without damaging the bark. Sticky traps containing a pheromone can be put up to trap the male moths, starting shortly after petal-fall.

Biological Control: Several natural predators and parasites attack borer eggs and larvae, but they do not control the pest. Dispensers can be purchased that release a mating disruption pheromone called Isomate-P. They should be hung in trees in early June, before moths fly. This control is effective in large commercial orchards, but less successful in smaller plantings or backyard trees where mated females can fly in from outside.

Raspberry Crown Borer

Pennisetia marginata

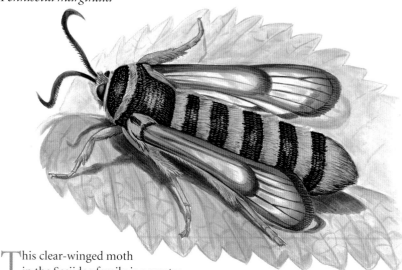

This clear-winged moth in the Sesiidae family is a master of insect mimicry. The adult mimics the feared yellow-jacket wasp, a crafty adaptation that protects this pest from predators.

Complete development takes two years. Adults fly from mid-August into September and feed on nectar and pollen of flowers such as asters. Within a few days, females start depositing single eggs, usually two to three per plant, on the undersides of leaves. They can lay from 130 to 150 eggs during their short lives. In late September and early October, the larvae hatch and crawl to the root crown, burrowing under the bark to form a blister-like hibernation chamber just below the soil. In spring, the larvae bore into new and old canes, feeding into autumn and hibernating in the feeding chambers. They continue to feed the following spring. In July, mature larvae burrow upward and outward, forming pupal chambers near the surface of the cane. In August, the pupae work their way through the bark and the adults emerge.

ID: *Adult:* black body with yellow banding on abdomen; clear wings have brown borders. *Larva:* white grub-like worm with dark head and thoracic shield; 3 pairs of thoracic legs; series of 8 small hooked appendages on abdominal segments 3–6.

Size: *Adult:* wingspan 25–30 mm. *Larva:* body length 25 mm.

Habitat and Range: larvae feed on *Rubus* species throughout the province.

Scouting: Watch for weak or spindly canes and signs of boring and girdling, such as sawdust and callus or galls. Prune out suspect canes and look for white grubs in root collars. Adults are rarely encountered.

Cultural/Physical Control: Remove infested stalks from the ground up. Burn, smash or squish cane bases to kill or dislodge larvae.

Biological Control: Predators include parasitic wasps, predatory beetles and birds. A biological spray containing the predatory nematode *Steinernema carpocapsae* is used around the bases of the canes to control larvae and pupae. Spray at night on moist soils to prevent desiccation of the nematodes.

Peach Twig Borer

Anarsia lineatella

The Peach Twig Borer is a moth whose larvae attack peach, plum, apricot and nectarine trees. Larvae bore into buds and developing shoots, causing them to wilt and die. Wilted shoots are often called "shoot strikes" or "flags." Larval feeding on fruit creates oozing holes and cavities at the stem end.

Young larvae (caterpillars) overwinter on host trees in a tiny cell called a hibernaculum in branch and twig crotches, pruning wounds or deep cracks in bark. A small, cylindrical, reddish brown tube of frass sticks out from the bark at each overwintering site. In early spring, the larvae emerge and crawl up to new shoots, blooms and developing fruit, where they burrow and feed. They then pupate, giving rise to the first adult generation, called "brood moths," which lay eggs on leaves, twigs and young, green fruit in May and June. From June to August, the summer caterpillars burrow into ripening fruit at the stem end. These larvae pupate in protected areas on the tree or in the fruit cavities, and a second generation of adults emerges in late

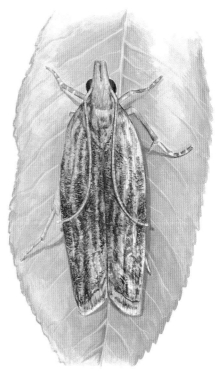

summer. These adults produce the next generation of caterpillars, which feed for a short time in September before burrowing into the wood for winter.

ID: *Adult:* small moth with dark grey, mottled forewings and pale grey underwings; palps extend out from head and look like a snout. *Larva:* Young: white with dark brown head; Older Instar: reddish brown to chocolate brown with narrow, white, ring-like bands between dark segments and dark brown or grey head.

Size: *Adult:* wingspan 8–11 mm. *Larva:* body length up to 12 mm.

Habitat and Range: primarily in southern Interior fruit-growing regions.

Scouting: Look for frass tubes in the crotches of twigs and branches in winter. Check developing buds, shoots and fruit at bloom for young larvae. The ring-like bands distinguish Peach Twig Borer larvae from other caterpillars that attack stone fruit.

Cultural/Physical Control: Cut off wilted shoots and infested branches and destroy larvae. Seal infested fruit in a plastic bag and dispose or freeze solid before composting. Remove frass tubes in late fall and winter.

Biological Control: Sprays with B.t.k. will kill larvae if applied at bloom, before they tunnel into twigs or fruit. Peach Twig Borers have several natural enemies including parasitic wasps and some species of ants. A dormant or delayed dormant (pre-bloom) spray with horticultural oil helps control this insect. Mating disruption pheromones are effective in commercial orchards but are less so in small plantings.

Lilac Leaf Miner

Caloptilia syringella

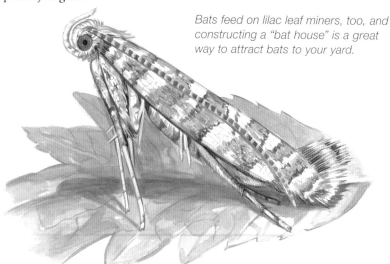

Bats feed on lilac leaf miners, too, and constructing a "bat house" is a great way to attract bats to your yard.

The Lilac Leaf Miner, also known as the Lilac Slender-moth, is a common pest of lilac and was introduced from Europe. It now can be found across Canada anywhere lilac is grown.

A brown or shrivelled leaf on a lilac may be an indication that there is a Lilac Leaf Miner larva inside; this miniscule moth is so small that its larvae can live inside a leaf. The damage caused by the larvae is cosmetic and does not kill the plant. This moth often has two generations per year.

Adults emerge in late May and early June. Eggs are laid in groups of 5 to 10 on the underside of a leaf near a vein. The eggs hatch, and the larvae enter the leaf, creating a series of mines. As the larvae grow, the mine begins to appear blister-like. Older larvae leave the mine, roll the leaf and continue feeding. Once mature, these little guys drop to the ground on silken threads and pupate in the duff. The second generation emerges in August, and the cycle repeats with their pupae overwintering. The first generation tends to attack the shrub's lower foliage, but the next generation moves up to higher leaves.

ID: *Adult:* narrow, brown-mottled wings; forewings have some black and silver markings. *Larva:* yellowish worm with a brownish head.

Size: *Adult:* wingspan 10 mm. *Larva:* body length 7–8 mm.

Habitat and Range: throughout the province; larvae feed mainly on lilac, but also on ash.

Scouting: Tree or shrub has an unhealthy appearance. Foliage may appear scorched, having reddish dried patches, especially in late summer. Early in the year, leaves appear discoloured, sometimes yellowish. Look closely at blister-like tunnels on the leaf, or unroll a rolled leaf to see if there are larvae within.

Cultural/Physical Control: Keep trees healthy during an outbreak by watering them during dry conditions and fertilizing them every spring. As long as the area is a reasonable size, you should be able to control infestations by picking infected leaves off by hand.

Biological Control: Many natural predators exist for this introduced species including parasites, diseases and birds such as warblers.

Speckled Green Fruitworm

Orthosia hibisci and others

Speckled Green
Fruitworm Moth

Fruitworm adults are among the first moths to emerge and are an indication that spring truly has arrived. There are records of them flying as early as February, not long after the snow has melted.

Adults appear in late February and fly into May. Eggs are laid during this period and hatch just after the host's leaves begin to flush. Larvae are primarily defoliators but get their name from the damage they do to fruit during a large outbreak. They do not bore into fruit but chew on flower petals, developing fruit and stems. Larvae mature early in summer, often the last week or two of June. They drop to the ground and burrow 5–10 centimetres into the soil, where they pupate. There is one generation per year.

ID: *Adult:* brown-winged, robust-bodied moth. *Larva:* green to bluish green overall with dorsal, mid-dorsal and lateral white stripe along body, which is covered in white speckles; some caterpillars are smoky green with similar markings and more distinct white striping.

Size: *Adult:* wingspan 40 mm. *Larva:* body length 25–35 mm.

Habitat and Range: throughout the province; larvae are generalists, feeding on apple, pear, aspen, willow, birch, poplar, cherry, gooseberry, elm, maple, oak and even spruce, larch and Douglas-fir.

Scouting: Watch for localized defoliation of host trees. Defoliation tends to be patchy and is rarely widespread. Larvae are often solitary feeders.

Cultural/Physical Control: Tree mortality rarely occurs during an outbreak because many trees are adapted to defoliation by insects. If there are only a few larvae, it is likely all right to let them be.

Biological Control: Predacious and parasitic wasps, parasitic tachinid flies and other predatory insects feed on these larvae, as well as many birds. Leaving the appropriate habitat for these beneficial animals is key to avoiding and controlling outbreaks. Plant wildflowers and shelterbelts, and leave areas of naturalized woodlands intact.

Carpenterworms & Carpentermoths

Acossus spp., *Prionoxystus robiniae*

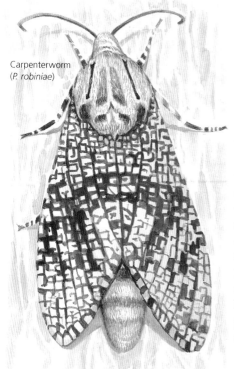

Carpenterworm
(*P. robiniae*)

Carpenterworms have up to four-year life cycles and often do not kill their hosts, though heavily infested trees riddled with tunnelling become weak and may break off in windstorms. The three main species in British Columbia, the Carpenterworm (*P. robiniae*), Poplar Carpentermoth (*A. centerensis*) and Aspen Carpentermoth (*A. populi*) have similar life cycles.

Adults emerge in June. Females lay up to 800 eggs, a couple at a time, in crevices and wounds on branches and trunks. Larvae hatch in about 10 days and burrow through the bark into the cambial layer of the tree, constructing tunnels that extend into the heartwood. Larvae push sawdust and frass out of tunnel openings. After a few years, larvae mature and pupate in May. The pupae wriggle to the surface, and adults emerge outside.

ID: *Adult:* Carpenterworm: male has grey-mottled forewings and yellow-orange hindwings; female is larger than male and has grey hindwings. Carpentermoth: smoky black forewings and grey hindwings. Aspen Carpentermoth: light grey forewings with some black markings; light grey body. *Larva:* white to green body sparsely covered with short, stout hairs; brown head and thoracic shield.

Size: *Adult: P. robinae:* wingspan 50–75 mm (females up to 85 mm). *A. centerensis:* wingspan 40–50mm. *A. populi:* wingspan 50–70 mm. *Larva: P. robiniae* and *A. populi:* body length 50–75 mm. *A. centerensis:* body length 40–50 mm.

Habitat and Range: Carpenterworm: throughout the province; feeds on poplar, aspen, cottonwood, green ash, mountain ash, elm and oak. Carpentermoth and Aspen

Carpentermoth: more prevalent in the parkland and boreal areas because they feed only on poplar species.

Scouting: Check trunks, especially at their base, for holes with sap mixed with sawdust and frass extruding from them. Look for sunken areas on the trunks resulting from extensive tunnelling and sapwood feeding.

Cultural/Physical Control: Keep trees healthy, pruned and watered. Wrap bases of trees with burlap to prevent adults from emerging and laying eggs. Leave wraps on for up to 4 years. Dig out larvae near the surface with a knife. Poke wire into tunnels to kill larvae. Remove heavily infested trees.

Biological Control: Natural controls include parasitic wasps and nematodes, diseases and predatory birds. Downy and hairy woodpeckers spend days working over an infested tree.

Sod Webworms

Chrysoteuchia topiaria, Parapediasia teterrella, Tehama bonifatella and others

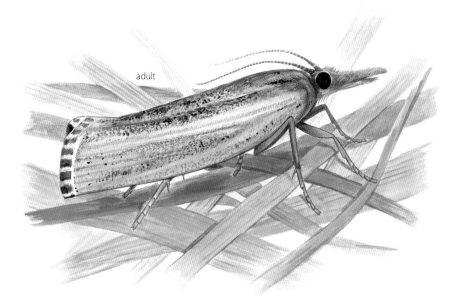

adult

Ever wonder what those little white moths are that fly up whenever you walk across the lawn? They are known as lawn/grass moths or sod webworms and include a number of different moth species in the family Crambidae. In British Columbia, the most common lawn pests are the Cranberry Girdler (*C. topiaria*), the Bluegrass Sod Webworm (*P. teterrella*) and the Western Lawn Moth (*T. bonifatella*; formerly called *Crambus nevadellus*).

Although lawn moths seem to have multiple broods, in fact they have overlapping generations, with adults appearing from mid-June to early September. Adults are active in mid- to late summer and are busy flying

Also Known As: Lawn Moths

ID: *Adult:* Crambidae moths: slender brown and white body; resembles a grass seed when sitting with wings folded around the body; mouthparts protrude, resembling a snout. Bluegrass Sod Webworm: small, whitish grey moth. Cranberry Girdler: whitish body has pale, golden-tipped forewings with an arching white line and smoky grey hindwings. Western Lawn Moth: beige forewings with mottled brown markings and straw-coloured hind wings. *Larva:* Bluegrass Sod Webworm: rows of light brown spots in rings on a greenish grey body; dark head. Cranberry Girdler and Western Lawn Moth: creamy white, yellowish to dark-bodied worm with dark spots and coarse hairs; head tends to be brown.

Size: *Adult:* wingspan 15–20 mm. *Larva:* up to 20 mm.

Habitat and Range: Bluegrass Sod Webworm: southern British Columbia wherever grasses grow; larvae feed on many species of grass including common lawn and pasture grasses; most sod webworm larvae feed only on the blades of grass plants. Cranberry Girdler and Western Lawn Moth: larvae feed in the soil, where they eat crowns and roots of grasses, cranberries and even conifer seedlings such as Douglas-fir, true fir and spruce.

Sod Webworms (continued)

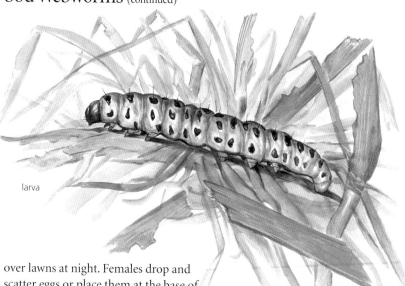

larva

over lawns at night. Females drop and scatter eggs or place them at the base of a grass stem. Larvae emerge from the eggs in approximately a week and begin feeding. They could be called "mini-loggers," since they cut down individual blades of grass at night like loggers in a forest. They haul the blade into a silken nest they have constructed and begin feeding. The silken nests of most sod webworm species are built in the thatch layer and are usually flush with the ground. Larvae hibernate within the nests and resume feeding in spring. In summer, once they are mature, larvae build a silken cocoon in the soil to pupate. Larvae chew bark and wood of cranberry stems and Douglas-fir, true fir and spruce seedlings near the soil line.

Other North American sod webworms that are less frequently encountered or are not recorded as pests in British Columbia are the Great Sod Webworm (*Pediasia trisecta*), the Striped Sod Webworm (*Fissicrambus mutabilis*) and the Vagabond Sod Webworm (*Agriphila vulgivagella*).

Scouting: Webworm damage may resemble damage from other lawn insect pests, diseases or even dog urine, so proper identification is critical. Look for the larvae themselves or the presence of silken threads or feeding chambers in the thatch. During the day, moths may fly up when you walk across or mow the lawn; they can be seen at dusk flying over the grass, laying eggs. A large number of birds picking at the lawn may indicate the presence of webworms. If you suspect webworms, soak the grass with a solution of 6 tablespoons of liquid dish soap in 8 litres of water and wait a few minutes: the webworm larvae will come to the surface.

Cultural/Physical Control: Keep your lawn healthy. Healthy lawns are better able to withstand and recover from sod webworm damage. Switch to a different variety of grass or groundcover if outbreaks are frequent.

Biological Control: A number of predators and parasites attack webworms. Ground beetles often scamper through grasses and munch on any webworm they encounter. Birds such as American robins and sparrows spend the entire spring and summer hunting for webworms and other insects in our lawns. Predatory nematodes exist naturally in soils and will kill a few larvae. These nematodes can even be bought commercially. For the best results, spray them on a moist lawn in the evening or at night.

Western Spruce Budworm

Choristoneura occidentalis

The Western Spruce Budworm feeds primarily on Douglas-fir, though it will feed on a variety of conifer species. Young trees and seedlings can be severely deformed or killed. Feeding on mature trees can result in slow growth and top-kill. Damaged trees often attract bark beetles and wood-rotting fungi, which combine to finish them off.

Adults emerge from July to early August and mate; the females lay eggs about 7 to 10 days later. Green eggs are laid on the underside of needles in one to three overlapping rows, like shingles. Eggs hatch in about 10 to 12 days. The young larvae do not feed but seek shelter under bark scales or among lichens on the tree, where they spin a silken tent in which to hibernate for the winter. In April, the larvae emerge and tunnel into one-year-old needles and buds to feed. When the new growth flushes out, the larvae spin loose webs of silk that bind shoots together as they feed on the new needles, male flowers and small conelets. In western larch, they tunnel into terminal and lateral shoots, causing them to break off. The larvae pupate in the web or elsewhere on the tree, and adults emerge about 12 to 18 days later.

ID: *Adult:* small moth; grey or orange-brown forewings with light bands or streaks and a white dot on each wing margin. *Larva:* dark brown to black head and collar; olive green, tan or dark brown body; each body segment has 2 pairs of ivory white dots.

Size: *Adult:* wingspan 22–28 mm. *Larva:* body length 25 mm.

Habitat and Range: throughout most of southern BC, including the south coast, southern Interior and Vancouver Island.

Scouting: Look for mining and tunnelling on needles and buds in April before bud-break.

Webbing and larvae appear on new shoots in May and on reddish brown shoot tips on damaged trees in mid-summer.

Cultural/Physical Control: Prune damaged shoots and branches before larvae pupate in July. If the leader is damaged, a new one can often be trained.

Biological Control: A variety of predators, feed on budworms, and they have over 40 known species of wasp and fly parasites to keep them in check. Large outbreaks in forest stands when the climate is favourable usually end only when the budworm runs out of food.

Obliquebanded Leafroller & Blueberry Leaftier

Choristoneura rosaceana, Croesia curvalana

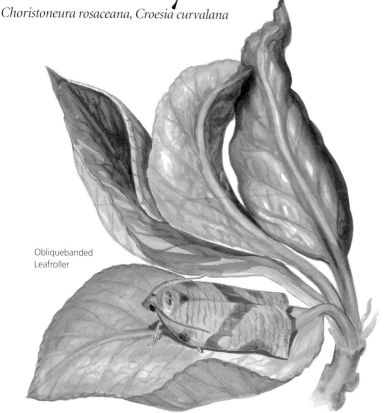

Obliquebanded
Leafroller

L eaf-rolling is a behaviour that both camouflages and shields caterpillars from predators. British Columbia has a wide variety of leaf-rolling Lepidoptera. The Oblique-banded Leafroller (*Choristoneura rosaceana*) and the

---

ID: *Adult:* Obliquebanded Leafroller (OBLR): varies from light tan to dark brown with darker bands on forewings; poor fliers; usually seen at dusk. Blueberry Leaftier: mottled, brown wings with 2 yellowish white spots on forewings, a large, triangular yellow patch behind head and a yellowish white band around outer edge of wings. *Larva:* OBLR: light to dark green with black band behind brown or black head. Blueberry Leaftier: yellowish green, often with dark stripe down back; dark brown head and thoracic shield.

Size: *Adult:* OBLR: wingspan 10–22 mm (females somewhat larger). Blueberry Leaftier: wingspan 15 mm. *Larva:* OBLR: up to 20–30 mm long. Blueberry Leaftier: 12–15 mm long.

Habitat and Range: OBLR: throughout southern British Columbia on a variety of deciduous fruit and ornamental trees and shrubs. Blueberry Leaftier: throughout the province on wild and commercial blueberries, cranberries, huckleberries and other *Vaccinium* species.

Blueberry Leaftier (*Croesia curvalana*) are two of the most commonly encountered species.

Leaftier and leafroller caterpillars look similar but can be distinguished by the way they roll the leaves. The leaftier caterpillar binds two or more leaves together with strands of silk and feeds inside the tied leaves. The leafroller caterpillar rolls or folds one leaf, then binds it with strands of silk and feeds within the fold. Most leafrollers and leaftiers are Tortricid moths, but some are Noctuids.

The Obliquebanded Leafroller feeds on leaves, buds, shoots and young fruit of a wide range of fruit trees and berry crops, as well as broadleafed trees and shrubs such as maple, hawthorn, crab apple and dogwood. It is a damaging pest across Canada. The late instar larvae overwinter in a hibernaculum (a temporary cocoon) in a protected area on the tree or in leaf litter. In spring, the female lays a mass of greenish, scale-like eggs on the upper surface of the host plant leaves. Eggs look black just before they hatch. Larvae go through six instars, and there are two generations per year (other leafroller species may have one to three generations per year). The Obliquebanded Leafroller usually pupates inside the rolled leaf on the plant; other leafroller species pupate in leaf litter on the ground.

Young Blueberry Leaftier larvae burrow into developing flower buds of blueberry, huckleberry, cranberry and other *Vaccinium* species. Older larvae feed on flowers and roll leaves. Other leaftier species feed on various ornamental, fruit and berry plants, including cypress, in British Columbia. Mature larvae drop to the ground to pupate in leaf litter. Most leaftiers overwinter as eggs in leaf litter at the base of the host plant, and there is usually only one generation per year.

Trichogramma wasps are parasites of leafroller and cutworm eggs. They are reared and released in commercial berry fields in the Fraser Valley to control the Obliquebanded Leafroller.

Scouting: Look for egg masses on leaves in spring. Look for defoliation and rolled leaves. Rolled leaves may have larvae or pupae inside.

Cultural/Physical Control: Prune plants appropriately in winter and avoid excess nitrogen, which results in lush foliage.

Biological Control: Predators include predacious and parasitic wasps, parasitic tachinid flies and other predatory insects. Predacious ground beetles are commonly observed pulling larvae out of their protective nests. Many birds such as vireos, woodpeckers and warblers also feed on leafrollers.

Bruce Spanworm & Winter Moth

Operophthera bruceata, O. brumata

They defoliate and slow the growth of yard and landscape trees. Larval feeding on apple, pear and berry leaves, blossoms and fruit can reduce fruit set. The Bruce Spanworm (*O. bruceata*), native to North America, is found across Canada. In aspen forests, severe outbreaks can last a couple of years. The very similar Winter Moth (*O. brumata*) was introduced to the west and east coasts from Europe and occurs in coastal BC.

Adult moths appear in large numbers in late October and early November. The wingless adult females lay eggs in cracks and crevices on host plants. The eggs overwinter, the larvae emerge in early spring and feed on new buds and foliage from March to early June. They then drop to the ground on silken threads, burrow up to 25 centimetres deep in the soil, construct an earthen cell and pupate.

These caterpillars, often called inchworms, spanworms or loopers, belong to the Geometriidae family. Larvae have two pairs of prolegs at the front and four pairs of thoracic legs at the back. They move by bringing the thoracic legs up to the prolegs and arching their back.

ID: *Adult:* male has light brown body and semi-transparent wings with brown and grey bands on forewings; female is wingless and furry, covered with large, dull brown scales. *Larva:* 1st instar: pale yellow body. 2nd to 4th instars: either light green or dark brown, with white longitudinal stripes on body.

Size: *Adult:* Male: wingspan 25–30 mm. Female: body less than 10 mm. *Larva:* 15 to 20 mm long.

Habitat and Range: throughout the province; larvae feed on blossoms and leaves of hardwood trees and woody shrubs including aspen, apple, pear, balsam poplar, Manitoba maple, blueberry, currant, saskatoon and rose.

Scouting: Infested plants have numerous larvae on the leaves. Caterpillars move with an "inchworm" motion.

Cultural/Physical Control: Keep trees healthy and prune appropriately. Pick small numbers of larvae off by hand. For a large outbreak, wrap bases of host trees with a wide sticky strip to prevent females from laying eggs high up on the tree. Do this in late summer or early autumn before adults emerge.

Biological Control: Predators include parasitic wasps and flies, predatory insects and birds. B.t.k. is an effective foliar spray.

Uglynest Caterpillar

Archips cerasivoranus

It is when a garden shrub is draped with a silky tent that we come to know the Uglynest Caterpillar. In severe cases, the nest appears so abruptly that it may induce panic. As the name suggests, this caterpillar's nest is an ugly sight, though the adult moth is rather attractive. This species rarely causes significant damage.

The adults emerge from late July into September. Egg masses are laid on the host plant, and do not hatch until late spring. The gregarious larvae climb to the top of the plant to build a silken nest that engulfs branches and leaves. Nests become quite unsightly, often growing larger and larger and accumulating frass. The nest protects the larvae, and if the larvae are disturbed, they wiggle backwards deeper into it. Larvae pupate randomly starting in June and lasting into September, building silken pupal cells around the edge of the nest.

Like tent caterpillars, this species is considered to be a social insect. Larvae work together to form an elaborate silken nest that protects them from predators and the elements. The nests also absorb and trap heat. By living together, this species has become quite successful.

ID: *Adult:* reddish head and body; red wings have touch of yellow and iridescent sheen. *Larva:* dark head and green to yellow body with dark spots.

Size: *Adult:* wingspan 20–24 mm. *Larva:* body length 20–23mm.

Habitat and Range: throughout the province on pin, choke and ornamental cherries.

Scouting: Watch for the silken tents in spring and for egg bands in late autumn and winter.

Cultural/Physical Control: Deal with hatchlings early in spring before they form huge nests. Pull apart the nests, squish the larvae and leave the stragglers for the birds. Remove eggs bands in autumn and winter.

Biological Control: Predators include predacious and parasitic wasps, parasitic tachinid flies and other predatory insects. One researcher observed a hornet that would chew a hole in the nest and ambush the larvae that came to repair the hole. Birds also home in on these nests and pull out larvae. Cool days and rainy weather can lead to a build-up of diseases.

Tent Caterpillars

Hyphantria cunea, Malacosoma spp., *Tolype dayi*

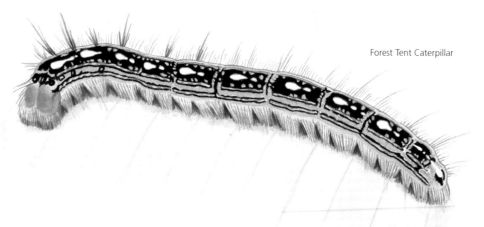

Forest Tent Caterpillar

We have at least five species of tent-making caterpillars in British Columbia. The Forest Tent Caterpillar (*M. disstria*) and the Western Tent Caterpillar (*M. californicum pluviale*) are the most common species. The Prairie Tent Caterpillar (*M. californicum lutescens*) occurs only in the southern Interior, and the Conifer Webworm (*T. dayi*) infests Douglas-fir, ponderosa and lodgepole pine and occasionally spruce in the south coast and southern Interior. The Fall Webworm (*H. cunea*) makes tents in a wide variety of hardwood trees and woody shrubs such as blueberries. Tent caterpillars are always present throughout the province. However, approximately every 10 years, tent caterpillars have a regional outbreak. For example, the Richmond/Delta area may be having an outbreak while populations in other areas of the province remain at their usual levels.

The life cycles of the different tent caterpillar species are very similar, and

---

ID: *Adult:* brown, robust, furry-bodied moth. Forest Tent Caterpillar: 2 dark brown bands on forewings. Prairie and Western Tent caterpillars: 2 white bands on forewings. Fall Webworm: wings all white or covered with grayish brown to black spots. *Larva:* covered in fine light-coloured hairs. Forest Tent Caterpillar: mature is dark with wide, bluish lateral stripes, thin yellow lateral stripes and a row of white, keyhole-shaped dorsal markings along black back. Prairie Tent Caterpillar: dark bodied with broken white dorsal line and powder blue sides. Western Tent Caterpillar: dark bodied with broken white dorsal line rimmed by orange markings. Fall Webworm:

black head, yellowish green body with black dorsal stripe; long white hairs emerging from black and orange spots on each side. Conifer Webworm: grey body with dark, diamond-shaped markings along dorsal line, distinct black and orange marking across third body segment; spiky white hairs emerging from each side.

Size: *Adult:* Forest, Western and Prairie Tent caterpillars: wingspan 35–45 mm. Fall Webworm: 25–42 mm. Conifer Webworm: 32 mm. *Larva:* Forest, Western and Prairie Tent caterpillars: body length 45–55 mm. Fall Webworm: up to 25 mm. Conifer Webworm: up to 34 mm.

Trees being eaten by tent caterpillars also fight back. During an infestation, hybrid poplars produce volatile chemicals that attract tent caterpillar parasites.

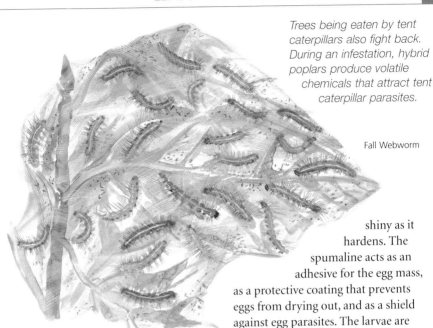

Fall Webworm

shiny as it hardens. The spumaline acts as an adhesive for the egg mass, as a protective coating that prevents eggs from drying out, and as a shield against egg parasites. The larvae are fully developed about a month after eggs are laid and overwinter in this form. The female Fall Webworm lays up to 1500 eggs in a mass on the underside of leaves and covers the eggs with white hairs from its abdomen. It overwinters as a pupa in a silken cocoon under bark. The Conifer Webworm is believed to overwinter as an egg. Larvae hatch the following spring, right around when the leaves of their host plants flush. The larvae are gregarious and feed together.

there is one generation per year. The short-lived adults emerge and take flight in July or August. Forest Tent Caterpillar females lay an egg mass containing between 150 to 200 eggs in a silvery grey mass that wraps around a small twig or branch. Western and Prairie Tent Caterpillar egg masses do not encircle the stem and are often laid near the bottom of their hosts. Female moths cover the egg masses with a frothy, silvery substance known as spumaline that turns dark and

Forest Tent Caterpillars do not form silken tents but leave a silken trail

Habitat and Range: Forest Tent Caterpillar: throughout the province; feeds on aspen, oak, ash, maple, basswood, birch, elm and poplar. Prairie Tent Caterpillar: aspen parkland and prairie regions in the southern Interior. Western Tent Caterpillar and Fall Webworm: across British Columbia including the boreal forest; hosts include pin and choke cherries, hawthorn, hazelnut, maples, willows, poplars, blueberries, huckleberries and a variety of other deciduous hardwoods and woody shrubs. Conifer Webworm: primarily Douglas-fir and Ponderosa pine but also lodgepole pine and Engelmann spruce.

Scouting: Watch trees for severe defoliation, silky webbing or masses of caterpillars. Look for egg bands beginning in late July.

Cultural/Physical Control: Pick or gently scrape egg bands off twigs and branches. In early spring, the larval colonies can be squished.

Biological Control: Not all animals dislike tent caterpillar outbreaks; certain birds and insects feast on them. There are over 40 species of parasites and predatory insects that feed on tent caterpillars. These range from predacious ground beetles, which have been observed climbing into trees and

Tent Caterpillars (continued)

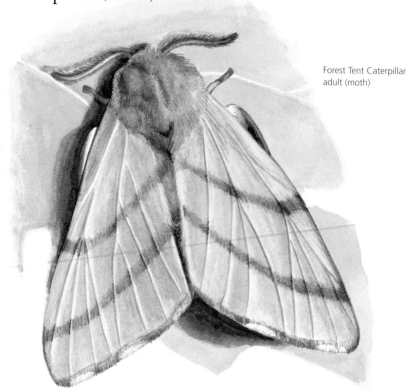

Forest Tent Caterpillar adult (moth)

wherever they go. During outbreaks, there are silken lines everywhere. When resting, these caterpillars bunch together on a silken pad on a branch. Western and Prairie Tent Caterpillars construct silken tents in the crotches of their tree hosts, returning to them to rest or during bad weather. Forest Tent Caterpillars mature in about 5 to 6 weeks, whereas Western and Prairie Tent Caterpillars take about 6 to 8 weeks. This development varies because it depends on weather conditions. Once mature, the larvae spin a silken cocoon, pupating shortly after. Forest Tent Caterpillars emerge from their cocoons in about 10 days and the other two species emerge after about three weeks.

breaking into silken tents to feed on caterpillars, to parasitoid tachinid flies (*Sarcophaga aldrichi*). Tachinid flies are sometimes called the "friendly fly." They thrive during outbreaks and can suppress tent caterpillar populations by 80 percent. The female drops a newly hatched maggot onto the caterpillar cocoon, and the maggot burrows in and feeds on the pupae. Birds love outbreak years, too, and their young may be raised almost entirely on tent caterpillars. During outbreaks, diseases caused by viruses, bacteria and fungi build up. A combination of all these factors leads to the extreme population crashes of tent caterpillars. The year after an outbreak, tent caterpillars that survive are being hunted by hundreds of creatures. It is tough to find a single caterpillar the following year after the population collapses.

Silverspotted Tiger Moth

Lophocampa argentata

larva

The Silverspotted Tiger Moth is one of the most common defoliators of Douglas-fir trees in south-coastal BC. It also attacks western hemlock, fir, lodgepole pine, Sitka spruce and western red cedar. Small tents containing these black, hairy caterpillars are a common sight on landscape trees in winter and early spring. This member of the tiger moth family, Arctiidae, often attacks single trees in open areas. Usually one to three, but sometimes more, tents can occur on a single tree. However, the damage is usually cosmetic because buds are not affected and will flush out again the next spring.

Adults emerge in mid-July to mid-August. The females lay their green eggs in clusters on needles and twigs.

Eggs hatch from mid-August to mid-September, and first and second instar larvae feed inside a 5 to 10 centimetre-long web or tent. Third and fourth instar larvae overwinter in the tents, which reach about 10 to 20 centimetres in length, and even feed from time to time during the winter. Feeding increases in early spring (February to March) as the temperature warms. Needles can be completely stripped from infested branches. In mid-April, larvae leave the tent but continue to feed. In May and June, they climb down off their host plants and wander off in search of a sheltered pupation site on the ground. There is one generation per year.

ID: *Adult:* yellowish brown with silvery white spots on forewings. *Larva:* black body covered with dense tufts of black, reddish brown and yellow hairs.

Size: *Adult:* wingspan 45 mm. *Larva:* body length up to 37 mm.

Habitat and Range: South-coastal BC on Douglas-fir, lodgepole pine, grand fir, amabilis fir, Sitka spruce and western red cedar; often on single trees in open areas in urban landscapes and parks.

Scouting: This is the only defoliating caterpillar found in large numbers on host trees in the winter and early spring. They can be quite common but do not cause any permanent damage. Infestations usually occur on scattered trees and do not spread.

Cultural/Physical Control: It is usually best to do nothing, but infested branches can be pruned out and destroyed, if necessary. Take care not to touch the caterpillars' hairs with your bare skin or get them in your eyes.

Biological Control: Several parasites and parasitoids, especially tachinid flies, usually cause large outbreaks to collapse in one or two years. B.t.k. (*Bacillus thuringiensis kurstaki*) can be sprayed on ornamental trees, but control is rarely needed.

Armyworm Moth & Army Cutworm

Pseudaletia unipuncta, Euxoa auxiliaris

Armyworm Moth

There are two species referred to in the literature as army worm. The larvae of these moths in the family Noctuidae march in groups in search of food once they have eaten everything at their original site, much like the Bertha Armyworm (*Mamestra configurata*), which feeds on canola in the Peace River region of British Columbia.

The Armyworm Moth (*P. unipuncta*) has an old genus name of *Mythimna* and some literature refers to it as *M. unipuncta*. Armyworm adults emerge in late May to June. The female lays rows of eggs along the underside of leaf blades and can lay up to 1400 eggs.

ID: *Adult:* Armyworm: pale brown forewing with a central white spot often highlighted by an orange patch; smoky grey hindwing. Army Cutworm: variably coloured forewing can be a patchwork of yellow and brown or sometimes solid yellow-brown; smoky grey hindwing. *Larva:* Armyworm: pale green to brown with orange, brown and white lateral, dorsal and subdorsal stripes. Army Cutworm: pale brown with pale and dark lateral, dorsal and subdorsal stripes.

Size: *Adult:* Armyworm: wingspan 35–45 mm. Army Cutworm: wingspan 40–45 mm. *Larva:* both species are about 40 mm long.

Habitat and Range: primarily in the parkland and prairie areas of the southern Interior and Peace River regions. Armyworm: feeds on corn, grasses such as oats, wheat and barley, and other forages. Army Cutworm: feeds on corn, sunflowers and a variety of vegetables and grasses.

Perennial sunflower (*Helianthus salicifolius*)

Larvae hatch in a couple of weeks and feed nocturnally in groups. They are "climbing cutworms," which means they climb up the plant and feed on the foliage instead of cutting the plants off at the soil line. Larvae mature in about one month's time, pupating in the soil. The next generation hatches in mid-summer. There are usually two generations, with the second generation overwintering as larvae and pupating in spring.

Army Cutworm (*E. auxiliaris*) adults emerge in summer and feed briefly before seeking shelter in higher elevations and cooler locations until autumn. They return in September and mate, with pregnant females bearing 1000 to 3000 eggs, which are laid in late autumn on open ground and disturbed soil amongst host plants. Eggs hatch shortly after, and larvae feed briefly and then overwinter in soil, emerging the following spring to feed on new shoots. Larvae mature in May and pupate in the soil at a depth of about 5 to 16 centimetres. They remain there for approximately one month.

Scouting: In early spring, emerging garden plants may be broken or snipped off. Foliage will also be slightly or heavily eaten.

Cultural/Physical Control: Cultivate your garden in spring and autumn to expose hibernating larvae and pupae to predators and the elements.

Biological Control: Natural controls include parasitic wasps, tachinid flies and other predatory insects.

Root Maggots

Delia spp.

Cabbage Root
Maggots

Adult root maggots feed on nectar of wild flowers. Cabbage Root Maggot (*D. radicum*) larvae feed by shredding roots of crucifers, whereas Onion Maggot (*D. antigua*) larvae prefer the roots of onions.

Root maggots overwinter as pupae in the soil. Adults emerge in early spring to feed on nectar of wild flowers. They live for five to six weeks, and females lay up to 200 eggs singly or in small batches at the base of host plants. Females

ID: *Adult:* resembles house fly but slightly smaller; grey with dark stripe down abdomen. *Larva:* whitish maggot that tapers towards head end, with no legs or distinct head capsule.

Size: *Adult:* 7 mm. *Larva:* 10 mm.

Habitat and Range: widespread across southern British Columbia.

Scouting: Onion Maggot females tend to lay eggs in bunches; the larvae move from plant to plant, so damage in the garden is often patchy. Onion Maggots also attack garlic,

leek and chives. Larvae begin feeding on root hairs, eventually moving into the taproot. Damage to seedlings is most destructive, often resulting in death of the plant. Second-generation feeding rarely results in plant death but does reduce yield and marketability of produce. Damage can be recognized by wilting and yellowing of the leaves. White sticky traps have proven effective in detecting the onion maggot fly. Commercial growers use sprays only if a certain threshold level is reached, as determined through monitoring. Larvae of both generations of the Cabbage

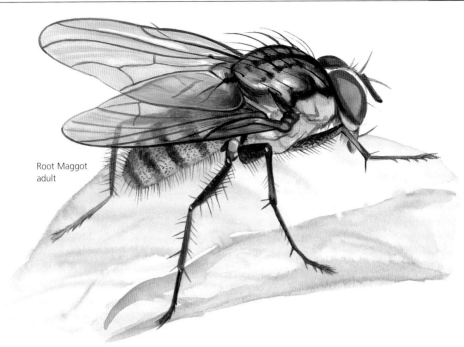

Root Maggot adult

prefer cool, moist soil for egg laying. Dry, hot conditions are not conducive to egg laying or larval survival, often forcing larvae into above-ground stem tissue. Larvae hatch and develop in three to four weeks. Pupation during summer lasts two to three weeks, and second generation adults emerge to lay eggs again. This second generation overwinters in the pupal stage. Onion Maggots may have up to three generations per year, whereas Cabbage Maggots have only two generations.

The Cabbage Root Maggot has been studied to better understand its egg-laying behaviour. The female does a spiral descent to a host plant, senses if it is acceptable as a host and then takes off. She repeats this three more times before laying her eggs. If at any time she lands on a non-host plant, she will fly away to start the process all over again. Therefore, planting susceptible crops in a monoculture will increase root maggot pressure, whereas planting in mixed rows or randomly with other crops will greatly reduce root maggot pressure.

Maggot tunnel and burrow into tubers of radish, turnip and rutabaga, exposing the tuber to increased risk of disease infection.

Cultural/Physical Control: Damaged or diseased plants are preferred egg-laying sites for Onion Maggots, so remove these plants to reduce the number of adults visiting your garden. Similarly, be sure to remove all culls in autumn. Rotating crops will reduce but not eliminate the problem because root maggot adults are good fliers. Growing plants under row cover cloth (spun polyester fabric that allows light and water to penetrate) will keep maggot flies out while allowing light and aeration.

Biological Control: Many predators, parasitoids and pathogens suppress root maggots. You may have seen flies at the tops of grasses, clinging to the seedhead in a death grip. These flies are infected with the fungus *Entomophthora muscae*. The fungus causes the fly to move to a high point, ensuring the spores will disperse over a wider area to increase the chance of infecting other flies. A rove beetle, *Aleochara bilineata*, is a parasitoid of the pupae.

Crane Flies

Tipula spp.

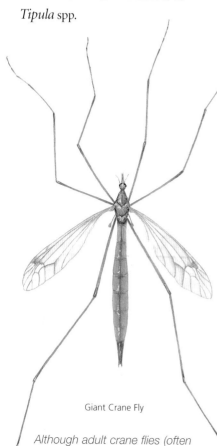

Giant Crane Fly

Although adult crane flies (often called mosquito hawks) are large and imposing, they are completely harmless because the adults of most species do not feed.

Larval crane flies, known as leatherjackets, feed on roots and crowns of turfgrass, vegetables and tree seedlings. There are more than 1500 species of crane fly in North America, most of which are benign decomposers in soil and wetlands. The most common pest species is the European Marsh Crane Fly (*T. paludosa*), which is widespread across southern British Columbia. Another European species, *T. oleracea* was identified in the Pacific Northwest in 1998.

Crane fly larvae overwinter in the soil, resume feeding in spring for a short time and then pupate. Adults emerge throughout the summer to mate and lay eggs in soil and turf. Moist soil conditions are essential for egg survival. Adults are very short lived and are non-feeding. Larvae feed throughout summer and autumn and move down in the soil to overwinter. *T. paludosa* has one generation per year while *T. oleracea* has two.

ID: *Adult:* slender-bodied and long-legged, looking remarkably like an enormous mosquito. *Larva:* long, brown, cylindrical and legless; has thick tentacle-like appendages on its posterior end for breathing.

Size: *Adult:* 15–25 mm. *Larva:* 5–20 mm.

Habitat and Range: most commonly found in moist soils or wetland habitats.

Scouting: Adults are clumsy fliers that will come to lights and are often encountered indoors. The larvae remain below sod level during the day, feeding on the roots and crowns of turfgrass and other plants at night.

They are also known to feed on crucifers and tree seedlings. Look for tunnels in root zone and shredding of the plant crown. Persistent surface moisture in soils is a welcome condition for crane fly egg laying.

Cultural/Physical Control: Allow the soil to dry between watering. Dethatch the lawn on a regular basis to prevent the accumulation of decaying organic matter.

Biological Control: Generalist predators such as ground beetles and rove beetles routinely control crane flies.

Fruit Flies

Euphranta canadensis, Rhagoletis spp.

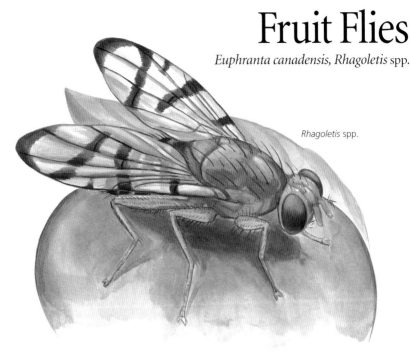

Rhagoletis spp.

Fruit fly larvae tunnel into fruit, consuming the pulp and then the seeds. Fruit flies are host specific, with the Cherry Fruit Fly (*R. cingulata*) and the Black Cherry Fruit Fly (*R. fausta*) attacking sour cherry and pin cherry. The Currant Fruit Fly (*E. canadensis*) attacks black, red and white currants and gooseberry. A new pest to BC is the Apple Maggot (*R. pomonella*), which attacks apple, crab apple and hawthorn.

Fruit flies overwinter as pupae in soil at the base of the host plant. Adults emerge in early summer, usually coinciding with flowering. Adults will feed for up to 10 days before laying eggs in developing fruit. Eggs soon hatch, and larvae tunnel into the fruit. Prior to harvest, larvae drop out of the fruit to pupate in the soil. There is only one generation per year.

ID: *Adult:* small, dark-bodied fly with distinctive dark pattern on wings, used to distinguish species. Currant Fruit Fly: light brown body and wing markings. *Larva:* legless maggot that tapers from rear to front.

Size: *Adult:* 3–5 mm. *Larva:* 1–4 mm.

Habitat and Range: Currant and Black Cherry fruit flies: province-wide; hawthorn and pin cherry serve as reservoirs for fruit flies. Apple Maggot: confirmed in the Abbotsford/Langley area.

Scouting: Females pierce green fruit to draw fluid to feed on; punctures appear as small holes ringed in dead, brown tissue. Some

puncture wounds have eggs deposited in them; eggs are elongate and rice-grain shaped, and lie just under the outer skin of the apple. Larval feeding appears as meandering tunnels. Affected fruit ripen rapidly and fall prematurely.

Cultural/Physical Control: Pick up fallen fruit daily; shallow cultivation below the plant in autumn will expose pupae to winter. Remove pin cherry and hawthorn.

Biological Control: Robber flies and aerial predators prey on adults. Once inside fruit, this species has few enemies. Most predation occurs on the pupae in the soil by ground beetles, rove beetles, etc.

Carrot Rust Fly

Psila rosae

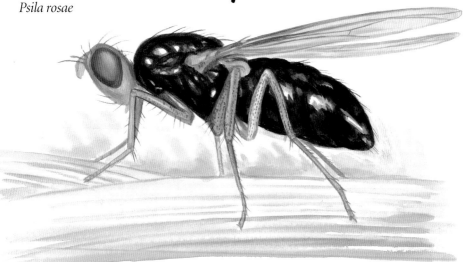

The Carrot Rust Fly (*P. rosae)* is commonly found in south-coastal British Columbia and central and eastern Canada. The larvae feed on the roots of carrot, celery, parsley, dill and parsnip.

Carrot Rust Flies overwinter as pupae in soil at depths as low as 10 centimetres. Adults emerge in May and June and move to sheltering plants to mate and feed. Females lay eggs as the base of carrot plants in the evening. Larvae hatch out and feed on the root hairs and roots, eventually leaving the root to pupate in the soil. A second generation of adults may be seen emerging in late July and early August to lay eggs. There are two generations per year in central Canada and BC.

In the pursuit of an integrated control strategy, two parasitoids were released for protection of commercial carrot crops in BC and Ontario. Unfortunately, neither became established.

ID: *Adult:* reddish head; yellow legs. *Larva:* tiny whitish maggot.

Size: *Adult:* 6 mm. *Larva:* 1–5 mm.

Habitat and Range: found throughout southern British Columbia; female prefers moist soils to lay eggs; carrots near plantings that offer shelter are attacked more often.

Scouting: Infestations are difficult to detect by looking at the foliage. Often, larvae feeding in the root results in disease infection, and this is what the gardener detects. Early instar larvae feed on the root hairs, whereas later instar larvae move into the root proper, especially the basal third.

Cultural/Physical Control: The most effective course of action is to prevent the adults from laying eggs by using a floating row cover after seeding. Ensure the edges are securely sealed at the soil line and leave enough fabric to allow the plants to grow. The cover can be removed in July. You can also delay seeding until late June to escape the first generation of adults.

Biological Control: Egg predators such as rove beetles and ground beetles suppress rust fly populations.

Tachinid Flies

Voria ruralis and others

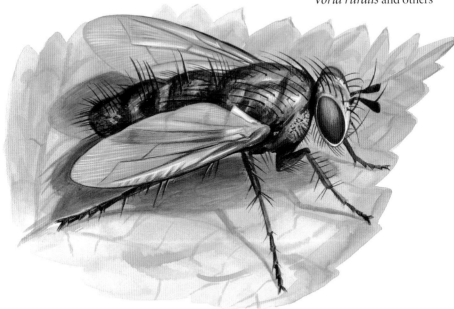

Larval tachinids feed on host insects from the inside, out. Adult tachinids feed on nectar. There are upwards of 1300 species of tachinid in North America. *V. ruralis* is a parasitoid of the Cabbage Looper. Other species parasitize caterpillars on many ornamentals.

Tachinid adults lay their eggs in the host insect, on the host near the head, or on plant material. If laid on the plant, the eggs either hatch and the larva seeks out a host insect or the eggs are meant to be eaten by the host insect and then hatch inside the host. Larvae will kill the host as a result of their feeding. Some species pupate inside the host insect, while other species drop to the ground and pupate in the soil. In British Columbia, most tachinids overwinter as pupae.

ID: *Adult:* resembles house fly but has stout spines at tip of abdomen (for defence when laying eggs on an uncooperative victim). *Larva:* whitish, legless grub lacking a distinct head capsule.

Size: *Adult:* 2–20 mm. *Larva:* 1–10 mm.

Habitat and Range: widespread across the province; preferred hosts are larvae of moths, sawflies and beetles, and adults of beetles and true bugs.

Scouting: You may be able to see a small egg, appearing much a like a tiny grain of rice, attached near the head of a caterpillar.

Parasitized insects tend to be sluggish, cease feeding and then simply die. You might find wrinkled caterpillars with a gaping hole where the larva or adult has emerged.

How to Attract: Tachinids are likely the most unsung heroes of your garden. They are highly host specific, meaning they are finicky about what they attack, usually restricting themselves to only one species of host. If beetles, sawflies or caterpillars are in your garden, tachinid flies will find them. They are quite capable of devastating a host population. Avoid using broad spectrum insecticides.

Hover Flies

Syrphus ribesii and others

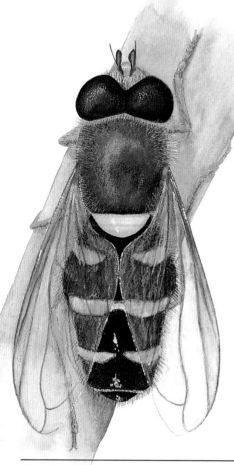

Adult hover flies do not harm plants. Larvae (maggots) feed on a range of foodstuffs including putrefying manure and old, rotten trees, but they are best known for eating aphids and other insects. These flies, also called syrphid flies, are often referred to as hover flies or flower flies because of the adults' hovering flight and their preference for flowers as a source of nectar. There are over 800 species of hover fly in North America, many of which, such as *S. ribesii,* are found in British Columbia.

Hover flies overwinter as larvae, pupae or adults, depending on the species. Eggs are laid, in the case of predatory hover flies, near the prey. There are usually four larval instars, followed by pupation on the plant or in the soil. There is usually only one generation per year.

The hover fly's striking colour, resembling a bee, is adopted as a form of mimicry to fool potential predators into thinking they will get a sting, when, in fact, the hover fly adult is harmless.

ID: *Adult:* readily recognized by its black and yellow colours and characteristic habit of hovering in flight; some species are very hairy, often mistaken for bees, whereas others are hairless and could pass for wasps or yellow jackets. *Larva:* flat, legless, green or brown maggot.

Size: *Adult:* 5–40 mm. *Larva:* 2–12 mm.

Habitat and Range: some hover fly larvae prefer decaying or even putrid matter; many species are found on plants across the province.

Scouting: Adults are commonly observed hovering in front of flowers, where they collect pollen and drink nectar. Larvae of predator species are commonly found wherever aphids

are, such as on undersides of leaves. Do not be alarmed to find maggots on your plant's leaves; they are likely hover flies and will do no harm to your plants.

How to Attract: A yard or garden with many flowering plants will attract hover flies, and you will experience all the benefits of this pollinator and predator. They are the first "bees" to visit in spring and the last to leave in autumn. If pollination were not enough of a reason to adore these flies, the larvae are voracious predators of aphids and other soft-bodied insects. You may be lucky enough to observe a larva hoist an aphid high in the air in what appears to be a show of triumph.

Robber Flies

Laphria spp., *Promachus* spp. and others

Beeish Robber Fly

Adult and larval robber flies are predators of other insects. Adult robber flies feed on anything up to their own size, including beetles, other flies, bees and wasps. The larvae feed on other insect larvae in the soil. Robber flies can be found across the province but are particularly abundant in dry sandy areas (*Promachus* spp.) and open woodland areas (*Laphria* spp.).

Adult robber flies may lay their eggs in soil, on foliage or in cracks and crevices in bark, or they may drop them randomly during flight, depending on the species. Larvae inhabit soil and leaf litter, burrowing down to overwinter. The larvae resume feeding in spring and then pupate. Adults emerge in early summer.

A feature unique to robber flies is a stout group of hairs on the front of the face called a mystax. The hairs serve to protect the face from thrashing limbs and wings of captured prey. Mystax—funny name for a moustache...

ID: *Adult:* can be a robust, bee-like fly or have elongate abdomen and stout thorax; eyes and pointed mouthparts are very well developed. *Larva:* legless and cylindrical with dark head capsule.

Size: *Adult:* 5–50 mm. *Larva:* 3–25 mm.

Habitat and Range: widespread across the province. *Laphria* spp.: prefer open woodland habitats, perching on foliage to scan for prey. *Promachus* spp.: often observed in sandy areas.

Scouting: Adults take their prey on the wing during the sunniest part of the day. You might see an adult perched on a leaf with its hapless prey impaled on its mouthparts. The larvae search for prey in soil and leaf litter.

How to Attract: Providing flowering plants for a refreshing drink of nectar and shrubs and trees for perches will entice robber flies into your yard.

Gall Midges

Dasineura spp., *Contarinia* spp.

Rose Midge (larva)

Several species of gall midges attack plants. Most are very host-specific; for example, the Rose Midge (*D. rhodophaga*) attacks only roses, and the Hemerocallis Gall Midge (*C. quinquenotata*) attacks only daylily flowers. Other common plant-feeding midges in British Columbia include the Apple Leaf Curl Midge (*D. mali*), the Blueberry Gall Midge, also called the Cranberry Tipworm (*D. oxycoccana*), and the Honey Locust Pod Gall Midge (*D. gleditschiae*). Most of these are introduced species from Europe.

ID: *Adult:* seldom seen; resembles fungus gnat and other tiny flies and can be tricky to identify; species can be identified by damage caused and by host plant. *Larva:* white, yellow or orange in different instars. Rose Midge: white.

Size: *Adult:* less than 1 mm. *Larva:* 1–3 mm.

Habitat and Range: throughout southern BC on a variety of plant species.

Scouting: Look for swollen, distorted, black, shriveled vegetative buds and flower buds. Young shoots and newly emerged leaves often appear twisted and distorted. Some midges attack only flower buds, others only vegetative buds, others both. Open a swollen bud carefully, and you will see the tiny maggots inside. A hand lens is very useful for getting a closer look.

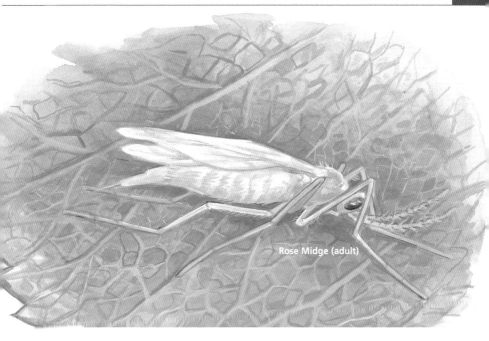

Rose Midge (adult)

Native gall midge species can be found on vine maple (*Acer circinatum*) and Pacific willow (*Salix lasiandra*). A recent European invader, the Swede Midge (*C. nasturtii*), attacks cabbage, rutabaga and other cole crops in Ontario but has not been found in BC.

All of these midge species are tiny Dipteran flies, less than half the size of a mosquito, and all have a similar life cycle. They usually overwinter as pupae in the soil. The female emerges in spring before bud break and, with a long, needle-like ovipositor, deposits her eggs inside the rolled-up leaf and flower buds before they open. The eggs hatch, and the larvae (legless maggots) feed inside the buds. Maggots go through three instars and a pre-pupal stage. Infested buds become swollen and distorted. After 5 to 10 days, the maggots drop to the ground to pupate in the soil, or, in the case of the Blueberry Gall Midge, the maggots pupate on the bud or leaf surface. A new generation of adults emerges, mates and lays more eggs.

After the maggots leave them, the infested buds blacken, shrivel and eventually drop off. Usually, the first thing a gardener notices is a lack of blooms and new shoots on the plants.

On plants that flower and produce new shoots all season long, such as roses, a new generation of adults emerges about every two weeks. The Rose Midge can be found in buds from January to October, but there are usually two peak adult flights: one in early June and another in mid-August. On plants that flower only once a season, such as daylilies, there may be only two generations per year.

Cultural/Physical Control: Pick off damaged blooms as soon as they appear in spring to prevent maggots from completing their life cycle.

Biological Control: A few natural parasitic wasps attack midge maggots, but they don't provide effective control.

Leafminers

Liriomyza spp., *Gracillaria syringella*

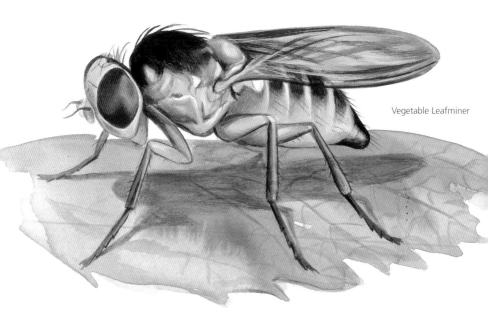

Vegetable Leafminer

Adult leafminers puncture the leaf surface to feed on oozing plant sap and to insert eggs into the leaf tissue. Larvae mine leaf tissue between the upper and lower surfaces. The Vegetable Leafminer (*L. sativae*) attacks tomato, lettuce, celery, beans, potato, onion, pepper and squash. What is often mistakenly called the Serpentine Leafminer or Chrysanthemum Leafminer, but should be referred to as the "unofficial" Serpentine Leafminer (*L. trifolii*) attacks chrysanthemum and other flowering plants. The "official" Serpentine Leafminer or Cabbage Leafminer (*L. brassicae*) attacks mustard, broccoli and nasturtium. The Pea Leafminer (*L. huidobrensis*) attacks peas and is distinct from the other species in that the mines are more visible from the underside of the leaf than from above. The Lilac Leafminer

ID: *Adult:* shiny, black and yellow fly. *Larva:* pale green, slightly flattened, legless maggot.

Size: *Adult:* 2–3 mm. *Larva:* 1–3 mm.

Habitat and Range: mostly restricted to southern British Columbia.

Scouting: Adult feeding punctures look like stippling on the upper leaf surface. Larval feeding starts as a thin meandering mine but may end up as a solid area of mined tissue. Most adult feeding and egg laying occurs in the morning.

Cultural/Physical Control: Pick off leaves that have visible mines. Remove weeds because many, such as lamb's-quarters, dandelion, goldenrod and chickweed, serve as alternate hosts for leafminers.

Biological Control: Two parasitic wasps are available commercially for use against leafminers in greenhouses.

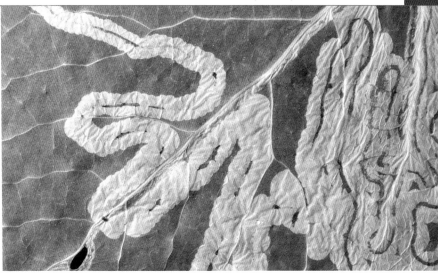

Mines (leaf damage)

(*G. syringella*), an introduced species, feeds on the leaves of lilac, green ash and privet.

The Lilac Leafminer is the only leafminer that is capable of overwintering in Canada outside of a greenhouse. The other species likely escape from a nearby greenhouse or are blown in with storm systems from the United States. Once here in summer, females lay eggs in leaf tissue. Females can live up to two or three weeks and deposit up to 400 eggs. The eggs hatch in a couple of days, and larvae mine inside the leaf, taking four to seven days to mature. The larvae cut a hole in the leaf and drop to the soil to pupate. There may be two or more generations per year, depending on how warm or cool the summer is.

Male leafminers depend on females to puncture leaf tissue to provide meals for them. Both sexes will drink nectar from flowers but do best when feeding on leaf sap.

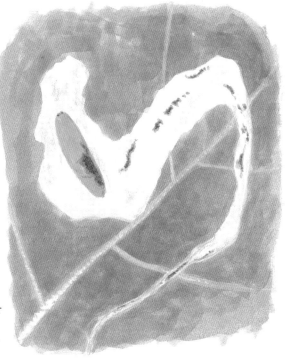

Leafminer larva in a mine

Fungus Gnats & Shore Flies

Bradysia spp., *Scatella* spp.

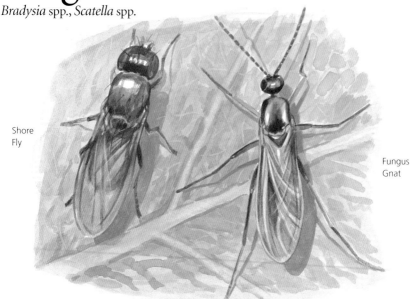

Shore Fly

Fungus Gnat

Fungus gnats (*Bradysia* spp.) and shore flies (*Scatella* spp.) are small, dark flies seen wherever there is moist, rotting vegetation, algae or soil with a content of organic matter.

They don't generally damage outdoor crops, but gnat larvae chew on roots of greenhouse vegetables and ornamental plants and can transmit pathogenic microorganisms that cause root rot. High populations of fungus gnat larvae damage house plants and seedlings in cold frames and greenhouses. Shore fly larvae rarely chew on roots, but the adults leave fecal matter on leaves of greenhouse plants. Fungus gnat eggs are tiny and rarely seen. The larvae go through four instars and feed and pupate in the soil. There are many generations per year.

Midges and small gnats such as march flies often swarm above rotting vegetation, but their larvae eat only rotted vegetation and algae. Fungus gnats walk on soil or potting media, or make short flights. Shore flies fly better than fungus gnats.

ID: *Adult:* Fungus gnat: small, fragile-looking, black fly with slender legs and antennae longer than body; weak flier, usually seen walking or making short flights; clear to light gray wings with Y-shaped vein. Shore fly: stout, black fly with short legs and short, bristle-like antennae. *Larva:* Fungus gnat: small, white or transparent, legless maggot with a shiny, black head. Shore fly: brownish yellow, legless maggot lacking a distinct head; dark-tipped, forked breathing tube at hind end. **Size:** *Adult:* 1–2 mm. *Larva:* 1–2 mm.

Habitat and Range: throughout the province.

Scouting: Look for adults and larvae in moist environments. Use yellow, sticky cards to monitor adult populations in greenhouses.

Cultural/Physical Control: Reduce watering, remove standing water and control algae. Cut houseplants back and re-pot into clean pots with fresh growing media.

Biological Control: *Hypoaspis* predatory mites, *Atheta* rove beetles and predatory wasps are available for commercial control of larvae and pupae in the soil.

Mosquitoes
Aedes spp., *Culex* spp., *Culiseta inornata* and others

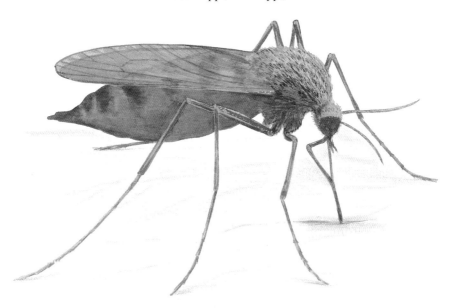

Most adult female mosquitoes require a blood meal. Some specialize on birds, some on mammals, and some on amphibians, reptiles, birds and mammals. Larval mosquitoes dine on bacteria, decaying organic matter and even proteins dissolved in water. There are approximately 50 species of mosquito in British Columbia of which *Aedes* species are the most common. The most pestiferous is *A. vexans*, followed closely by *A. strictus*,

A. spencerii, and *A. dorsalis*. A big lumbering species seen early in spring is *Culiseta inornata*. A major threat by virtue of its ability to transmit West Nile Virus is *Culex tarsalis*. Mosquitoes can be found everywhere standing water is found.

There are three main life history strategies found among mosquitoes. *Culiseta inornata* overwinters as an adult, emerging early in spring to feed and mate. Eggs are laid in permanent

ID: *Adult:* slender, delicate fly with long antennae and proboscis. *Larva:* has bulging thorax and slender abdomen ending in forked structure for breathing and salt exchange.

Size: *Adult:* 5–10 mm. *Larva:* 2–3 mm.

Habitat and Range: found everywhere water is to be had, from snow melt pools and sloughs to depressions in farm fields and even in discarded tires.

Scouting: Adults tend to stay out of hot sun, preferring to rest in vegetation, coming out at dusk to feed. Larvae can be observed near the edge in shallow still water bodies. The earliest mosquito is likely *Culiseta inornata*. *A. spencerii* is also out early in spring and it is typically an ankle biter. *A vexans*, *A. strictus* and *A. dorsalis* are more common in May, June and July. *Culex tarsalis* is most abundant in warm, wet weather in summer and early autumn.

Mosquitoes (continued)

and semi-permanent ponds. The larvae go through four instars, filtering food out of the water. They pupate in the water and emerge as adults at the water surface. There can be as many as three generations per year. *Culex tarsalis* also overwinters as an adult. Other species overwinter as eggs and hatch in snowmelt pools. These species typically have only one generation per year. *A. spencerii* overwinters as an egg and hatches in snowmelt pools but is also capable of hatching later in rain-fed pools, therefore, it will have two or three generations per year. *A. vexans* overwinters as an egg but does not hatch until the warm rains of summer. This species can develop very quickly in sun-warmed roadside ditches. Eggs of *A. vexans* have been recorded to last up to seven years before hatching and they are therefore very drought resistant.

Only about 10–13 of the mosquito species in BC, primarily Culex *spp., can transmit West Nile Virus (WNV). West Nile Virus has not been found in British Columbia as of 2007, but the threat is not trivial. It is a virus that affects the brain and brain stem. Most cases have no symptoms, but a few infected people have contracted West Nile Neurological Syndrome (also known as West Nile Fever), which is akin to a bad flu but can persist for weeks or months and, in some cases, symptoms are similar to encephalitis and may result in paralysis or death. The disease is carried in many different birds. Many species of mosquito feed on birds throughout spring and early summer, amplifying the number of birds infected with the virus. In July,* Culex tarsalis *populations increase, and this species feeds on birds and humans, acting as a bridge for the virus. This period poses the greatest hazard for us to contract the disease, especially in southern BC. Why risk infection? Use repellent and avoid being outdoors at dusk. WNV is a serious disease that demands you to be serious about avoiding it.*

Cultural/Physical Control: The best way to manage mosquitoes is to eliminate the larvae by draining ponds and, especially for *Culex tarsalis*, containers such as plant pots, old tires and birdbaths. You can reduce adult numbers by cutting the lawn low and not having thick vegetation for them to use as resting sites. Now, I have just described the ideal mosquito-free yard—a barren waste-land. Instead of this extreme, you could use repellent and long-sleeved clothing. We take for granted having screens on our windows and doors—why not go one step further and wear mosquito-netting clothing?

Biological Control: Larval and pupal mosquitoes have a host of aquatic predators, including dragonfly and damselfly nymphs, fish, frogs and predaceous diving beetles. Birds, dragonflies and damselflies, empid flies, seemingly anything that flies and hunts, dines on adult mosquitoes. Encourage birds and dragonflies to visit your yard by providing a birdbath or water feature (be sure to check it for mosquito larvae). Larval mosquitoes can be controlled using a bacterial agent called *Bacillus thuringiensis* var. *israelensis* (B.t.i.). It is a stomach poison for flies and only flies.

Gall Wasps

Diplolepis bicolor, D. rosae, Neuroterus saltatorius

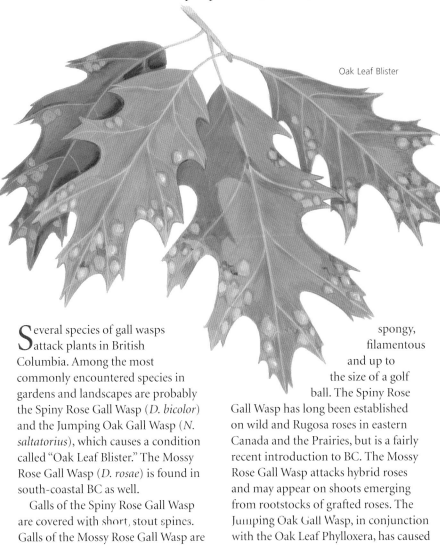

Oak Leaf Blister

Several species of gall wasps attack plants in British Columbia. Among the most commonly encountered species in gardens and landscapes are probably the Spiny Rose Gall Wasp (*D. bicolor*) and the Jumping Oak Gall Wasp (*N. saltatorius*), which causes a condition called "Oak Leaf Blister." The Mossy Rose Gall Wasp (*D. rosae*) is found in south-coastal BC as well.

Galls of the Spiny Rose Gall Wasp are covered with short, stout spines. Galls of the Mossy Rose Gall Wasp are spongy, filamentous and up to the size of a golf ball. The Spiny Rose Gall Wasp has long been established on wild and Rugosa roses in eastern Canada and the Prairies, but is a fairly recent introduction to BC. The Mossy Rose Gall Wasp attacks hybrid roses and may appear on shoots emerging from rootstocks of grafted roses. The Jumping Oak Gall Wasp, in conjunction with the Oak Leaf Phylloxera, has caused

---

ID: *Adult:* small, dark brown wasp. *Larva:* small, white, worm usually seen inside galls.

Size: *Adult:* 1–2 mm. *Larva:* 1 mm or less.

Habitat and Range: southern Vancouver Island and the Gulf Islands, the Lower Mainland and the Fraser Valley.

Scouting: Hard, round, spiny galls on wild and Rugosa rose canes are an indication that you have Spiny Rose Gall Wasps in your garden. If you see spongy, swollen galls on hybrid roses and rootstocks, you probably have Mossy Rose Gall Wasps. Jumping Oak Gall Wasp larvae feed on new leaves in spring and cause leaf blisters in late summer and fall.

Gall Wasps (continued)

Mossy Rose Gall
Wasp galls

significant dieback of Garry oak forests on Vancouver Island.

On roses, small, white larvae overwinter in cavities within the galls and can be seen when galls are cut open. Adult wasps emerge in spring and lay eggs on leaves and shoots. Larvae crawl into new shoots and young, woody twigs and create the hairy or spiny galls. There is one generation per year.

Larvae of the Jumping Oak Gall Wasp create swollen, white, blister-like galls on the margins of oak leaves. Leaves appear scorched. The galls fall the ground in June and July. Movement of larvae within the galls produces a soft, swishing sound, like raindrops, in the leaf litter. The larvae overwinter in the galls, and adult wasps emerge in March or April to lay eggs in new leaf buds. These larvae feed and pupate on the new leaves. About one month later, the next generation of adults emerges and lays eggs on the lower surface of the oak leaves. As these larvae feed, they induce the plant cells to form the blister-like galls in which they overwinter.

Cultural/Physical Control: Spiny Rose Gall Wasps cause little or no injury to Rugosa roses and generally can be ignored. For Mossy Rose Gall Wasps, prune out and dispose of galls in fall; freeze or crush larvae before putting them in the compost pile. Be sure to cut out all galls because each gall can produce 30–40 adults in spring. For Jumping Oak Galls, keep trees healthy and vigorous; pick off leaf galls when seen and rake up leaf litter and bury it or dispose of it off-site.

Biological Control: None known.

Raspberry Sawfly

Monophadnoides geniculatus

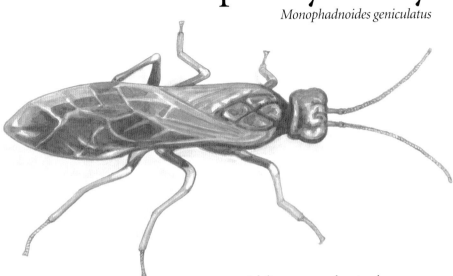

Gardeners and farmers with raspberry patches often encounter these interesting-looking sawflies. The larvae are skeletonizers, and large numbers can sometimes defoliate an entire raspberry patch, leaving nothing but leaf stems and veins (called "leaf skeletons"). Like all sawflies, they are not true flies at all but are members of the Order Hymenoptera, which includes ants, wasps and bees. Sawflies are in the family Tenthredinidae.

Adults emerge and mate when raspberries are blooming. Females lay eggs in leaf tissue. Larvae hatch and feed on the underside of leaves, but during heavy infestations they may also feed on flowers and newly formed raspberries. Leaf damage starts off as tiny holes, but as larvae grow, the holes become larger and longer. Full-grown larvae drop to the ground and build cocoons in the surrounding soil, where they hibernate in a prepupal stage. Pupation occurs the following spring. This species only has one generation per year.

ID: *Adult:* winged, black and yellow body with red to orange markings on legs. *Larva:* light green body covered in white spiny bristles; yellowish head.

Size: *Adult:* wingspan 6 mm. *Larva:* body length 12 mm.

Habitat and Range: throughout the province, primarily in areas that also have wild raspberries and other Rubus species.

Scouting: During spring and summer, look for small to large, ovate holes in leaves. Examine the underside of leaves for the small, spiny, white to greenish larvae.

Cultural/Physical Control: Larvae can be picked off leaves and squished by hand. This can be quite effective, especially in small areas with a small infestation.

Biological Control: Predators of these pesky sawflies range from parasitic wasps, predatory spiders, beetles and other insects to many insectivorous birds. Plant a variety of nectar-producing flowers to attract parasitic wasps, and keep some native bushes intact to attract many predators.

Birch Leaf Miners

Fenusa pusilla, Profenusa thomsoni

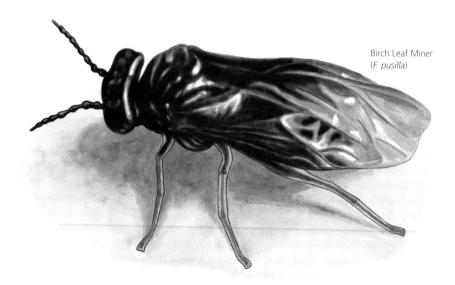

Birch Leaf Miner
(*F. pusilla*)

Birch leaf miners arrived in North America from Europe and quickly spread westward into the Prairie Provinces and British Columbia. The two main species in BC are the Birch Leaf Miner (*F. pusilla*) and the Ambermarked Birch Leaf Miner (*P. thomsoni*). Both are small, black sawflies and are parthenogenic, meaning that males are not required for reproduction (so are rare in North America). As their names suggest, the larvae spend their lives within birch leaves, where they cause unsightly dead spots on the foliage, and in extreme cases, dead leaves. Although a heavily infested tree appears dead and has a rusty appearance, leaf miners damage the owner's ego more than the tree itself—the damage they cause is basically cosmetic and does not kill the tree. In extreme cases, however, damage may hinder tree growth.

The Birch Leaf Miner has two generations in one year. The adult sawfly emerges in late May or early June.

ID: *Adult:* winged, dark-bodied sawfly. Birch Leaf Miner: black with yellow legs. Ambermarked Birch Leaf Miner: black with white legs. *Larva:* Birch Leaf Miner: white body with brown head and a large, dark patch plus 3 dark spots on underside of thorax. Ambermarked Birch Leaf Miner: light-coloured head and 2 dark dashes on thorax.

Size: *Adult:* wingspan 2.5–3.5 mm. *Larva:* body length 5–8 mm.

Habitat and Range: throughout the province primarily on paper birch.

Scouting: Look for brown blotches with black markings on the underside, leaves containing whitish larvae and overall brown or rust-coloured foliage.

The female cuts slits with her ovipositor into the upper surface of leaves, where she deposits an egg. The larva hatches and feeds on the tissue between the leaves' epidermal layers. In some cases, there can be several larvae feeding within the same mine. The little worm continues to feed into its fourth instar. The non-feeding fifth instar drops to the ground, pupating in an earthen cell a few centimetres deep in the soil. The second generation hatches two weeks later, and the cycle repeats. In southern parts of the province in warm years with late-season frosts, a third or even fourth generation can occur, but in most of the province this species normally completes only two generations, overwintering as pupae in hibernation cells under fallen leaves.

Ambermarked Birch Leaf Miner females emerge in July and lay eggs in central slits along leaf veins. This species has five feeding instars with a sixth non-feeding stage that hibernates in the soil in a prepupal stage and pupates in spring. Mines often have several larvae and contain dark frass deposits.

The control of this species by a parasitic wasp is one of the great success stories of biological control in North America. A native species of parasitoid wasp (Lathrolestes luteolator) has started to feed on the Ambermarked Birch Leaf Miner and has significantly reduced the leaf miners' numbers.

Cultural/Physical Control: The best treatment is to keep your birch trees healthy. Water the trees when conditions are dry, and ensure your have healthy soil. Organic fertilizers may be used in spring to give the trees a boost so they can withstand a bit of defoliation and recover quickly.

Biological Control: Parasites and predators are valuable allies in helping to control birch leaf miners. Warblers, vireos and chickadees love to work through the branches of our birch trees and pull these unwanted pests from the leaves. Parasitic wasps also are of great benefit and have substantially reduced their number.

Cottonwood Sawfly

Nematus currani

Sawflies are members of the order Hymenoptera, and adults look like small wasps or bees, though they don't sting. Sawfly larvae resemble hairless caterpillars (the larvae of moths and butterflies) but have six or more pairs of stubby prolegs on their abdomen while caterpillars have five or fewer pairs. Sawfly larvae usually feed in large groups and can quickly defoliate a tree. Repeated attacks may cause trees to weaken and die.

Adults emerge in early spring before bud-break. They lay eggs on new shoots, and larvae can be seen feeding in large groups in April or May. Defoliated trees usually put out a new flush of growth in August. Larvae pupate and overwinter in spun cocoons. There is one generation per year in most of the province, except in the Fraser Valley, where a second generation of larvae may be seen feeding on the new growth in late August or early September.

The Cottonwood Sawfly is one of many sawfly species that attack broadleaf and coniferous trees in British Columbia. Several species, including the Cottonwood Sawfly, are native to western North America, but others, such as the European Pine Sawfly (*Neodiprion sertifer*), are introduced.

ID: *Adult:* black, wasp-like body; orange spots on head; yellow and black legs. *Larva:* hairless, greenish yellow body; yellow head.

Size: *Adult:* 6–7 cm. *Larva:* 1–2 cm.

Habitat and Range: black cottonwood and hybrid poplar in the southeastern Fraser Valley, Kamloops and Cariboo regions; larvae are usually in clusters on new growth.

Scouting: Clusters of small, yellowish green larvae feed in new shoots in spring. There may be a second generation in late August in the Fraser Valley. Larvae consume the entire leaf tissue except the main veins.

Cultural/Physical Control: Cut off infested branches and destroy larvae.

Biological Control: Several natural predators and parasites attack the Cottonwood Sawfly but do not control it. Home garden "leaf shine" sprays containing neem oil are very effective on sawfly larvae. Insecticidal soap will kill young larvae on contact; more than one application is usually required.

Pear Slug
Caliroa cerasi

This glistening, black, leaf skeletonizer resembles a slug. It is an introduced species from Europe and is commonly observed feeding on the leaves of fruit trees, creating brown patches.

Adults emerge in late spring after the host trees leaf out. Females insert an egg into the leaf, which creates a blister in response. About 10 to 15 days later, slug-like larvae hatch and begin feeding on the upper leaf surface. They continue to feed for two to three more weeks, skeletonizing the leaves. Mature larvae drop to the ground and spin cocoons in the duff, where they pupate. A second generation of adults emerges in late July. This is when the most damage to tree leaves can occur. Mature larvae drop to the ground in fall, pupate in the soil and remain there until spring.

ID: *Adult:* black-and-yellow-bodied wasp. *Larva:* immature looks like glossy, dark slug with a swollen head; mature is yellowish green.

Size: *Adult:* wingspan 10 mm. *Larva:* body length 10–12 mm.

Habitat and Range: throughout the province on fruit trees, cotoneaster, hawthorn and mountain ash.

Scouting: Watch for signs of leaf skeletonizing in mid- to late June and again in late July and early August.

Cultural/Physical Control: The most common method used to control these slugs is to take a garden hose and blast them off the leaves using high pressure. Be careful to use a water stream that is strong enough to blast off larvae but not the leaves. Larvae can also be picked off by hand and squished or dropped into soapy water.

Biological Control: There are many beneficial critters that help control these little pests. Predators range from birds to parasitoid wasps, which often keep the pear slug numbers at lower levels.

Ants

Formica spp., *Pogonomyrmex* spp., *Camponotus* spp. and others

Harvester Ant

Some species of Wood and Field ants practise slavery by stealing ant pupae of other species and raising them as their own. The emerging adults think they are at home and work for their captors with no complaints. That is why you may see black and red ants working together in the same mound.

Ants are scavengers and, in some cases, predators of other insects. Wood or Field Ants (*Formica* spp.) are common in both field and woodland habitats. Harvester Ants (*Pogonomyrmex* spp.) are found in open grassland habitats. Ten species of Carpenter Ants (*Camponotus* spp.) inhabit decaying wood such as tree stumps and rotten building materials in BC, but the most common species are the Black Carpenter

ID: *Adult:* narrow waist between thorax and abdomen; long, elbowed antennae on head. Wood and Field ants: can be all red, all black or have red head and thorax and black abdomen. Harvester Ant: can be all red or all black. Carpenter, Black Garden and Pavement ants: are all black except the Red and Black Carpenter Ant, which has a reddish-brown thorax. *Larva:* enclosed in a pearly white cocoon.

Size: *Adult:* Carpenter ants: 12 mm. Wood and Field ants: 4–8 mm. Pavement Ant: 2–4 mm. *Larva:* 2–8 mm.

Habitat and Range: Carpenter ants: nest in decaying wood, often invading homes if the

lumber is water-damaged. Wood and Field ants: build nests in the ground, often creating large mounds. Harvester Ant: seed eater that builds large mounds and covers them with plant material to act as heat regulators. Garden Ant: nests in soil, creating small mounds. Pavement Ant: typically nests under paved walkways and stepping stones.

Scouting: Mounds are conspicuous by the displacement of soil and possible disruption around roots of shrubs and flowers. Foragers use a chemical scent to mark the path to food sources, so you may often see lines of ants marching along. Carpenter ants do not use chemical trails. Wood, Field, Pavement and

Ant (*C. pennsylvanicus*) and the Red and Black Carpenter Ant (*C. herculeanus*). The Pavement Ant (*Tetramorium caespitum*), introduced from Europe, is common in the Pacific Northwest and builds nests along foundations and under sidewalks and stepping stones. The Black Garden Ant (*Lasius niger*) is widespread in urban areas.

Ants are social insects with one to many queens responsible for laying eggs in the heart of the colony nest. Larvae are cared for and fed by worker adults. The larvae pupate within the nest. Adult ants are sterile and serve many roles within the colony, ranging from nursery attendant and servant of the queen to housekeeper, guard and forager. Queens overwinter in the nest. New queens are produced in spring (Carpenter Ants) or autumn (all others). They go on a nuptial flight and then disperse, drop their wings and found a new colony or overwinter to start fresh in spring. Colonies may persist for years.

Wood Ant

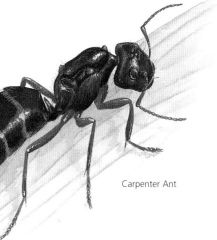

Carpenter Ant

Carpenter Ants do not sting; instead, they bite and are capable of spraying formic acid from their rear. Harvester Ants can inflict a painful sting. Carpenter Ants can be detected by looking for piles of sawdust alongside tree stumps or wooden structures that are in contact with or near the ground. Wood and Field ants will tend to aphids for their honeydew. The ants patrol the host plant, defending aphids from all attackers, which can exacerbate your aphid problems.

Cultural/Physical Control: Physically disturb the mound repeatedly and you might convince the ants to move to another locality. Pouring boiling water into the mound will achieve the same result but will harm plant roots. You can disrupt the march of ants into your home by observing the path they take into your house and washing the path with soap and water to eliminate their chemical highway markers.

Biological Control: Birds, beetles, wasps and other insects all feed on ants. However, ants are voracious predators in their own right. Having an ant colony nearby will reduce the pest problems you have in your garden. Ants are also good at mixing soil and removing plant debris. Overall, ants are beneficial and should be dealt with only if in direct conflict with your lawn or garden.

Honey Bee

Apis mellifera

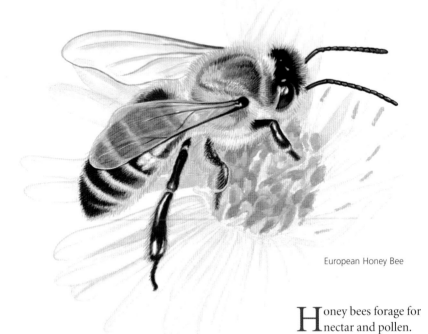

European Honey Bee

One of only two Nobel Prizes awarded for discoveries involving insects deals with how bees communicate with each other. In 1923, Karl von Frisch described the "waggle dance" of honey bees that allows worker bees to exchange the whereabouts of good foraging sites. Through the dance, the bees learned not just where the site was located but also what kind of flowers and how productive the site is.

Honey bees forage for nectar and pollen. They do no damage to plants; instead, they serve a vital role in pollinating flowers, especially tree fruits, which have heavy, sticky pollen. Honey bees are raised for honey production as well as their pollinating services. The European Honey Bee (*A. mellifera*) was introduced to North America by European colonists. The Africanized Bee (a hybrid species) or "killer bee" is not in Canada. This bee has a bad reputation that is largely undeserved. Africanized Bees just

ID: *Adult:* fuzzy, black and yellow, and has elbowed antennae. *Larva:* plump, whitish legless grub without a noticeable head capsule.

Size: *Adult:* 15–20 mm. *Larva:* 5–10 mm.

Habitat and Range: widespread across the province, though most are domesticated by beekeepers.

Scouting: Honey bees are most active on warm, sunny days, rarely venturing out in cloud and never in cold or drizzle. You can measure how industrious a honey bee has been by the size of the pollen load she carries on her hind legs.

Honey bees are essential for fruit pollination and have a place in all gardens, ornamental or producing; healthy espaliered apple tree, *Malus* (above).

have a much wider "personal space" so are thought to attack out of nowhere, when, in fact, you have come too close to their hive. Africanized Bees also send out more workers to defend their hive than European Honey Bees, hence the severity of attacks by Africanized Bees is usually much greater.

Honey bees are social insects that live in a hive. A single fertile queen establishes the colony and cares for the early brood of larvae, collecting pollen to mix with honey into "bee bread" to feed the young. Once sterile workers emerge, the queen is relegated to strictly egg-laying duty. Young adult bees care for the larvae and pupae and maintain the hive, while older bees defend the hive and forage for food. In time, some larvae are fed "royal jelly" from birth until pupation and become new queens who go on a nuptial flight to mate with males, or drones. If the colony is big enough, the old queen will take some drones and workers with her in a swarm to found a new hive; otherwise, she is ousted by the new queen. Hives are perennial provided there is enough stored honey and the hive is adequately sheltered to survive winter.

How to Attract: Honey bees require nectar and pollen all summer long so a diverse garden is their best friend. If you can ensure a steady supply of blooms throughout summer, you will be able to enjoy their determined pollinating activities for a long time. Honey bees are not aggressive unless you threaten their nest. Workers will be dispatched to defend the nest and die in the process (their stinger is barbed and, when inserted, it stays along with the venom sack, so that the victim continues to get a dose even after the bee is gone). Honey bees suffer many stresses, including disease, robber flies, hive-attacking beetles and mites, and lack of blooms. Recent problems with colony decline are being vigorously investigated; however, similar declines have occurred several times over the last century.

Leafcutter Bees

Megachile spp.

Alfalfa Leafcutter Bee

Leafcutter bees in the genus *Megachile* use leaves, whereas mason bees, in the genus *Osmia*, do not cut leaves but use mud instead to fashion their nests. Leafcutter bees are widespread across British Columbia. The Alfalfa Leafcutter Bee (*M. rotundata*) was introduced for alfalfa pollination.

Leafcutter bees are not social; instead, fertile females carry the entire load of rearing. Adults emerge from the overwintering pupa in spring to construct cells out of leaf material in natural voids, or they excavate holes in rotten wood. The cells are lined with leaf material and provisioned with nectar and pollen. Females can produce 30 or 40 eggs and require a cell for each one. Nests tend to contain six to eight cells each. The larvae hatch to feed for the remainder of summer and pupate before winter comes. There is only one generation per year.

Most leafcutter bees saw semicircular disks out of leaves for use in building their nests.

ID: *Adult:* similar to a honey bee but slightly flattened and black and white or black and grey. *Larva:* plump, whitish legless grub without a noticeable head capsule.

Size: *Adult:* 12–18 mm. *Larva:* 3–10 mm.

Habitat and Range: found province-wide; females like to nest in natural voids in standing trees or in plants with pithy stems, such as roses. You can entice leafcutter bees into your yard by placing on a stand a 5 cm x 20 cm block of wood with holes varying from 3–5 mm drilled to a depth of 15 cm.

Scouting: You can distinguish between honey bees and leafcutter bees not just by colour, but also by the way they carry their pollen. Leafcutter bees carry their pollen on the underside of their abdomen, whereas honey bees carry it on their legs. Leafcutter bees collect leaf disks from rose, lilac, ash

and Virginia creeper. The damage is not harmful to the plant.

Cultural/Physical Control: Ideally you should encourage these bees into your yard because they will fly in cloudy and cool weather when honey bees are nowhere to be seen. Leafcutter bees are active early in spring, just when many of our native bush fruit are flowering and in dire need of their services. If numbers are so high that there is substantial damage to lilacs, for example, then covering the bush with a floating row cover will protect it. To prevent bees from nesting in rose stems, plug the end of cut stems with glue or wax.

Biological Control: Leafcutter bees are rarely so numerous that you might entertain thoughts of controlling them. However, there are parasitoids and blister beetles that will go after the nests.

Bumble Bees

Bombus spp.

Bumble bees are excellent native pollinators that do no harm to plants. They can be found throughout British Columbia. Most are in the genus *Bombus,* but members of the genus *Psithyrus* invade *Bombus* nests and lay eggs for the *Bombus* workers to raise for them.

A mated female bumble bee overwinters in a sheltered space, emerging in spring to begin colony establishment. She will locate an abandoned rodent burrow or similar cavity and construct a wax pot to provision with honey, and then lay eggs nearby on a bed of pollen. A wax sheet is laid overtop for protection. Once the first brood has emerged, the founding female remains in the nest to lay more eggs near additional honey pots constructed by her offspring. Egg laying continues all summer, and in autumn the queen will produce unfertilized eggs that yield males to mate with new daughters that were allowed to turn into queens. It is these late-emerging queens that overwinter to found new colonies in spring. The old queen and her sterile daughters die off with the coming of winter. Unlike honey bees, bumble bee colonies last only one season.

ID: *Adult:* large, very hairy, black and yellow body with elbowed antennae. *Larva:* plump, whitish legless grub without a noticeable head capsule.

Size: *Adult:* up to 25 mm. *Larva:* 5–20 mm.

Habitat and Range: widespread across the province.

Scouting: New queens establish nests in abandoned rodent burrows. It is comical to watch bumble bees come lumbering in for a gentle landing at the entrance to their nest. Bumble bees are good natured, allowing us to get quite close to them when they are foraging or coming and going from the nest. They are active very early in spring and late into autumn.

Cultural/Physical Control: Bumble bees are beneficial and should not be considered for control. Although their sting is very painful, the stinger is not left in the victim, and bumble bees are usually very docile and approachable.

Biological Control: None warranted.

Solitary Bees

Megachile spp., *Osmia* spp.

Orchard Mason Bee

The Hornfaced Bee (*O. cornifrons*) was introduced to eastern North America from Japan in the 1960s as a fruit tree pollinator. It is not known to be established in BC. If introduced in artificial nests, it may survive in warm, southern areas of the province. However, its introduction is controversial because it may compete with native solitary bees for food and nesting sites, and introduce foreign predators and parasites.

The Blue Orchard Bee nests in holes in the ground in sheltered areas and overwinters as an adult inside the cocoon. The bees emerge in spring or early summer when flowers are in bloom. After mating, females forage for pollen and nectar. Females have a pollen-brush on the underside of their abdomen called a scopa, which the males lack. Each female finds a pre-existing hole suitable for nesting and deposits her eggs in cells, sealed with mud. Mason bees are so-called because they build a separate cell for each egg. There is usually one generation per year.

There are many species of solitary bees in BC. They are important pollinators and are wonderful insects to encourage in your garden. They are not aggressive, and their sting is mild. Some species, such as the Alfalfa Leafcutter Bee (*M. rotundata;* see p. 180), which was introduced from Europe in the 1930s, and the native Orchard Mason Bee, also called the Blue Orchard Bee (*O. lignaria*), can be purchased commercially and reared in artificial nests. You may have seen mason bee houses, which resemble birdhouses, in yards, gardens, orchards and berry patches.

Rearing mason bees can be a fun science project for children. Starter kits and "observation nests" can be purchased with clear panels that allow one to observe the bees develop from babies to adults.

ID: *Adult:* dark, metallic blue-black body.
Size: *Adult:* 12 mm.
Habitat and Range: throughout the province in open areas with nectar flowers.
Scouting: Watch for females to locate natural nests.

How to Attract: Set out empty artificial nests in your garden, backyard or patio and native mason bees will colonize them.

Parasitoid Wasps

Family Braconidae and Ichneumonidae

When I think of sci-fi movies, I am reminded of parasitic wasps. These amazing creatures are one of the most beneficial species that inhabit our gardens, but their life cycle is rather gruesome. Some Ichneumonid females walk along tree trunks until they sense the vibration of a boring beetle grub or moth caterpillar within. Then, with extreme precision, the females acrobatically curl their abdomen and coil their long ovipositor directly above the surface of the trunk. They drive their ovipositor through the bark and the inner wood, directly into the unsuspecting larvae. After laying an egg, the females pull out their ovipositor and continue hunting. An immunity-suppressing virus often accompanies the egg. The weakened grub or caterpillar becomes a buffet for the hungry wasp larva,

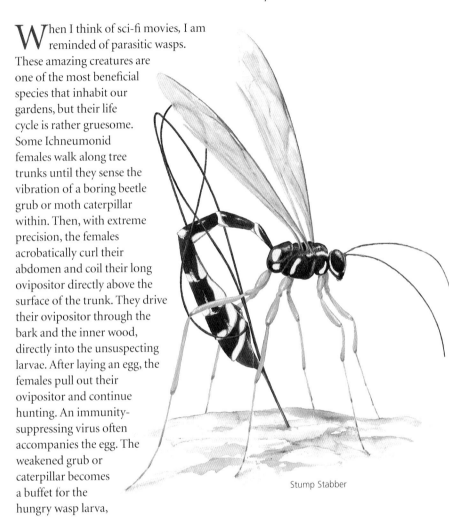

Stump Stabber

ID: *Adult:* varied bodies, but ant-like with 2 sets of wings; some adult females have abnormally long ovipositors projecting from tip of abdomen. *Larva:* whitish, maggot-like worm.

Size: variable

Habitat and Range: throughout the province in all habitats and gardens.

Scouting: Watch for small, black wasps feeding on nectar or buzzing in garden vegetation. They are most often observed during pest outbreaks. Also keep an eye out for wasps sitting on plant leaves. They are easily spotted wiggling their antennae as they smell for prey.

How to Attract: Adults are attracted to nectar-producing flowers. Minimize or eliminate the use of harmful insecticides to keep their populations healthy.

Parasitoid Wasps (continued)

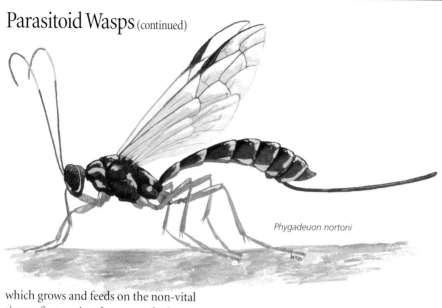

Phygadeuon nortoni

which grows and feeds on the non-vital tissues first, saving the organs for last. The prey continues to feed, and often dies as the wasp larva emerges from its body, just like in the movie *Alien*. Sometimes the prey will pupate and die with an adult wasp emerging later.

Thread-waisted Wasp

Some Braconid wasps complete their life cycle within the egg of the prey. Others attach their eggs to the body of the prey caterpillar. They can suppress a pest's population by as much as 30 percent! Then, a combination of other parasitoid wasps and other predators and disease can virtually eliminate the pest. Tent caterpillars, for example, build up huge populations that almost vanish the following year.

Amazingly, some wasps parasitize other wasps, which is known as hyperparasitism. A parasitoid's larva feeding inside a caterpillar isn't always safe. There are smaller wasps that seek them out, insert their ovipositors through the caterpillar and into the wasp larva.

Yellow Jackets

Dolichovespula maculata, Vespula spp.

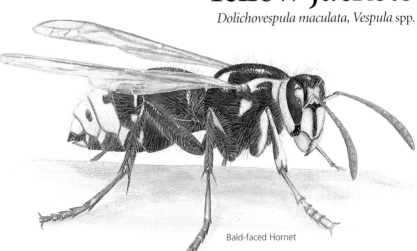

Bald-faced Hornet

Yellow jackets are known by a number of names including wasps and hornets. They get their name from the yellow or white striping on their black bodies. The two main genera of these wasps in our region are *Dolichovespula* and *Vespula*. In our gardens, we often encounter both genera, but the yellow jackets (*Vespula* spp.), with their distinctive yellow and black banding, are the most common. The Bald-faced Hornet (*D. maculata*), also called the White-faced Hornet, is the other commonly encountered species in BC. It is the big black and white one that is often seen in our yards or gardens. It is not a true hornet but is more closely related to the yellow jacket wasps. Both species build paper nests, which they defend ferociously.

We don't have to look hard to find these nerve-racking wasps in the garden. They tend to be attracted to sweet substances and can be found feeding on aphid honeydew or flowers, or crashing our garden parties in late

ID: *Adult:* Yellow jacket: black with yellow bands. Bald-faced Hornet: black with white bands. *Larva:* white grubs.

Size: *Adult:* wingspan 12–20 mm. *Larva:* body length is variable.

Habitat and Range: in gardens and landscapes throughout the region.

Scouting: It is not hard to find these guys; they are in most yards and gardens.

Cultural/Physical Control: Prevention is often the best method to deal with these dangerous insects. Keep your yard free of rotting fruit, decaying garbage, food and empty pop or beer cans. You can trap famished queens before they build nests in spring. Lure traps can be purchased from gardening stores, or you can make your own. For a water trap, use a pail filled with soapy water, with a small piece of meat (liver, fish, etc.) suspended by a string 2.5–5 cm above the water. When a wasp comes to grab a piece of food, it falls into the water and drowns. Place a piece of screen over the bucket so only wasps can get in and to prevent other critters from stealing your bait.

Small, early spring nests are the easiest to deal with. If you have a bee allergy or sensitivity, hire a professional. Colonies are relatively inactive after dark, so that is the best time to take action. Wear a long-sleeved shirt, pants and any other attire that can reduce the risk of

Yellow Jackets (continued)

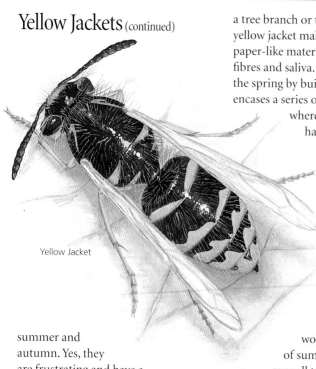

Yellow Jacket

a tree branch or the eavestrough. The yellow jacket makes a nest out of a paper-like material composed of plant fibres and saliva. This new queen starts the spring by building a small nest that encases a series of up to 45 larval cells where eggs are laid. Larvae hatch and develop in the cells, maturing into sterile female workers. The queen and her new workers begin expanding the colony, which can become quite large and may have hundreds of workers towards the end of summer. The workers take over all tasks except laying eggs. Adults feed on nectar, pollen and smaller insects, while larvae are fed chewed insects. In the late summer, the queen lays eggs that develop into new queens and reproductive males who leave the colony to mate. The males die and the new queens search out suitable hibernation sites, while the rest of the colony perishes after the first hard frost.

summer and autumn. Yes, they are frustrating and have a nasty sting, but they are beneficial as insect predators and minor pollinators.

The pregnant female queen overwinters as the only survivor from the previous year's colony. When she comes out of dormancy in spring, she seeks a suitable nest site that can range from a rodent burrow or a crack in a wall to an exposed paper nest under

---

being stung. Small external nests can be removed by hand. Approach the nest quietly and cautiously, and slip a bag over it from below. The top of the nest can then be detached using a knife or paint scraper and the bag immediately sealed and disposed of. Large nests should not be controlled using this method—hire a professional. Do not knock a nest down because the queen will only build a new one or join another local colony. Do not seal entrances of underground nests or nests in walls; the yellow jackets will only chew themselves a new entrance and may end up emerging on the opposite side of the wall.

Remember that yellow jackets are beneficial predators. If the nest is in an area where it is not

a hazard to people, leaving it alone is the easiest solution. Remind everyone of its presence and perhaps mark the nest's location.

Biological Control: Because of their aggressive nature, yellow jackets have few predators. Robber Flies (Family Asilidae) feed on them, and some of our larger spiders most likely feed on hornets and wasps trapped in their webs. Other animals like shrews and voles may tackle an injured or sick wasp that is crawling on the ground. In the winter, bees, mice and other insectivores, including bears and racoons, often ravage the nests. Chickadees, for example, are commonly seen hanging from an old hornet's nest in autumn, looking for abandoned larvae and pupae.

Other Bugs
of
Garden Interest

Spruce Spider Mite

Oligonychus ununguis

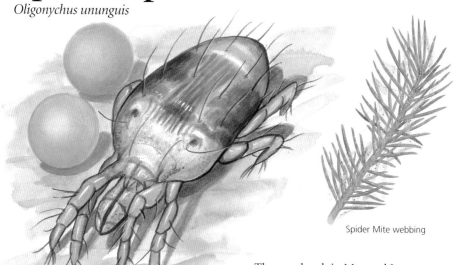

Spider Mite webbing

The Spruce Spider Mite feeds on chloroplasts in needle cells of spruce and many other conifers, causing needles to brown and drop. This spider mite is common in nurseries and landscapes across the province. Alberta spruce (*Picea conica* 'Alberta') is very susceptible.

The Spruce Spider Mite overwinters in the egg stage on branches of spruce.

The eggs hatch in May and June, yielding six-legged larvae that feed on new foliage and shoots. The larvae moult into eight-legged proto- and then deutonymphs, and then into eight-legged adults. From egg to adult can take as little as nine days in warm weather. Adults live for up to one month and can lay up to 50 eggs. There may be as many as six generations per year, with feeding pressure greatest in August and September.

ID: *Adult:* 8 legs; moderately hairy with pale front and dark rear. *Larva and nymph:* resemble adult, only smaller; larva has only 3 pairs of legs.

Size: *Adult:* 0.5 mm. *Larva:* 0.1–0.2 mm. *Nymph:* 0.2–0.4 mm.

Habitat and Range: throughout southern British Columbia; host plants include spruce, Douglas-fir, balsam fir, cedar, hemlock, larch, pine and juniper.

Scouting: Look for webbing among the branches and needles. Tap a branch over a white piece of paper to better see the mites. Needles will appear yellow and have black flecks on them—this is mite waste. Mites are most abundant on drought-stressed open trees in hot summers. Feeding can result in loss of needles, death of twigs and limbs and, in extreme cases, death of the tree.

Cultural/Physical Control: Open, dry trees are most susceptible, so closing in the canopy with multiple plantings will help raise the humidity within the branches. A strong pressure jet of water will easily dislodge the mites, but this action needs to be repeated to be effective for season-long control.

Biological Control: Many insects feed on spider mite eggs—they are the caviar of the insect world. Thrips, pirate bugs, damsel bugs, lacewings, lady beetles, all sorts of predators enjoy a tasty spider mite egg. Predator mites are very effective in suppressing spider mite populations so avoiding use of pesticides will conserve their numbers.

Eriophyid Gall Mites

Aceria fraxiniflora, Eriophyes spp., *Vasates quadripedes* and others

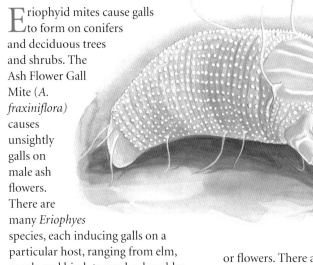

Eriophyid mites cause galls to form on conifers and deciduous trees and shrubs. The Ash Flower Gall Mite (*A. fraxiniflora*) causes unsightly galls on male ash flowers. There are many *Eriophyes* species, each inducing galls on a particular host, ranging from elm, maple and birch to poplar, boxelder, mountain ash and cherry. The Maple Bladder Gall Mite (*V. quadripedes)* also induces galls on leaves, in this case, maple. The Pine Rosette Mite (*Trisetacus gemmavitians)* causes large, round galls on the twigs of Jack pine.

In general, gall mites overwinter as fertilized adult females in bark crevices or leaf and flower buds. They emerge in spring and move to leaves or flowers. There are two nymphal stages and then the adult, which lives for up to one month. There can be several generations per year. A special case arises for species of gall mite on plum and chokecherry. No summer females are produced; instead, males and overwintering females emerge from spring eggs. Therefore, although the overwintering female produces a gall, there is only one generation per year.

ID: *Adult:* extremely tiny, elongate mite with 2 pairs of legs near head; pale to white in colour. *Nymph:* identical to adult, only smaller.

Size: *Adult:* 0.2 mm. *Nymph:* 0.1 mm.

Habitat and Range: widespread across British Columbia; most species are very host specific, infesting only one or a few species of tree; hosts include hardwood trees and shrubs.

Scouting: Gall mites damage plants in a number of ways. They can be free-living vagrants, and the damage they cause resembles that of spider mites. They can form what are called erinea, or patches of velvet, on upper or lower leaf surfaces. Gall mites can also produce bladder galls, small pouch-like growths on the upper surface of a leaf. Lastly, larger, woody galls can be formed out of flowers and on limbs. Whatever the form of the damage, it is rarely seriously harmful to the plant. Most galls are merely unsightly.

Cultural/Physical Control: Once the gall is formed, all you can do is prune off the affected limb, flower or leaf. Treating a tree with horticultural oil in early March may reduce the number of overwintering females.

Biological Control: Once the mites have formed their erinea or gall, they are well protected. Generalist predators such as predatory mites, thrips, and pirate bugs prey on free-living mites.

Ticks

Dermacentor andersoni, Ixodes pacificus

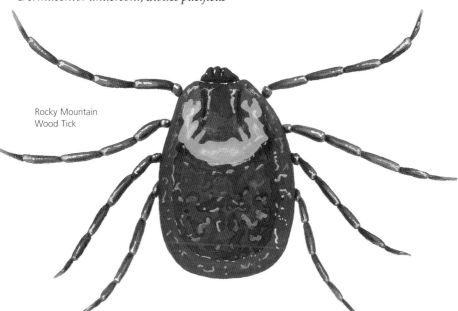

Rocky Mountain
Wood Tick

Ticks take a blood meal from suitable vertebrate hosts. There are more than 20 species of tick in British Columbia. The Rocky Mountain Wood Tick (*D. andersoni)* feeds on mice, squirrels, rabbits and other small mammals as a larva and nymph, and on cattle, sheep, horses, dogs, deer and humans as an adult. The Western Black-legged Tick (*I. pacificus*) is common on the islands and along the mainland coast and Fraser River and feeds on humans, deer, cats and dogs. Other common ticks in BC include the Brown Dog Tick (*Rhipicephalus sanguineus*), which feeds on dogs, coyotes and rarely on humans as an adult; and the Winter Tick (*D. albipictus*), which

---

ID: *Adult:* Rocky Mountain Wood Tick: slightly egg-shaped, but flattened; 8 legs; head/thorax region is white with dark markings; male has hard plate covering entire upper surface of body, whereas female's hard plate covers only front one-third. Western Black-legged Tick: female is red and black; male is smaller and black. *Larva and nymph:* identical to adult, only smaller.

Size: *Adult:* 5 mm. *Larva:* 1 mm. *Nymph:* 1–3 mm.

Habitat and Range: Rocky Mountain Wood Tick: dry interior hills and grasslands east of the Coast Range Mountains and north to Williams Lake. Western Black-legged Tick: in grass, forests, scrub and brush on Vancouver Island and the Gulf Islands, along the mainland coast north to Powell River and east along the Fraser River to Yale and north to Boston Bar.

Scouting: Larvae, nymphs and adults "quest" for hosts by clinging to grass with 2 pairs of legs reaching to the air, awaiting a passing host. The risk of getting a Western Black-legged Tick is greatest in spring and early summer and the Rocky Mountain Tick in June through July. After a day spent hiking or working in "tick country," you should conduct a tick check on your body.

feeds on moose, horses, deer and cattle during the winter, but not on humans.

Adult ticks lay masses of eggs, up 6500, in the soil in spring. The larvae hatch in June and July (Rocky Mountain Wood Tick) or spring and early summer (Western Black-legged Tick) and climb grasses to await a passing host. After a blood meal, the larvae drop to the ground to moult into the nymphal stage. If the weather is hot, the nymphs will overwinter; if not, they will feed again and moult to the adult stage and overwinter as adults. The entire life cycle can take up to three years, depending on how warm or cool the summer is and host availability.

Males blood feed but do not swell up very much. In contrast, females can take one or more days to gorge themselves and nearly triple their size, from 5 mm to 12 mm.

Rocky Mountain Wood Tick

Cultural/Physical Control: Ticks roam the host for several hours before settling down to feed. They prefer protected sites such as at the waistband, armpits and neckline. If they have begun to feed, you need to have the tick voluntarily remove its mouthparts to prevent excess saliva being injected or secondary infection. Grasp the tick as near to the skin as possible, using tweezers, and slowly, evenly pull the tick away, being careful not to rip off the head. Do not use heat or salt or gasoline because these will cause the tick to salivate, thereby increasing risk of disease transmission. The Western Black-legged Tick transmits a microorganism called *Borrelia burgdorferi* that causes Lyme Disease. There have been about 60 cases of Lyme Disease in BC in the past decade, and health officials believe Lyme Disease-carrying ticks may be present throughout the province. Symptoms include headache and muscle and joint aches, fever and fatigue. A bull's-eye rash may appear on skin, and a creeping paralysis starts from the feet and legs and moves upward. Infected people may take months or years to recover. The Rocky Mountain Wood Tick is capable of transmitting Rocky Mountain Spotted Fever and Lyme Disease, as well as being responsible for tick-borne paralysis. In tick-borne paralysis, as long as the tick is feeding near the base of the head, a creeping paralysis will occur. Remove the tick and the paralysis will recede. Rocky Mountain Spotted Fever, which can be fatal, has rarely been reported in British Columbia.

Biological Control: Ticks combat natural enemies and the elements by playing a numbers game...out of 6500 eggs at least a few should live to reproduce. There is not much you can do for control except wear repellent and long pants or gaiters while in grasslands and brush or wooded areas.

Spider Mites

Tetranychus spp.

Two-spotted Spider Mite

When spider mites feed, they puncture the cell wall and suck out the chloroplast, the organelle responsible for photosynthesis. The remainder of the cells' contents bleeds out. Surrounding cells detect the leaking fluid and respond by committing suicide (technically called apoptosis) to remain intact, which hopefully will stop whatever ruptured their neighbour. A larger feeding wound than the spider mite originally made results, hence the characteristic stippled appearance from such a small mite.

Spider mites suck the chloroplasts out of plant cells on the undersides of leaves. The Two-spotted Spider Mite (*T. urticae*) is the most common spider mite you will encounter in British Columbia. It infests many different plants including flowers, shrubs and trees. The Pacific Spider Mite (*T. pacificus*) and McDaniel Spider Mite (*T. mcdanieli*) are more commonly found infesting fruit trees.

ID: *Adult:* Two-spotted Spider Mite: roughly parallel-sided; mildly hairy; 2 large, dark lateral spots. Pacific Spider Mite: spots tend to blend together into a broad band, and may have a couple of small spots posteriorly. McDaniel Mite: uniformly dark on rear two-thirds. *Nymph:* 8 legs; resembles adult, only smaller.

Size: *Adult:* 0.3–0.5 mm. *Nymph:* 0.1–0.3 mm.
Habitat and Range: across the province on many flowering, shrub and tree hosts. Two-spotted Spider Mite: has been recorded from over 1200 different plant species; prefers arid conditions. McDaniel Spider Mite: prefers moist conditions. Pacific Spider Mite: prefers arid conditions.

In autumn when the weather cools, food quality declines and day length shortens, spider mite adults go into diapause, a form of hibernation. The mite turns a reddish colour, its shell becomes thicker and its metabolism slows down, allowing the mite to survive even severe winters. In spring, the mite reverts back to the active form, laying up to 100 eggs over its two-week lifespan. The eggs hatch into six-legged larvae, then moult into proto- and then deutonymphs before

Spider Mite damage

becoming adults. The period from egg to adult can be as short as five days or as long as 25 days, depending on how warm or cool the summer is. There can be many generations per year. Spider mites disperse by walking, catching a ride on insects and other animals and by ballooning, whereby they secrete a line of silk that gets caught up in the wind to carry them away.

Scouting: Spider mites spin silk to tie food together, ensnare potential predators, make a nice microhabitat, disperse pheromones and tie down potential mates. This silk is not formed into a spider-like web; rather, it is more dispersed. Look for moving dots that seem to float in the air, when actually they are walking along the silken lines. Smaller black dots are their excrement. Leaf tissue appears to be speckled or stippled as a result of their feeding. Tap plants over a white sheet of paper to better see the mites.

Cultural/Physical Control: Given that they prefer dry conditions, a more closed canopy that promotes humidity will discourage Two-spotted and Pacific spider mites. Alternatively, you can easily dislodge the mites with a strong jet of water.

Biological Control: Predatory mites, thrips, pirate bugs, lacewings and lady beetles are all on your side to manage spider mites. Conservation of these beneficial animals will go a long way to suppressing spider mite problems.

Crab Spiders

Coriarachne spp., *Misumena* spp., *Ozyptila* spp., *Xysticus* spp.

These amazing spiders sit for hours on a flower waiting for unsuspecting prey. With lightening speed, they lunge forth, grab their victim and give it a deadly, venomous bite. The digestive enzymes in the venom break down the insect's innards into a soupy liquid that is sucked out by the spider. These little guys are harmless to humans—their tiny fangs can't penetrate our skin. The female lays her fertilized eggs in a nest made of a folded-over leaf woven with silk. She defends her nest from predators and often dies before the eggs hatch. The young spiderlings emerge from the nest in about two to three weeks.

Goldenrod Crab Spider

The best way to describe a crab spider is as a deadly assassin. Crab spiders do not spin webs to capture or wrap their prey. They are ambush spiders. Crab spiders are quite common in BC, but because of their ability to camouflage themselves, they are not often observed. If gardeners carefully check their flower heads, they may come across a small, camouflaged spider patiently waiting for a meal.

Crab spiders can change colour like chameleons. For example, the Goldenrod Crab Spider changes its body colour from white to yellow to match the flower it is sitting on.

ID: *Adult:* body colour often matches surroundings; has bellybutton-like dot on underside of abdomen that marks where spinerettes are; front legs are longer than back legs and are held out to the side in crab-like posture. Goldenrod Crab Spider *(M. vatia)*: female is white to yellow with 2 reddish streaks on abdomen; male tends to be darker, in shades of grey, brown and red. Other species and genera resemble male *M. vatia* but vary in colour, size and pattern. *Immature:* similar to adult but smaller.

Size: *Adult:* body length up to 1 cm; the legs spread much wider; males are smaller than females.

Habitat and Range: throughout the province in gardens and wild areas.

Scouting: Look in newly opened flowers, such as yarrow and goldenrod, with plenty of insect activity. An awkwardly positioned insect hanging or sitting on a flower may indicate a spider's presence. Some species hunt in the leaf litter or on trees or logs.

How to Attract: Plant flowers that attract insects, especially white or yellow flowers and nectar-producing flowers. Avoid the use of harmful insecticides.

Wolf Spiders

Pardosa spp.

Wolf Spider

Folks often jump when they see these spiders unexpectedly dart through the gardens. Fast moving and commonly encountered, this group of spiders basically outruns its prey like a wolf, hence the name "wolf spider." Wolf spiders are all from the spider family Lycosidae, which makes up about eight percent of the world's spider fauna. As with all our spiders, wolf spiders are extremely beneficial to us. They are at the top of the food chain in the insect world and prey on pretty much any insect they are able to overpower. They are pouncers, leaping on their unsuspecting prey and injecting them with deadly venom. One of the more commonly encountered wolf spiders is *P. moesta*, which loves open areas such as gardens and farm fields.

Adult males and females breed in spring, with males dying shortly after. The females later appear with egg sacs that are carried until they hatch in the summer. Hatch time varies and warm summers lead to earlier emergence of spiderlings. Each eggs sac holds about 45 to 50 eggs, and this mass of tiny spiderlings, exact replicas of adults, quickly disperses after emergence. They immediately start helping gardeners and farmers by feeding on tiny insects. As they grow, they moult and shed their skin a few times until they reach maturity, which takes about two years. They pass the first winter as tiny spiderlings and the second winter as full-size immature sub-adults. Gardeners can often tell that spring isn't far off when they observe sexually maturing sub-adults running over melting patches of snow in March and April.

ID: *Adult:* brown, ground dwelling spider with long, thin legs; female is sometime observed carrying a blue to white coloured egg sac. *Spiderling:* similar to adult, but smaller.

Size: *Adult:* body length 4–6 mm. *Spiderling:* 1–2 mm.

Habitat and Range: throughout the province in a wide range of habitats.

Scouting: Search throughout the garden and yard, around farms and pretty much anywhere there are open areas with debris for these spiders to hide in and plenty of insects to eat.

Jumping Spiders

Family Salticidae

Boreal Jumping Spider
(*Phiddipus borealis*)

These amazing creatures are the acrobats of the garden circus. They are seen high up in the vegetation or scampering across the ground. One identifying characteristic of a jumping spider is that, if you try and poke it, the spider will often launch itself out of sight in a flash.

Jumping spiders are in the family Salticidae, which makes up about 10 percent of the world's spider fauna. They are probably the most overlooked spiders in Canada because of their elusive behaviour. To find these guys in the garden, head out on a warm, sunny day and scan sunny patches on tree trunks, or look for them perched in the canopy of garden plants. These spiders have excellent vision and have two large eyes that give them binocular capabilities. They can see prey or predators from far away. One neat experiment that can be done in the backyard demonstrates how alert jumping spiders. If a pen tip is held in front of a jumping spider and moved slowly back in forth, the spider will move its body, following the pen with its eyes.

Jumping spiders are similar to other spiders in their life cycles. Mating occurs in spring, eggs are laid in eggs sacs in late spring and the eggs hatch in summer. Jumping spiders overwinter as spiderlings, maturing and reproducing the following spring.

ID: *Adult:* stout body with short legs; female often rather drab brown; male can be somewhat more brightly coloured; abdomen often has colourful cryptic patterns; middle 2 eyes are large and distinguish this species from other types of spiders. *Immature:* similar to adult but smaller.

Size: *Adult:* body length 3–10 mm.

Habitat and Range: throughout the province in gardens and natural areas.

Scouting: Look at sunny patches on tree trunks and in garden vegetation. They may also be found on sidewalks and buildings, and in any place where the may be able to capture a meal.

How to Attract: To maintain healthy populations of jumping spiders, avoid the use of harmful insecticides.

Orbweavers

Araneus spp.

Folks often get excited when they encounter these large spiders. Fully grown females are twice the size of the males and can be the size of a loonie. Commonly called garden spiders, orbweavers create large, symmetrical webs. They are usually encountered in late summer. The easiest way to remove an orbweaver is to chase it into a cup or jar; if you are brave, carry it gently by hand to a nearby fence or shrub. Try to relocate it to a spot where, its new web will be beneficial to you. Orbweavers are harmless to humans and are often hugely beneficial to gardeners, devouring numerous insects including plenty of pesky ones. Several species are common in BC, which has about half of the almost 100 species of orbweaver spiders in Canada. A common species in the southern Interior is the Western Plains Orbweaver (*A. gemmoides),* also known as the Cat-faced Spider or Jewel Spider; the Roundshouldered Orbweaver (*A. gemma*) occurs on the south coast and Vancouver Island.

Mating occurs in autumn. The female produces an egg case and then dies. The egg case overwinters, often tucked away in a protective crevice. In spring after the eggs hatch, the spiderlings climb to

Araneus spp.

a high spot and release silken threads that the wind catches, carrying them to their new homes. This is known as ballooning. The spiderlings build webs and begin to feed, maturing by autumn.

Charlotte in Charlotte's Web *is an orbweaver.*

ID: *Adult:* Western Plains Orbweaver: plump, brown body with large, lighter brown abdomen often marked with dark brown and white, giving the appearance of cat face (or arrow on some specimens). Roundshouldered Orbweaver: similar, but with light-coloured dorsal line down middle of abdomen. *Immature:* similar to adult but smaller.

Size: *Adult:* body length 6–7 mm (male) or 14–15 mm (female).

Habitat and Range: throughout the province in gardens and farmyards; can be quite common in maturing farm crops.

Scouting: Look for huge orb-shaped webs on fences, shrubs or porches in late summer and autumn. The spider is never far, often tucked away in a silken chamber off to the side of the web.

How to Attract: Don't use harmful insecticides.

Northern & Western Black Widow

Latrodectus spp.

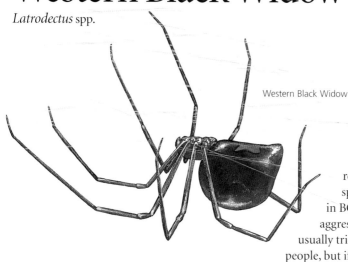

Western Black Widow

The Black Widow is one of the most well-known and notorious spiders, and folks are often surprised to know it exists in BC. This spider is a member of Cobweb Spider family (Theridiidae), which makes up about eight percent of the world's spiders. It builds a rather messy looking web that basically clogs the entrance to a hole or crevice, so that any insect or small creature that enters becomes entangled.

This spider can be considered a beneficial species because it eats plenty of pest insects. It also happens to be the deadliest spider in North America, though there have been no deaths as result of this spider recorded in BC. It is not an aggressive spider and usually tries to avoid people, but if you are working in an area where the Black Widow is known to exist, wear gloves when you retrieve wood from a woodpile or are working in a barn, an unfinished basement or an outdoor building moving stuff around.

Mating occurs in spring and, yes, females sometimes, though rarely, devour their mates. Later that spring, an egg case containing 250 to 700 eggs is produced and placed in a sheltered location with constant humidity. Spiderlings hatch in mid- to late spring and quickly disperse. Adults overwinter and can live up to three years. Females spend most of their life at their nest.

ID: *Adult:* glossy, black body; long legs; red mark on underside of abdomen resembles an hourglass. *Immature:* similar to adult but smaller.

Size: *Adult:* 5 mm (male) or 12 mm (female).

Habitat and Range: warm, dry habitats in the southern Interior and southern Vancouver Island; most commonly observed in sheltered locations such as animal holes, woodpiles and any other dark crevice or hole.

Scouting: Look for these spiders and their webs in abandoned badger and ground squirrel holes, in woodpiles and in outhouses. Only the females bite.

Cultural/Physical Control: Gently remove webs and spiders from locations where contact with humans or pets may occur; otherwise, leave them alone.

Biological Control: None known.

Centipedes
Lithobius spp.

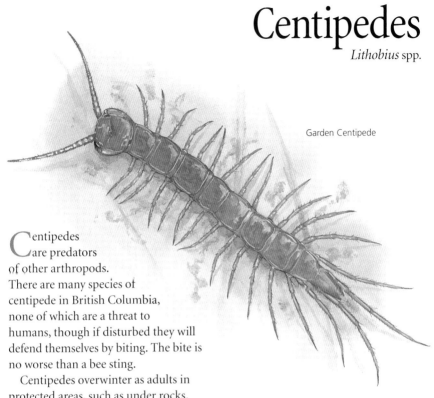

Garden Centipede

Centipedes are predators of other arthropods. There are many species of centipede in British Columbia, none of which are a threat to humans, though if disturbed they will defend themselves by biting. The bite is no worse than a bee sting.

Centipedes overwinter as adults in protected areas, such as under rocks. They lay eggs in soil from spring onwards. The immatures undergo several moults and may take as long as one year to mature. Some centipedes have been reported to live five or six years.

Not all centipedes live up to their name by having 100 pairs of legs. One of the most common centipedes in British Columbia has only 15 pairs.

ID: *Adult:* many-legged, flattened, red or orange body with curved pincers and long antennae on head. *Immature:* resembles adult, only smaller; only 1 pair of legs per segment, which usually stick out laterally.

Size: *Adult:* 20–40 mm. *Immature:* 5–20 mm.

Habitat and Range: widespread throughout the province; prefer moist, dark areas, including basements.

Scouting: Active at night, centipedes prefer damp, dark places to search for prey and feed on insects that are smaller and slower than they are. You can often find them under stones or wood and in corners of damp basements.

Cultural/Physical Control: Remove the source of damp conditions by ensuring good air circulation and drainage and repairing leaks. Remove piles of debris or trash that serve as hiding places for centipedes. Repair cracks or holes in the foundation, window frames, weather stripping and screens to prevent entry from outside.

Biological Control: Centipedes are fast-moving, top predators of the insect world and have very few natural enemies, except mammals such as mice and shrews. Centipedes in turn prey on spiders and carpet beetles indoors and earthworms and insects outdoors. If you find them indoors, it means you have insects for them to feed on. Use the presence of centipedes as a wake-up call to "bug-proof" your house.

Millipedes

Julus spp.

Cyanide Millipede

Although the name millipede means "a thousand legs," these arthropods, in fact, have only from 30 to 100 pairs. Because they have two pairs of legs on each segment, they appear to have many more, hence the "thousand leg" moniker.

Millipedes have biting/chewing mouthparts that they use to feed on decaying vegetation. There are many species of millipede in British Columbia. These arthropods serve a very useful role in breaking down material and opening up soils.

Millipedes overwinter as adults, late-instar immatures, or as eggs. Adults mate in autumn and lay eggs in soil or under debris. In spring, the eggs hatch and go through 7 to 10 moults before becoming adults. The life cycle may take up to two years, with adults living for four to five years.

ID: *Adult:* dark, elongate and cylindrical with legs on each of many segments. *Immature:* initially looks like white worm but grows progressively longer and darker to resemble adult.

Size: *Adult:* 25–40 mm. *Immature:* 5–30 mm.

Habitat and Range: province-wide in moist soils.

Scouting: Millipedes are active at night, feeding on any kind of plant material that is soft, such as decaying vegetation, tender roots and mature fruit. They are commonly seen in mature strawberry fruit that is touching the ground. Like the armadillo, they curl up to protect their soft underbelly when disturbed.

Cultural/Physical Control: Raise fruit off the ground. Remove debris and rotting vegetation.

Biological Control: These arthropods rarely pose a threat to healthy plants. Few animals prey on millipedes because some millipedes have the ability to excrete a noxious gas in self-defence.

Pseudoscorpion

Chelifer cancroides

Pseudoscorpions are essentially scorpions with a rounded abdomen and without the tail.

They are predators of small arthropods. There are several species of pseudoscorpion in British Columbia, but the most common species to be found in or around the home is *C. cancroides*.

The adult female pseudoscorpion builds a nest out of leaf litter and silk in which to lay eggs. She remains in the nest and nurtures the immatures until they are in the third instar, whereupon mother and young leave the nest. It takes approximately one year to go from egg to adult, and adults may live up to five years.

ID: *Adult:* light brown to whitish, round-bodied arthropods; 2 long, clawed appendages at front. *Immature:* similar to adult, but smaller.

Size: *Adult:* 3–5 mm. *Immature:* 1–3 mm.

Habitat and Range: widespread in southern British Columbia; favour protected sites such as animal nests or the shelter of rocks.

Scouting: Often overlooked because of their small size, pseudoscorpions hunt for prey in leaf litter and under bark. When observed indoors, they are usually found in the bathroom, where it is humid and warm, and they most likely came in by hitching a ride on your clothing.

How to Attract: Given that these are beneficial predators, there is no need for control other than to gently pick up and release outdoors, any that you find indoors. Pseudoscorpions feed on springtails, mites and most small insects.

Springtails

Family Sminthuridae, Entomobryidae, Isotomidae and Onychiuridae

Collembolans, or springtails, have biting/chewing mouthparts they use to feed on fungi and decaying plant material. Springtails have a worldwide distribution, including Antarctica. The most commonly encountered springtails are in four families, Sminthuridae, Entomobryidae, Isotomidae and Onychiuridae. The defining character of springtails is a fork-like appendage arising from the underside at the rear, called a furcula. It is used to launch the springtails into the air as a means of escape from predators.

Springtails lay up to 400 eggs singly or in groups, depending on the species, in the soil or in leaf litter. Eggs hatch in a few days, and the immatures moult anywhere from three to eight times before becoming adults. Unlike other insects, the adults continue to moult, as many as an additional 40 times. Springtails live from one to five years.

ID: *Adult:* Onychiuridae: elongate and whitish with no furcula. Entomobryidae and Isotomidae: elongate, ranging in colour from blue or purple to grey; have well developed furcula. Sminthuridae: globular shape. *Immature:* identical to adult but smaller.

Size: *Adult:* 1–6 mm. *Immature:* 1–4 mm.

Habitat and Range: province-wide; most are leaf-litter or soil dwellers, though they can also be found on water, at margins of rivers and ponds and on trees; so common that densities of up to 60,000 per square metre have been found; may be the most numerous animal on the planet after nematodes.

Scouting: In spring, as the snow is melting, large masses of springtails can be seen on snow banks; it may be easier for these small creatures to travel over snow than through the rough terrain underneath. Any time you disturb soil, you should be able to see these small creatures. They are considered to be a positive indicator of soil health.

Cultural/Physical Control: In some cases, springtails will feed on seedlings and root hairs of young plants. In this case, let the soil dry down between watering.

Biological Control: Pseudoscorpions prey on springtails, and reducing the amount of organic matter in your soil will also keep springtail numbers lower. However, there is usually no need to control these creatures. Springtails are beneficial beyond their function in recycling and soil health; they also feed on disease fungi. Studies have demonstrated reduced disease incidence when springtails are present.

Harvestmen

Leiobunum spp., *Phalangium opilio*

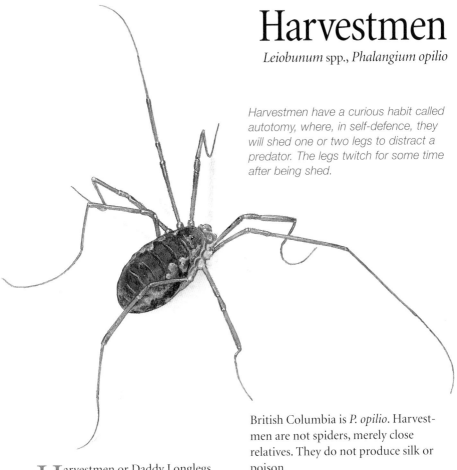

Harvestmen have a curious habit called autotomy, where, in self-defence, they will shed one or two legs to distract a predator. The legs twitch for some time after being shed.

Harvestmen or Daddy Longlegs have piercing mouthparts much like spiders to prey on small insects and mites. There are several species in the genus *Leiobunum*, but the most commonly encountered species in British Columbia is *P. opilio*. Harvestmen are not spiders, merely close relatives. They do not produce silk or poison.

Harvestmen overwinter in the egg stage, hatching out in spring. The immatures develop over summer, with adults noticeable in July. There is only one generation per year.

Also Known As: Daddy Longlegs

ID: *Adult:* spider-like but with seemingly only 1 body segment instead of 2, and only 2 eyes; exceptionally long, thin legs. *Immature:* identical to the adult but smaller.

Size: *Adult:* 4–6 mm. *Immature:* 1–4 mm.

Habitat and Range: widespread across the province; prefers grassy margins.

Scouting: You will most often encounter Harvestmen in the fringe of grass next to your home or crawling up the wall. Adult Harvestmen are most noticeable in August and September.

Cultural/Physical Control: The evil weedwhacker is the archenemy of the Harvestman. Removing the fringe of grass around fences and walls destroys their preferred habitat. You should leave that fringe as a first line of defence against insects entering your home.

Biological Control: Harvestmen are effective predators, eating small insects and mites and scavenge dead insects and plant debris. There is no need for biological control of these creatures.

Sowbugs & Pillbugs

Porcelio laevis & P. scaber

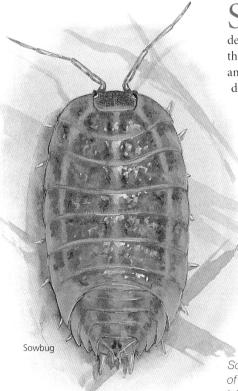

Sowbug

Sowbugs (also known as wood lice or pillbugs) are detritivores, feeding on decaying plant material. Occasionally they will feed on seedlings, roots, leaves and fruit in contact with soil but rarely do serious damage to plants. They do not bite. The sowbugs *P. laevis* and *P. scaber* are becoming increasingly common in British Columbia in moist soils and under decaying vegetation, wood and bark. Both species of sowbug were introduced from Europe.

The female sowbug retains eggs and young immatures in a marsupium on her underside for a couple of months. It may take up to one year for a sowbug to go from egg to adult. Adults may live up to three years.

Sowbugs are one of the few members of the class Crustacea (which includes lobster, shrimp and crab) to invade land. In general, insects are considered to be the lords of the land while crustaceans rule the oceans.

ID: *Adult:* armadillo-like, flattened armour plates; bluish grey overall; 7 pairs of legs; 2 long and 2 short antennae in front and short, paired appendages protruding out back. *Immature:* same as adult but smaller.

Size: *Adult:* 5–12 mm. *Immature:* 3–10 mm.

Habitat and Range: throughout southern British Columbia, in moist soil and woody debris in urban gardens and landscapes; often found along foundations, decks, planters and window boxes where it is cool and damp; slowly expanding to rural and natural areas.

Scouting: Sowbugs are active mostly at night and on damp cloudy days; you will find them escaping the sun under rocks and debris. Occasionally they will venture into your home.

Cultural/Physical Control: Plant seeds deeply and do not water until the first true leaves emerge. Water early in the day, and lift foliage and fruit off the ground. Remove debris that sowbugs use for shelter.

Biological Control: Being a recent introduction, they are not on the menu of many predators. There are reports that dog hair sprinkled on the ground will keep sowbugs away from tasty plants.

Gray Garden Slug

Agriolimax reticulatus

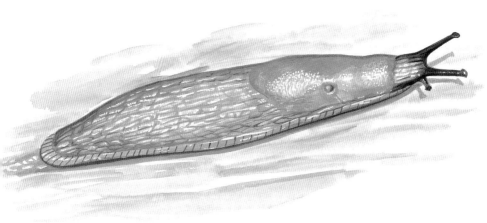

Given that slugs move slowly, there is not a lot of opportunity to get out and meet a mate. Therefore, slugs are hermaphroditic—they have both sets of reproductive organs; however, they still have to exchange sperm with another slug. So, every slug they meet is a mate—no need to wander around endlessly looking for Mr. or Miss Right.

The Gray Garden Slug feeds on a wide variety of garden plants, rasping away the soft tissues of leaves and fruit. This slug was introduced from Europe but has found its way across Canada.

Slugs lay eggs in the soil or under debris all season long. Primarily eggs, but also immatures and adults, are capable of surviving the winter.

ID: *Adult:* grey, elongate, slimy, fleshy body; 1 long pair of antennae on upper part of head and 1 short pair of antennae on underside of head. *Immature:* identical to the adult, only smaller.

Size: *Adult:* 1–3 cm. *Immature:* 5–20 mm.

Habitat and Range: require moist conditions so are restricted to wetter areas, especially pampered gardens.

Scouting: Slugs are most active between 3 and 6 AM, climbing onto low vegetation. Feeding can be recognized by the characteristic shredding of tissue by immatures and ragged holes made by adults. Their travels are revealed by the dried slime trail on soil and plants.

Cultural/Physical Control: There are many ways to reduce slug pressure in your garden.

You can set out 10 cm X 10 cm pieces of plywood onto the soil. Slugs will gather under the wood for protection and all you have to do is collect and dispose of the slugs each morning. You can also trap slugs in shallow pans of old beer sunk into the soil, or a half-grapefruit rind turned upside down on the soil surface. Traps should be serviced daily. Jagged barriers of sand, sharp rock, crushed egg shells or diatomaceous earth spread around plants or as a border to the garden will discourage travel by slugs. Simple sanitation in the yard, such as removing debris suitable as hiding places for slugs, will limit slug populations. Physical barriers such as screening or bands of copper around plants are also effective.

Biological Control: Magpies, ground beetles and marsh flies all prey on or parasitize slugs.

Earthworms

Aporrectodea tuberculata, Eisenia fetida, Lumbricus spp.

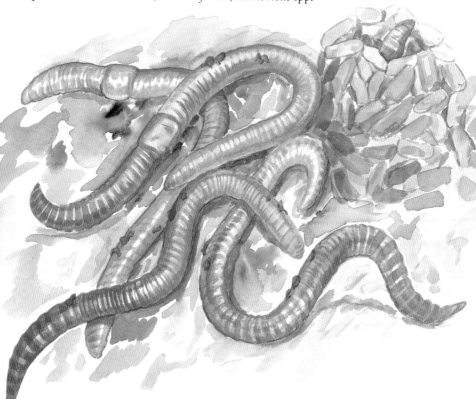

Worms consume decaying organic matter. The Dew Worm (*L. terrestris*) is originally from Europe and digs long vertical tunnels, as deep as 3 metres, and forages for food horizontally in and around the root zone, with occasional exit mounds formed at the soil surface to void waste material. The Red Worm (*L. rubellus*) is more common in forests and feeds in

ID: *Adult:* elongate pink to reddish body; segmented, with collar near front end; no legs or identifiable head. *Immature:* identical to adult except no clitellum and smaller in size

Size: *Adult:* 5–25 cm. *Immature:* 1–5 cm.

Habitat and Range: originally wiped out in northern North America by the last glacial period, but have been reintroduced by humans, either deliberately (fisherman's bait) or inadvertently (in soil, root balls, containers brought in from the US or Europe); dew worms are most commonly found in urban areas and near popular fishing spots; other earthworms occur province-wide.

Scouting: Most worms are at peak activity in wet springs and again in autumn. The Dew Worm leaves large mounds with castings (its waste) on the surface. Other worms do not make such conspicuous mounds. Burrows near the surface cause the ground to be

Red Wriggler compost worms

the leaf litter layer, forming meandering burrows. The Canadian Dew Worm (*A. tuberculata*) is very common, feeding well underground. The Red Wriggler (*E. fetida*) is a favourite of composters, who use the worm to rapidly break down organic matter for use in the garden.

In general, earthworms, being hermaphrodites, exchange sperm to fertilize their eggs. Eggs and sperm are cast off in a cocoon, hatching in three weeks. There are anywhere from 2 to 20 worms in each cocoon, and 20 to 40 cocoons are produced yearly. It takes approximately one year for immature worms to mature. Adult worms can live as long as nine years.

Contrary to popular belief, earthworms do not get flushed out of the soil during a rainstorm to drown on the surface. Instead, the lubricating properties of rain make surface travel possible. It is simply unfortunate if an earthworm wanders into a puddle (more likely the puddle forms around them, earthworms not being known for a speedy gait) or is stranded on concrete or asphalt as the rain stops and the water evaporates.

lumpy and uneven, leading to scalping of sod caused by a lawn mower with the blade set too low. There is much debate on the merits/demerits of earthworms. Although they rapidly turn over organic matter and mix and aerate the soil, they also substantially change the local plant community by removing smothering litter layers that limit what can grow in an area.

Cultural/Physical Control: Top-dressing with sand and infrequent deep watering to drive roots down will discourage earthworms from feeding too near the surface. Removing thatch in the lawn will disrupt their burrows.

Biological Control: Many birds and insects feed on earthworms.

Where to Scout

Species	Trees	Shrubs	Herbaceous Plants	Grasses/Lawns	Leaf Litter/Soil	Ponds/Wetlands	Open/Sunny Areas	Woodlands	Roots/Crown	Flowers	Foliage/Fruit	Stems/Branches	Trunk/Bark
Dragonflies & Damselflies • Odonata													
Meadowhawks & Whiteface Dragonflies		•	•	•		•	•					•	
Mosaic Darners	•	•	•	•		•	•					•	•
Spreadwings			•	•		•	•				•	•	
Bluets			•	•		•	•			•	•		
Grasshoppers & Crickets • Orthopter													
Grasshoppers			•	•			•				•		
Field Crickets			•	•			•			•	•		
True Bugs • Hemiptera													
Ambush Bug			•	•			•	•		•	•		
Damsel Bugs	•	•	•	•			•	•		•	•	•	•
Plant Bugs or Lygus Bugs	•	•	•	•			•	•			•	•	
Stink Bugs	•	•	•					•		•	•		
Lace Bugs	•	•	•				•	•			•		
Boxelder Bug	•							•			•		
Minute Pirate Bug	•	•	•	•			•	•		•	•	•	•
Sucking Insects • Homoptera													
Aphids	•	•	•				•	•		•	•	•	
Cooley Spruce Gall Adelgid	•							•			•	•	
Mealybugs			•								•	•	
Scale Insects	•	•						•			•	•	
Oak Leaf Phylloxera	•							•			•		
Psyllids	•	•					•	•			•		
Whiteflies		•	•				•	•		•	•		
Leafhoppers	•	•	•	•			•	•					
Cicadas	•			•			•	•				•	
Spittlebugs	•	•	•				•	•			•	•	
Termites, Earwigs, Thrips & Lacewings													
Pacific Dampwood Termite	•				•			•				•	•
European Earwig			•	•	•			•		•	•		
Thrips	•	•	•				•	•		•	•		
Lacewings & Snakeflies	•	•	•	•			•	•		•	•	•	
Beetles, Weevils & Borers • Coleoptera													
Blister Beetle		•	•				•			•	•		
Flea Beetles			•				•				•		

Early Spring	Late Spring	Early Summer	Late Summer	Fall	Larva/Nymph	Eggs/Pupa	Adult	Damage	Beneficial	Pest	Page Number	Species
												Odonata • Dragonflies & Damselflies
	•	•	•				•		•		42	Meadowhawks & Whiteface Dragonflies
		•	•				•		•		45	Mosaic Darners
		•	•				•		•		46	Spreadwings
		•	•				•		•		48	Bluets
												Orthoptera • Grasshoppers & Crickets
	•	•	•		•		•			•	49	Grasshoppers
	•	•	•	•	•		•			•	50	Field Crickets
												Hemiptera • True Bugs
		•	•				•		•		51	Ambush Bug
	•	•	•		•		•		•		52	Damsel Bugs
•	•	•	•		•		•			•	53	Plant Bugs or Lygus Bugs
	•	•	•		•		•			•	54	Stink Bugs
•	•	•	•		•	•	•	•		•	55	Lace Bugs
	•	•	•	•			•			•	57	Boxelder Bug
•	•	•	•				•		•		58	Minute Pirate Bug
												Homoptera • Sucking Insects
	•	•	•		•		•			•	59	Aphids
	•	•						•		•	61	Cooley Spruce Gall Adelgid
	•	•	•		•		•	•		•	62	Mealybugs
	•	•					•			•	63	Scale Insects
	•	•	•		•	•		•		•	64	Oak Leaf Phylloxera
	•	•	•		•			•		•	66	Psyllids
	•	•	•		•	•	•	•		•	68	Whiteflies
	•	•	•		•		•	•		•	69	Leafhoppers
		•	•				•	•		•	70	Cicadas
	•	•			•			•		•	72	Spittlebugs
												Termites, Earwigs, Thrips & Lacewings
	•	•			•			•	•	•	73	Pacific Dampwood Termite
		•	•	•			•	•	•	•	74	European Earwig
	•	•	•				•			•	75	Thrips
	•	•	•		•	•	•		•		77	Lacewings & Snakeflies
												Coleoptera • Beetles, Weevils & Borers
	•	•					•		•	•	78	Blister Beetle
•	•	•	•				•	•		•	79	Flea Beetles

When to Scout | Look For

Species	Trees	Shrubs	Herbaceous Plants	Grasses/Lawns	Leaf Litter/Soil	Ponds/Wetlands	Open/Sunny Areas	Woodlands	Roots/Crown	Flowers	Foliage/Fruit	Stems/Branches	Trunk/Bark
Beetles, Weevils & Borers • Coleoptera													
Ground Beetles	•	•	•	•	•	•	•	•			•	•	•
Leaf-feeding Beetles	•		•				•	•		•	•	•	•
Sap Beetle (Beer Beetle, Picnic Beetle)		•	•	•			•			•	•		
Elm Bark Beetles	•							•					•
Carrion Beetles			•				•	•			•		
Click Beetles/Wireworms	•		•	•	•		•		•				
Bark Beetles (Mountain Pine Beetle)	•							•					•
Rove Beetles	•	•	•	•	•		•	•		•	•	•	•
June Beetles & European Chafer	•	•		•			•		•		•		
Dung Beetles				•			•		•				
Lady Beetles	•	•	•	•	•	•	•	•		•	•	•	•
Tiger Beetles					•	•	•	•					
Root Weevils		•	•		•		•		•		•		
Terminal Weevils	•						•	•				•	
Bronze Birch Borer & Jewel Beetles	•							•			•		•
Poplar Borer	•							•			•		•
Banded Alder Borer	•	•						•					•
Poplar & Willow Borer	•							•			•		•
Butterflies, Moths & Allies • Lepidoptera													
Swallowtails & Tiger Swallowtails	•	•	•			•	•	•		•	•	•	
Cabbage Butterfly			•				•				•		
Admirals	•	•						•		•	•	•	
Mourning Cloak Butterfly	•	•						•			•	•	
Azures & Blues			•	•			•	•		•			
Monarch			•				•			•	•		
Painted Lady			•				•			•	•		
Crescents			•				•	•		•	•	•	
Fritillaries			•				•	•		•	•		
Coppers		•	•	•		•	•	•		•	•		
Clouded Sulpher			•				•			•			
Gypsy Moth	•	•					•	•			•	•	•
Northern Pitch Moth	•							•				•	
Gallium Sphinx			•	•			•			•	•		
Satin Moth	•							•				•	•

	When to Scout				Look For							
Early Spring	Late Spring	Early Summer	Late Summer	Fall	Larva/Nymph	Eggs/Pupa	Adult	Damage	Beneficial	Pest	Page Number	Species
												Coleoptera • Beetles, Weevils & Borers
	•	•	•	•			•		•		80	Ground Beetles
•	•		•		•	•	•	•		•	81	Leaf-feeding Beetles
		•	•	•			•	•		•	83	Sap Beetle (Beer Beetle, Picnic Beetle)
		•	•	•			•			•	84	Elm Bark Beetles
•	•	•	•	•	•		•	•	•	•	85	Carrion Beetles
•	•	•			•		•	•		•	86	Click Beetles/Wireworms
	•	•	•	•			•			•	87	Bark Beetles (Mountain Pine Beetle)
•	•	•	•	•			•		•		88	Rove Beetles
	•	•	•		•		•	•		•	89	June Beetles & European Chafer
	•	•	•	•	•		•		•	•	91	Dung Beetles
•	•	•	•	•	•	•	•		•		92	Lady Beetles
		•	•	•			•		•		94	Tiger Beetles
	•	•	•	•			•	•		•	95	Root Weevils
•	•	•			•		•	•		•	96	Terminal Weevils
	•	•	•				•	•		•	97	Bronze Birch Borer & Jewel Beetles
		•	•				•	•		•	98	Poplar Borer
	•	•	•	•			•	•		•	99	Banded Alder Borer
•	•						•	•		•	100	Poplar & Willow Borer
												Lepidoptera • Butterflies, Moths & Allies
	•	•	•		•		•		•		101	Swallowtails & Tiger Swallowtails
•	•	•	•		•		•	•		•	103	Cabbage Butterfly
	•	•	•	•	•		•		•		104	Admirals
•	•	•	•	•	•		•	•		•	106	Mourning Cloak Butterfly
•	•	•					•		•		107	Azures & Blues
			•	•	•		•		•		109	Monarch
	•	•	•	•	•		•		•		111	Painted Lady
	•	•	•	•	•		•		•		112	Crescents
	•	•	•	•	•		•		•		113	Fritillaries
•	•	•	•	•	•		•		•		115	Coppers
•	•	•	•	•			•		•		117	Clouded Sulpher
•	•	•	•		•	•	•	•		•	118	Gypsy Moth
		•	•					•		•	120	Northern Pitch Moth
	•	•	•		•		•		•		121	Gallium Sphinx
		•	•		•		•	•		•	123	Satin Moth

Species	Trees	Shrubs	Herbaceous Plants	Grasses/Lawns	Leaf Litter/Soil	Ponds/Wetlands	Open/Sunny Areas	Woodlands	Roots/Crown	Flowers	Foliage/Fruit	Stems/Branches	Trunk/Bark
Butterflies, Moths & Allies • Lepidoptera													
Underwing Moths	•							•			•	•	
Large Aspen Tortrix	•							•			•		•
Cherry Bark Tortrix	•	•					•	•				•	•
Snowberry Clearwing			•	•			•	•		•			
Garden Tiger Moth	•	•	•				•	•			•		
Cypress Tip Moth	•	•					•	•			•	•	
Polyphemus Moth	•	•						•			•	•	
Plume Moths		•	•	•			•			•	•		
Codling Moth	•							•			•		
European Skipper			•	•			•			•	•		
Peach Tree Borer	•	•					•	•					•
Raspberry Crown Borer		•					•		•			•	
Peach Twig Borer	•						•	•				•	
Lilac Leaf Miner		•					•	•			•		
Speckled Green Fruitworm	•	•						•		•	•	•	
Carpenterworms & Carpentermoths	•							•					•
Sod Webworms & Lawn Moths	•			•			•		•		•		
Western Spruce Budworm	•							•			•	•	
Obliquebanded Leafroller & Blueberry Leaftier	•	•					•	•		•	•		
Bruce Spanworm & Winter Moth	•	•					•	•		•	•		
Uglynest Caterpillar		•					•	•			•	•	
Tent Caterpillars	•	•					•	•			•	•	•
Silverspotted Tiger Moth	•							•			•	•	
Armyworm Moth & Army Cutworm			•	•				•			•	•	
Maggots, Flies, Midges & Miners • Diptera													
Root Maggots			•		•		•		•	•			
Crane Flies			•	•			•		•				
Fruit Flies	•	•						•		•	•		
Carrot Rust Fly			•		•		•		•				
Tachinid Flies	•	•	•	•			•	•		•	•		
Hover Flies	•	•	•			•	•	•		•	•		
Robber Flies	•	•	•				•	•				•	•
Gall Midges	•	•	•				•	•		•	•		
Leafminers	•	•	•					•			•		

Early Spring	Late Spring	Early Summer	Late Summer	Fall	Larva/Nymph	Eggs/Pupa	Adult	Damage	Beneficial	Pest	Page Number	Species
												Lepidoptera • Butterflies, Moths & Allies
•	•		•		•		•		•		124	Underwing Moths
•	•	•	•		•	•	•			•	125	Large Aspen Tortrix
	•	•	•	•	•			•		•	126	Cherry Bark Tortrix
		•					•		•		128	Snowberry Clearwing
	•	•	•		•		•		•		129	Garden Tiger Moth
•	•				•	•		•		•	130	Cypress Tip Moth
	•	•	•		•		•		•		131	Polyphemus Moth
•	•	•	•	•			•				132	Plume Moths
	•	•						•		•	133	Codling Moth
		•	•				•			•	134	European Skipper
	•	•	•				•	•		•	135	Peach Tree Borer
	•	•			•			•		•	136	Raspberry Crown Borer
•	•	•	•	•	•		•	•		•	137	Peach Twig Borer
	•	•	•		•			•		•	138	Lilac Leaf Miner
•	•	•			•		•	•		•	139	Speckled Green Fruitworm
	•	•					•	•		•	140	Carpenterworms & Carpentermoths
	•	•	•		•			•		•	141	Sod Webworms & Lawn Moths
•	•	•	•				•	•		•	143	Western Spruce Budworm
•	•	•	•		•			•		•	144	Obliquebanded Leafroller & Blueberry Leaftier
•	•			•	•			•		•	146	Bruce Spanworm & Winter Moth
	•	•	•	•	•		•			•	147	Uglynest Caterpillar
•	•	•	•		•			•		•	148	Tent Caterpillars
•	•		•	•				•		•	151	Silverspotted Tiger Moth
•					•			•		•	152	Armyworm Moth & Army Cutworm
												Diptera • Maggots, Flies, Midges & Miners
•		•	•				•	•		•	154	Root Maggots
		•	•				•			•	156	Crane Flies
		•	•				•	•		•	157	Fruit Flies
	•	•					•	•		•	158	Carrot Rust Fly
	•	•	•			•	•		•		150	Tachinid Flies
•	•	•	•	•	•		•		•		160	Hover Flies
	•	•	•				•		•		161	Robber Flies
•	•	•						•		•	162	Gall Midges
	•	•	•				•	•		•	164	Leafminers

Where to Scout

Species	Trees	Shrubs	Herbaceous Plants	Grasses/Lawns	Leaf Litter/Soil	Ponds/Wetlands	Open/Sunny Areas	Woodlands	Roots/Crown	Flowers	Foliage/Fruit	Stems/Branches	Trunk/Bark
Maggots, Flies, Midges & Miners • Diptera													
Fungus Gnats & Shore Flies					•	•		•	•				
Mosquitoes			•	•		•		•			•		
Sawflies, Ants, Bees & Wasps • Hymenoptera													
Gall Wasps	•	•					•	•			•	•	
Raspberry Sawfly		•						•			•		
Birch Leaf Miners	•							•			•		
Cottonwood Sawfly	•							•			•		
Pear Slug	•	•						•			•		
Ants	•	•	•	•	•		•	•		•	•	•	•
Honey Bee	•	•	•				•	•		•			
Leafcutter Bees	•	•					•	•		•	•		
Bumble Bees	•	•	•				•	•		•			
Solitary Bees	•	•	•		•		•	•		•	•		
Parasitoid Wasps		•						•		•	•		
Yellow Jackets	•	•	•		•		•	•		•	•	•	
Other Bugs of Garden Interest													
Spruce Spider Mite	•	•					•	•			•		
Eriophyid Gall Mites	•	•					•	•		•	•	•	
Ticks	•	•	•	•		•	•	•			•	•	
Spider Mites	•	•	•				•	•			•		
Crab Spiders			•	•	•		•	•		•		•	•
Wolf Spiders			•	•	•		•						
Jumping Spiders	•	•	•		•		•	•		•	•	•	•
Orbweavers	•	•	•	•			•	•			•	•	
Northern & Western Black Widow					•			•					
Centipedes			•	•	•		•	•					
Millipedes			•		•			•			•		
Pseudoscorpions					•			•					•
Springtails					•	•		•	•				
Harvestmen			•	•	•		•						
Sowbugs & Pillbugs					•				•				
Gray Garden Slug			•		•						•		
Earthworms				•	•			•	•				

	When to Scout				Look For							
Early Spring	Late Spring	Early Summer	Late Summer	Fall	Larva/Nymph	Eggs/Pupa	Adult	Damage	Beneficial	Pest	Page Number	Species
Diptera • Maggots, Flies, Midges & Miners												
•	•	•	•				•		•	•	166	Fungus Gnats & Shore Flies
•	•	•	•				•			•	167	Mosquitoes
Hymenoptera • Sawflies, Ants, Bees & Wasps												
•	•	•	•		•		•	•		•	169	Gall Wasps
	•	•	•		•		•			•	171	Raspberry Sawfly
	•	•	•					•		•	172	Birch Leaf Miners
•	•		•				•	•		•	174	Cottonwood Sawfly
	•	•	•		•					•	175	Pear Slug
	•	•	•	•			•	•	•	•	176	Ants
	•	•	•				•		•		178	Honey Bee
	•	•	•				•	•	•	•	180	Leafcutter Bees
•	•	•	•	•			•		•		181	Bumble Bees
•	•	•					•	•	•		182	Solitary Bees
	•	•	•				•		•		183	Parasitoid Wasps
•	•	•	•				•		•	•	185	Yellow Jackets
Other Bugs of Garden Interest												
	•	•	•	•	•		•	•		•	188	Spruce Spider Mite
	•	•	•					•		•	189	Eriophyid Gall Mites
	•	•					•			•	190	Ticks
•	•	•	•	•	•		•	•		•	192	Spider Mites
	•	•					•		•		194	Crab Spiders
•	•	•	•	•	•		•		•		195	Wolf Spiders
•	•	•			•		•		•		196	Jumping Spiders
		•	•				•		•		197	Orbweavers
	•	•	•		•		•		•	•	198	Northern & Western Black Widow
•	•	•	•				•		•		199	Centipedes
	•	•	•		•		•		•	•	200	Millipedes
	•	•	•		•		•		•		201	Pseudoscorpions
•	•	•	•				•		•		202	Springtails
	•	•	•		•		•		•		203	Harvestmen
	•	•	•		•		•		•	•	204	Sowbugs & Pillbugs
•	•	•			•		•			•	205	Gray Garden Slug
	•	•	•	•	•		•	•	•	•	206	Earthworms

Glossary

abdomen: posterior-most major body region of insects, containing the digestive system and gonads

autotomy: the ability of certain animals to shed a body part as a defence mechanism (e.g., Daddy Longlegs shedding a leg)

borer: insect that chews into woody tissue of plants

B.t. (_Bacillus thuringiensis_): a bacterium that produces a protein toxic to insects. Different strains of the bacterium affect different kinds of insects, e.g., B.t.k. for caterpillars and B.t.i. for fly maggots. B.t. is considered a very effective and environmentally friendly pesticide.

cambium: in trees, the layer of actively dividing cells located between the wood (xylem) and the soft, green tissue (phloem) under the bark

cat-facing: a type of damage caused by insects feeding on developing seeds, which results in a lack of growth hormone in the plant and a lack of growth at the point of feeding, leaving a seam or scar while the surrounding tissue continues to grow

chrysalis: a term specifically referring to the pupal stage of a butterfly. A caterpillar changes into the butterfly within the chrysalis.

complete metamorphosis: the insect life cycle that progresses from an egg through at least three larval instars and a non-feeding pupal stage, ending in the adult stage. The immature or larval stage rarely resembles the adult form. The wings only develop during the major transformation undergone in the pupal stage.

cornicle: one of a pair of short tubes that stick out from the posterior end of an aphid's body; when attacked, droplets containing an alarm pheromone are often emitted from the cornicles

cuticle: the hardened outer shell of an insect

detritivores: animals that feed on detritus (decaying organic matter)

deutonymphs: the third developmental stage of mites and ticks

diapause: a state of dormancy in insects, used to survive winter

distal: furthest from the body

dorsal: top or uppermost surface of the body

ecdysis: shedding of the cuticle during the moult to the next instar

elytra: the first pair of wings on beetles that are modified into hardened wing covers

erinea: mite-induced plant hair growths

exudate: fluid matter, such as sap, resin or gum, that oozes from a plant, usually after injury

flocculence: waxy secretions from woolly adelgids feeding on conifers

forb: a non-woody flowering plant; includes most vegetables, herbs and garden flowers

frass: dry to semi-dry excrement of insects, in contrast to liquid "honeydew" secreted by aphids

furcula: an appendage at the rear of springtails, used to propel the springtail into the air to escape predators

gall: woody growth of plant tissue, usually induced by insect activity or secretions, to surround and protect the insect inside

gradual metamorphosis: the insect life cycle that progresses from an egg through at least one nymphal stage and ends in the adult stage. The immature or nymphal stage resembles the adult stage with the exception that the wings are not completely formed but are visible as developing buds.

haplodiploidy: a form of reproduction where unfertilized females give birth to male offspring and fertilized females give birth to female offspring

heartwood: the tissue of a tree at the centre of the main stem. Little or no fluid transport occurs here, in contrast to the sapwood where there is free-flowing water transport. The heartwood and sapwood combined make up the xylem of a tree.

hermaphrodite: the adult contains both male and female gonads and sex organs. It usually must exchange sperm with another of the same species to fertilize the eggs.

hibernaculum: a sheltered location or structure, such as a case or nest, in which an animal or insect hibernates for the winter

holarctic: a term describing the distribution of an organism, in this case, across the northern and arctic ecoregions of the planet

instar: the immature growth stage of an insect. There may be several instars between the egg and adult stages.

larva: the immature stage of an insect that undergoes complete metamorphosis

latrodectism: the clinical symptoms resulting from a neurotoxic venom from one of many spider species in the genus *Latrodectus*, which are commonly referred to as black widow spiders

marsupium: a broodpouch, used to carry eggs or young

moulting: formation of new cuticle followed by ecdysis; the growth process of an insect

nymph: immature stage of an insect that undergoes gradual metamorphosis

ovipositor: abdominal appendage on females used to deposit eggs

parthenogenesis: reproduction without mating; occurs in aphids and some other species

phytoplasma: wall-less bacteria that live in the phloem of plants and in insects. The damage they cause ranges from mild yellowing to death. Examples include aster yellows and western-X disease of *Prunus*.

proboscis: modified mouthparts of butterflies and moths, adapted for siphoning nectar from flowers

pronotum: the shoulder area immediately behind the head, often present as a hardened plate

prothorax: the first body segment behind the head, followed by the meso- and metathoracic segments

proximal: closest to the body

raptorial: a leg with an enlarged femur to facilitate grasping of prey, commonly seen in preying mantids and damsel bugs

scutellum: a triangular plate behind the pronotum; is commonly enlarged in stink bugs and plant bugs

skeletonizer: an insect that scrapes off the epidermal or surface tissues of a leaf

tachinid: a member of the Diptera family Tachinidae. These flies parasitize other insects and are considered to be beneficial.

thorax: the second major body region of an insect, located between the head and the abdomen. It is comprised of three segments with a pair of legs arising from each segment. The first thoracic segment is often strengthened dorsally and referred to as the pronotum. If the insect is winged, the first pair of wings arises from the second segment and the second pair of wings arises from the third thoracic segment.

ventral: lower or bottommost surface of the body

References

Acorn, J and I. Sheldon. 2006. *Butterflies of British Columbia.* Lone Pine Publishing, Edmonton.

Barnes, R.D. 1991. *Invertebrate Zoology* (Fifth Edition). Harcourt Brace Jovanovich Inc., Toronto.

Borror, D.J., C.A. Triplehorn and N.F. Johnson. 1989. *An Introduction to the Study of Insects* (Sixth Edition). Saunders College Publishing, Philadelphia.

Buddle, C.M. and D.P. Shorthouse. 2000. "Jumping spiders of Canada." *Newsletter of the Biological Survey of Canada* (Terrestrial Arthropods) 19(1): 16–18.

Cannings, R. 2002. *Introducing the Dragonflies of British Columbia and the Yukon.* Royal British Columbia Museum, Victoria.

Cerezke, H.F. 1992. *Large Aspen Tortrix.* Natural Resources Canada, Canadian Forestry Service. Northern Forestry Centre, Edmonton. Forestry Leaflet 21.

Cerezke, H.F. 1991. *Forest Tent Caterpillar.* Natural Resources Canada, Canadian Forestry Service. Northern Forestry Centre, Edmonton. Forestry Leaflet 10.

Corbet, P. 1999. *Dragonflies: Behavior and Ecology of Odonata.* Cornell University Press, New York.

Cranshaw, W. 2004. *Garden Insects of North America.* Princeton University Press. Princeton.

Duncan, R.W. 2006. *Conifer Defoliators of British Columbia.* Natural Resources Canada, Victoria.

Dunkle, S. 2000. *Dragonflies Through Binoculars: A Field Guide to Dragonflies of North America.* Oxford University Press, New York.

Edwards, C.A. (ed). 2004. *Earthworm Ecology* (Second Edition). CRC Press LLC, New York.

Eisner, T., M. Eisner and M. Siegler. 2005. *Secret Weapons: Defenses of Insects, Spiders, Scorpions and other Many-legged Creatures.* Harvard University Press, Cambridge.

Eisner T. 1994. "Integumental Slime and Wax Secretion: Defensive Adaptations of Sawfly Larvae." *J Chem Ecol* 20: 2743–49.

Elmhirst, J. (ed). 2000. *Home and Garden Pest Management Guide for British Columbia 2001 Edition.* British Columbia Ministry of Agriculture, Food and Fisheries, Victoria.

Evans, H.E. 1984. *Insect Biology.* Addison-Wesley Publishing, Reading.

Flint, M.L. and S.H. Dreistadt. 1998. *Natural Enemies Handbook: The Illustrated Guide to Biological Pest Control.* University of California Statewide Integrated Pest Management Project Publication 3386.

Fullard J.H., M.B. Fenton and J.A. Simmons. 1979. "Jamming Bat Echolocation: The Clicks of Arctiid Moths." *Can J Zool* 57: 647–49.

Gieles, C. 1996. *Microlepidoptera of Europe.* Vol 1. Pterophoridae. Apollo Books, Stentrup.

Hopkin, S.P. 1997. *Biology of the Springtails.* Oxford University Press, New York.

Howard, R.J., J.A. Garland and W.L. Seaman. 1994. *Diseases and Pests of Vegetable Crops in Canada.* Canadian Phytopathological Society and Entomological Society of Canada, Ottawa.

Ip, D.W. 1992. *Dutch Elm Disease.* Natural Resources Canada, Canadian Forestry Service. Northern Forestry Centre, Edmonton. Forestry Leaflet 19.

Langor, D.W. 1995. *Satin Moth.* Natural Resources Canada, Canadian Forestry Service. Northern Forestry Centre, Edmonton. Forestry Leaflet 35.

Layberry, R.A., P.W. Hall and J.D. Lafontaine. 1998. *The Butterflies of Canada.* University of Toronto Press, Toronto.

Marshall, S.A. 2006. *Insects: Their Natural History and Diversity.* Firefly Books Ltd., Richmond Hill.

Metcalf, C.L., W.P. Flint and R.L. Metcalf. 1962. *Destructive and Useful Insects* (Fourth Edition). McGraw-Hill Book Company, New York.

Pedigo, L. 1989. *Entomology and Pest Management.* Macmillian Publishing Company, New York.

Sargent T.D. 1976. *Legion of Night: The Underwing Moths.* University of Massachusetts Press, Massachusetts.

Solomon, J.D. 1995. "Guide to Insect Borers of North American Broadleaf Trees and Shrubs." *Agricultural Handbook 706.* U.S. Department of Agriculture, Forest Service, Washington, DC.

Triplehorn, C.A. and N.F. Johnson. 2004. *Borror and DeLong's Introduction to the Study of Insects* (Seventh Edition). Thomson Brooks/Cole, Toronto.

Index

Names in **boldface** type refer to the primary species accounts.

About the Authors

Janice Elmhirst

Janice Elmhirst grew up on a small, mixed dairy farm north of Belleville in southern Ontario. She obtained a B.Sc. (Agr.) with a specialty in Pest Management from the University of Guelph in 1982 and a Ph.D. in Botany (Plant Pathology) from the University of Toronto in 1988. As a post-doctoral fellow at Agriculture and Agri-Food Canada, Harrow, Janice helped to develop a biological control agent for plant diseases. From 1990 to 2002, she did applied research and extension in Integrated Pest Management for both the Ontario and British Columbia governments and headed the BC Provincial Pest Diagnostic Laboratory for four years. In 2002, she started her own company, Elmhirst Diagnostics & Research, which provides consulting services to the ornamental nursery industry.

Ken Fry

Ken Fry, entomology instructor at the School of Horticulture at Olds College, has been involved in insect pest management research, teaching and extension for over 12 years, including nine years as a research scientist at the Alberta Research Council. His research is focused on biological control of insect pests and integrated pest management. Ken has never met a bug he didn't like, or at least have a grudging respect for.

Doug Macaulay

Doug Macaulay's childhood fascination with insects led to a career as an agroforester and entomologist with Alberta Agriculture and Food, where he helps people farm with trees, reforest watersheds, manage woodlots and deal with insects and diseases. In his spare time, he works as an insect taxonomist, curating his collection of Alberta insects. He is also working on an identification key of the plume moths of Alberta and Western Canada, and surveying Lepidoptera and Odonata in Alberta parks in cooperation with the Alberta Lepidopterists' Guild and Alberta Parks and Protected Areas.